D1368050

Feminist Novelists
of the
Belle Epoque

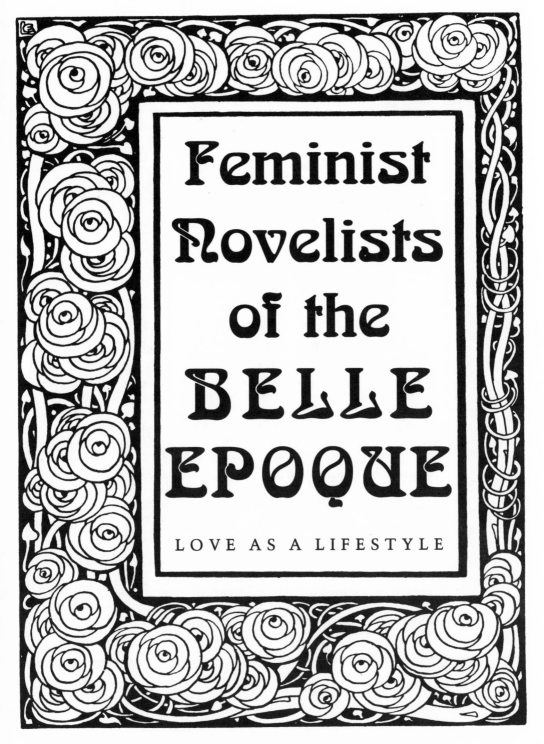

Feminist Novelists of the BELLE EPOQUE

LOVE AS A LIFESTYLE

Jennifer Waelti-Walters

INDIANA UNIVERSITY PRESS   BLOOMINGTON AND INDIANAPOLIS

Manufactured in the United States of America

Library of Congress Cataloging-in-Publication Data
Waelti-Walters, Jennifer.
Feminist novelists of the Belle Epoque: love as a lifestyle /
Jennifer Waelti-Walters.
p.   cm.
Includes bibliographical references.
ISBN 0-253-36300-4. — ISBN 0-253-20557-3 (pbk.)
1. French fiction—Women authors—History and criticism.
2. Feminism and literature—France—History—20th century.
3. French fiction—20th century—History and criticism. 4. Women and literature—France—History—20th century. 5. Sex role in literature. 6. Love in literature. I. Title.
PQ673.W34   1990
843'.912099287—dc20   89-45468
                                                                    CIP

1   2   3   4   5   94   93   92   91   90

For Jeanne Hyvrard
In memory of her foremothers

CONTENTS

PREFACE

The project which grew into this book came into being by accident while I was doing something else. One day as I was searching through the card catalog in the Bibliothèque Nationale (all those books which for one reason or another have never made it into the official bound volumes) I found a reference to J. Bertaut's *La Littérature féminine d'aujourd'hui* (1909) and ordered the text on impulse, thinking that it would be a critical disaster. To my surprise it was a businesslike little book, and the author was very enthusiastic about a number of contemporary writers, none of whom I recognized. The only names I knew in the whole volume were those of Colette and Anna de Noailles. So from curiosity I started to read some of the novels mentioned, to see what they were like. I started with Marcelle Tinayre because my university library had one or two of her works and found myself opening a novel in the late evening and reading until I finished it at 3 A.M. After I had done this several times I began to wonder why I enjoyed these novels so much, and upon analysis decided it was because they were the first books that I had ever read in French in which the heroines walked out at the end of the novels unpunished, unrepentant, not sick, not impoverished, but actually alive and autonomous.

This was a discovery; I was hooked. Some thirty novelists and one hundred fifty novels later the patterns of this book had fallen into place. I feel strongly that certain novelists should be saved from oblivion, that certain novels are still of great interest today, and that certain pieces of writing are unique in the expression of women's experience in French literature: the description of the birth in Lucie Delarue-Mardrus, *Marie fille-mère* (cf. chapter 4) and the orgasm in Colette, *L'Ingénue libertine* (cf. chapter 8), to give but two examples.

The major women writers of the Belle Epoque have a view of women as human beings struggling to survive against great odds. These beings have three apparently simple needs that are constantly refused to them: the right to work, the right to love, the right to be an independent human being on equal terms with men. Revolutionary though such changes would be, these novelists are not trying to create a revolution. They call for reform in practical ways in the public sphere and in the home so that women may survive physically and psychologically with autonomy and dignity, and they strive to make this clear in the various realms of women's activity important to turn-of-the-century women in France.

The result is a volume of basic gynocriticism: I am drawing attention to a particular body of material and attempting to present it in its own terms. This book offers a study of the most interesting novels by those novelists who between 1900 and 1914 conceived of a changing role for women. My aim is to bring the women novelists of the period to the attention of both anglophone and francophone readers interested in women's writing, in women's rights, and in social history. It is written in narrative style to make access to the material pleasant; this should not be taken to mean that it is a volume of plot summary, however. The descriptions given are carefully thematic and analytical in order to reveal both the concerns at issue and the structure of the novels. I have set aside all novelists who work within the accepted nineteenth-century views of women; this means that I have excluded many people who were much admired at the time and who are remembered with nostalgia by aging readers, critics, and booksellers to this day. It also means that I have included a number of determined socialist-feminists whose *romans à thèse* would be scorned by those who believe in the predominance of art and artifice in literature. I have quoted in French in an attempt to give the flavor of the various styles, as these novels are hard to come by; and I have provided a translation not only because they are even harder to find in English, but also because, as I said, I want to reach an anglophone audience as well.

This body of writing had been set aside and forgotten. Its reemergence from silence is important because, as we are all aware, knowledge about women cannot just be added to the knowledge we have about men to increase the total sum of information available. The new knowledge forces a reassessment of the old. Some of these women—Tinayre, Yver, Delarue-Mardrus, and Harry in particular—were very widely read indeed; Gide, Proust, et al., whether we acknowledge the fact or not, wrote within a literary context imbued with novels such as the ones I present, wrote perhaps against these women's ideas to a certain extent. Certainly when one considers the male-female relations in their work it is difficult to believe that Gide and Rachilde, for example, are living in the same political and social climate. As an experiment this year, I included Tinayre's *La Rebelle* in my twentieth-century-novel course, and we read it between Gide's *L'Immoraliste* and Proust's *Un Amour de Swann*. The students loved *La Rebelle* and were deeply concerned by the questions it raised; the unexpected advantage was that they went on to enjoy *Swann* much more than is usual for an undergraduate class. Tinayre had provided a solid base from which Proust could be understood and called into question. The whole course benefited from the addition.

I see this exploration as the first step in a reevaluation of the period by the juxtaposition of the moral and literary values of the women and men writing before the 1914–18 war in France. Next I hope to publish an anthology of extracts of feminist writings in order to make this period of French history more generally available to other scholars and students who wish to explore the field.

My thanks to the staff of the Bibliothèque Nationale, Paris, and the librarians of the Bibliothèque Marguerite Durand for their help in finding materials; to the University of Victoria and the Social Sciences and Humanities Research Council of Canada for leave and a Leave Fellowship without which the book would not have been written yet; to Mary Shelton for translating the quotations and to Lucie Miller and Johanne Grenier for typing and retyping the manuscript; to Mair Verthuy for her constant input and her hours in secondhand-book shops; to Catherine Ludet for listening indefatigably to the story of the "novel of the day"; to Claire Peverelli for tracing the death of Simone Bodève; to Maureen Scobie, Gwladys Downes, and Christine St. Peter for their comments on the manuscript; and to Jeanne Hyvrard for her thoughtful discussions of the importance of love in French society.

Feminist Novelists
of the
Belle Epoque

Away from the
Bourgeois Ideal

1 This book is about novels by women, not "silly novels by silly lady novelists," as George Eliot once wrote, but subversive novels by politically astute and socially conscious women. These are books which trace women's escape from the constraints of the nineteenth century and their emergence into the twentieth century as autonomous beings with values and concerns that we share today.

Out of the Nineteenth Century

Women's situation is a social matter, yet it is a matter that has been excluded from the study of society for most of historical time in the Western world. History, literature, and even the more modern studies offered by the social sciences provide us with little information. Two perceptions recur: woman is other; woman's sphere is the private and interior space of each man's home. There are exceptions to these generalities, of course, but they are for the most part true, especially in post-Napoleonic France.

It is a cliché to say that France is the country of love, but the cliché itself has come into being because the role of affective and sexual relationships is acknowledged to a much greater extent in public life (that is, in the male sphere) than it is in most other Occidental industrialized states. Love is one of the sources of power, one of the threads that form the political picture. Indeed I proffer a hypothesis that political struggles in France move on a continuum from domination to love; that is, from periods when those values generally recognized as male—war, wealth, law, control—predominate over those where there is a greater respect for women, a greater sense of equality between the sexes, and where the politics of the time are more concerned with the welfare of the governed than the ambitions of the governors.

The overt recognitions that women are an oppressed minority despite being a numerical majority in many societies, and that gender is a category that is as fundamental to social analysis as those of class, race, and religion, may seem for many to be recent phenomena, provoked in large measure by feminist scholarship,[1] but politicians have been exploiting their covert understanding that this is so for a long time, while feminist writers both female and male have been responding to them in their literature.

Not only did Napoleon situate himself and his government on the male-dominant extreme of the political spectrum, but he also fixed his perceptions in a legal code that has disempowered women ever since. Under the Napoleonic Code (1804) women were rendered inferior to men. A very little autonomy was left to unmarried women whose fathers were dead and to widows without male heirs, but most of the female population was reduced to servitude. The basic premise was that a married woman must always obey her husband.[2] She could not have a separate residence without his consent, and he controlled all her property and assets. Without his consent she could not buy, sell, mortgage, or have a bank account. She could not work without his permission, and any money she earned belonged to him. She had no legal authority over her children while her husband was alive, and he could commit them to someone else's care at his death. Children born in wedlock belonged to the husband; he could file maternity suits but a woman could not file paternity suits. Indeed women were declared incompetent to serve as legal witnesses of certificates of marriage, birth, or death. A wife's adultery could be punished by two years' imprisonment; the husband who caught his wife in *flagrant délit* and murdered her could be acquitted. Divorce for women was abolished.

The Napoleonic Code controlled women through love and sexuality. It regulated the relations between spouses and between parents and children. It prevented women from obtaining gainful employment so that most women were trapped economically and had to exchange sexual services to survive, be it within marriage or by public prostitution.

Throughout the whole of the nineteenth century feminists and social-ists struggled to move toward more "female" values, to restore some measure of equity in the political structures, to reestablish women's right to some measure of autonomy, some possibility of survival. The major issues were those of marriage, maternity, economic governance, and the right to work—namely, each woman's control over her own body.

The pleas and arguments against the Napoleonic Code began immedi-ately[3] and gradually grew until by the 1830s the idea that women have a useful role to play in society had become important. Women began to demand sufficient education to allow them to assume fully their human condition and protest the effect of social conditioning and pressure on the female character. They claimed that female nature is not to be gentle, subservient, and self-sacrificing as society pretends and requires.[4] It was at this period that women began to see women's liberation and the social participation that should ensue as necessary for the creation of a more just and egalitarian society.

This is the period of romanticism and of utopian socialist groups of various kinds—"Saint-Simoniens," "Fouriéristes," and "Communistes icariens," among others.[5] All the most influential social groups took women's roles into serious consideration, and all shared the concrete aim to create a society where all sorts of oppression, those of sex and class in particular, would be abolished and where all individuals would be free to fulfill their own potential for the good of the whole community. (Henri de Saint-Simon is reported to have stated on his deathbed, "L'homme et la femme, voilà l'individu social" [the man and the woman are together the social individual].) The women involved in these movements are not overawed by male doctrines. They seem to embrace them, learn political awareness, and work toward a development of their own feminist con-sciousness and a modification of male structures.[6]

Women of the 1830s had a clear idea of what they wanted and for what purpose. They claimed their rights to education for physical, material, and intellectual strength; to opinion on political and religious matters; and to legal right over their possessions. Their demands for total reform of education, equality in marriage, and a sexual liberation that would give rise to a new morality were still being made in much the same form in 1900. Then 1848 brings a new burst of feminist activity in the changing political climate, the focal point of which is the struggle for universal suffrage—the symbol of social equality and participation which women were not to obtain until 1944. In this period feminist consciousness tends to mirror the republican political concerns and so remains restricted to women's political rights and the extension to women of the civil rights implicit in the three principles of the French Revolution of 1789: liberty, equality, fraternity. There is no authentically female autonomous political movement. The struggle is now for an improved place for women in the existing male structures, for the extension of the allotted roles of wife and mother: improved education, the right to work, and the right to full participation in society outside the confines of home and family.

Socialist feminists and social activists formed their next alliance in the period leading up to the Commune of 1871, and the last decades of the century brought a number of reforms, though ultimately women still had little control over their own lives.[7]

The first Women's Rights Congress was held in 1878; in 1879 the reforms in women's education began. In 1880, a normal school for women preparing to teach in primary school was opened at Fontenay-aux-Roses, and in 1881 the normal school for secondary-school teachers was created at Sèvres. State high schools for girls (lycées) were created at the same period, though the school curriculum for boys and girls would not be identical until 1937. Schooling for children of both sexes became compulsory in 1889. The first woman lawyer was called to the bar in 1900; in 1898 Dr. Edwards-Pilliet replaced her husband in the chair of physiology at Laboisière hospital.

Women also made legal advances. In 1881 they obtained the right to open a savings bank account, in 1884 the right to divorce was reintroduced, and in 1897 women were recognized as legally competent to be civil witnesses. Married women gained control of their earnings in 1907, and finally in 1912 unmarried mothers could file paternity suits.[8]

The struggle lasted from the institution of the Napoleonic Code to the Belle Epoque, and during that time women reclaimed barely the minimum legal and civil rights necessary for their survival and for some sense of autonomy.

In 1900 the fight continued for the reform of the civil code and for the vote. Male socialists were still including female equality in their program but were rarely precise in the formulation of plans. Feminism was receiving favorable attention: in 1897–98 sociologist Jacques Flach lectured on the social and political condition of women at the College of France (a bastion of male scholarship to this day). Others began to publish on similar issues. Women were being named to local and national committees and commissions. There were a number of important congresses held in Paris on the rights of women,[9] and numerous women's newspapers—notably *La Fronde*, founded by Marguerite Durand—were publishing regularly.[10] Things appeared to be moving toward a more egalitarian society.

Nonetheless, the major theme of reform throughout the nineteenth century remains that of woman's role as mother. Whether the attitude be that of the Saint-Simoniens, who saw the mother as the savior of society or, in less exalted terms, as the guardian of the home, teaching her children purity and social values, and nurturing her husband; or whether it be described in political terms, in the context of the continued production and raising of citizens, the social perception of women as fulfilling one essential function remains the same. Hence, as we shall see, the centrality of the questions of love, marriage, and motherhood in the literature of the period and the continued concern with the inherent contradiction between the apparent importance of the mother per se and the treatment of mothers who do not fit into the institution of marriage as defined by bourgeois society in the nineteenth century.

Women in 1900 were still defined by their sexuality and controlled by it. Although they had more legal rights than they had in 1804, social attitudes toward them were only just beginning to change.

Away from the Bourgeois Ideal

By 1900 there was a small army of women writing novels for an audience mainly of women.[11] Aristocratic and bourgeois women bought yellow-covered books; working-class and country women cut the serials out of their husbands' newspapers, stitched the episodes together, bound them, and exchanged them with friends whose husbands preferred other newspapers.[12]

Most of these novels reinforce the traditional dichotomous images projected onto women in the Western world: woman as wife and mother or as whore. Pierre-Joseph Proudhon (1809–65), one of the most socialist theoreticians of nineteenth-century France and a violent antifeminist, categorizes women as "prostituées ou ménagères," either pleasing or useful to men. Léopold Lacour, a feminist reformer,[13] adds a further category; he says that women of the period are dolls, housekeepers, or prostitutes and that these three roles are the results of masculine despotism, against which modern women are struggling. Most French novels iterate this definition of the possible situations open to women and illustrate it in one way or another. French novels were well known abroad as those infamous yellow books in which adultery was both condoned and enjoyed—even when the novels were condemnatory in tone and intent—but they also made the very important statement, which I shall take up later, that women's desire was incompatible with the structures of nineteenth-century marriage.[14]

These "traditional" novels fall into several distinct categories with their own stock characters and styles. If we follow the class structure we begin with the social novels, usually written by aristocratic ladies with time on their hands. Gyp is the supreme example of such work; she wrote pert, satirical novels at the rate of two or three a year from 1868 until 1930.[15] For a similar public are the romantic novels by Gérard d'Houville, Camille Pert, Georges de Peyrebrune, et al., in which the language is lyrical, the heroine frequently a passionate Creole, and the story that of adultery.[16] A more exotic variant on these novels is provided by the writers who set their stories in North Africa, the Middle East, or Indochina; Miriam Harry is the best known of this group.

As we move down through society, we arrive at novels set in the provinces (Mme Claude Lemaître, Camille Marbo) and at tales of Parisian life such as those written by Jeanne Landre[17] and Liane de Pougy. Provincial girls tend to be seduced and lost, or married against their will to some unsuitable husband, whereas in the Parisian stories poor working girls and "petits rats de l'Opéra" (little dancers) are admired for their beauty, and become rich and famous courtesans. The final category, situated at the limits of literature and popular fiction, is that of tear-jerking, cliff-hanging adventure stories—Daniel Lesueur provides excellent examples—in which there often are a female medical student and an impoverished Russian.[18]

These novels are constructed around stereotypes which reinforce the popular conceptions and misconceptions about women, use the readers' expectations and assumptions without challenging or changing them in any way, and generally reimpress on women the distorted images of themselves that they have been taught to accept as accurate reflections of themselves and their kind.

In these novels, as one expects, half the women are virtuous and half are adulterous, and therefore wicked, rich, and passionate. Sinful women are usually half-foreign, poor wicked women tend to be connected to the theater, students are poor, fathers are often archaeologists, seducers are unhappy, ugly women have no hope, love is fate. And love is outside marriage. Pleasure is inevitably linked to the prostitute figure, who is agreeable to men, while the housekeeper figure lurks in the background.

Throughout the period the figure in relation to which all female characters were measured was the prescriptive image of the perfect bourgeois wife.[19] She was seen as the regulating power of the nineteenth-century social machine. Her proper sphere was the home, which was a nest and refuge for her husband to return to after his day's work, and this idea of the home as a nest was taken quite literally. The woman spent her time making cushions for her husband's head and embroidering footstools for his feet. Indeed, one of the ways by which a novelist told the reader that the context was a modern, autonomous, "hard" woman's home was by omitting to cover all available surfaces with antimacassars, chair backs, table runners, tassels, and so on. The enveloping quality of the prevalent interior decoration had both a physical and a psychological purpose.

A bourgeois wife was valued for her softness: she was gentle, quiet, and comforting. As her husband's shadow she had no opinion, no voice, no image but his. She must love and tend to her husband, meeting his every need. Her self-sacrifice counterbalanced his self-interest and self-advancement; her emotion, his reason; her dependency complemented his dominance. She had been brought up to feel no desire and have no corrupting knowledge or experience. All her virtues were self-effacing: patience, docility, good humor, flexibility. Her only means of obtaining anything she might want or need was by strategies of indirection and accommodation. In sum, she had been deprived of all sense of herself as an active, living being and of all power legal, economic, and personal. By a dowry her family had bought her a husband and sold her into subservience. As a way of preventing woman from being a threat or challenge to man, the system was beyond compare. The bourgeois wife belonged to her husband; possession was complete and exclusive. Thus were both family lineage and property protected. The husband had his rights; his wife had her place.

A wife loved her husband; a girl believed that romantic love would be her reward for a youth of self-control, self-effacement, and self-denial. Love was set up as the linchpin of society, and all the major circumstances of a woman's life were connected to it: her life with her parents, her choice of a husband, her relation to her children.

Given the prevalent assumption that women lived through their emotions, as well as the schooling in innocence, ignorance, and tractability received by most late-nineteenth-century girls, one would expect such a social system to work quite well in maintaining harmonious inequality. However, if the more astute women novelists are to be believed, this was not the case, and the failure of the system was built into the teaching on which it depended. Let us examine the components of the problem.

1. In the latter part of the nineteenth century, politicians in France became increasingly concerned about the low birthrate and worked very hard to valorize maternity to such an extent that the terms "wife" and "mother" were inseparable in the public mind.[20] The image of the future, whether the speaker were an unswerving traditionalist or a utopian socialist, was that of a family united around a stable, virtuous wife and mother. (It was the proposed relationship of wife to husband that differed considerably from speaker to speaker.) For most of the female population marriage meant motherhood sooner or later.

2. As marriages were arranged, most of them were *mariages d'inclination*, which meant at worst that the bride did not find her proposed husband repulsive and at best that she found him attractive; at worst that she had been sold to the highest bidder (socially speaking) and at best that the parents felt the families to be compatible. Warm affection was the strongest sort of love usually seen within marriage.

3. As a result of long centuries of traditional, religious, mythical, social, and literary misogyny in France, the implacable binary oppositions central to nineteenth-century thought and the prescriptive presentations of the ideal bourgeoise, most women were incapable, by 1900, of conceiving of themselves in any roles other than those of homemaker or prostitute. (Living alone was not in the scheme of things because no ordinary woman could function by herself; it was not possible for her to exist materially, whatever she did, without extra financial assistance, so she had to belong to some man either permanently or temporarily.)

4. Similarly inculcated into women was the belief that a good woman did not feel desire; her love was tender, affectionate, and compliant. A pas-

sionate woman was a bad woman; bad women were prostitutes; wives were not prostitutes. So wives were not passionate.

As the novelists of the period make extremely clear, such a system can hold in any family only until the wife either responds passionately to her husband or falls in love with somebody else. As soon as she experiences desire she must believe herself to have fallen. She then believes herself unworthy of her husband and, more important to society, an unworthy mother of her children. Thus she feels forced to choose not only between affection for her husband (if any) and love for another man, but also between love for her husband and for her children. The conditioning she has internalized will not allow her to see herself as a complex being, so she has to give up someone she loves, tearing herself apart as she does so. It is the constant struggle among conditioning, experience, and personal emotion in the lives of women who do not, will not, or cannot conform that is the theme of most of the novels in this study.

A sense of continual fragmentation dominates the writing of the women in this book. Because of the overbearing and exclusive possessiveness allowed to men of the period, most of the women characters feel that they can love only one person at a time: that person requires their entire being. In these terms every step in life is transformed into a choice toward one person against another: for a fiancé against a father, for a husband against a child. Every decision becomes a heartrending one.

When you add the assumption of self-sacrifice in women to the obligation to choose between affections, the potential for women to become total victims of abusive partners or parents becomes limitless. It is easy to see how a father could create or destroy a daughter by his behavior toward her. It is clear also why, in these novels, the close relationships are between father and daughter, mother and son. A father can give his daughter a measure of freedom and a future by giving her an education; a mother clings to her son because his masculinity validates her maternity and because he can protect her when his father is no longer there to do so. Also, we should take into account yet again that women have been taught that to have status they need to belong to a man; no mother can protect her daughter from the father, no woman has any public power to transmit to another, and very few have any tradition of private support within the family. In these circumstances it is not surprising to find that all the authors, however strong, autonomous, and feminist they may be, give their feminist characters sons who can perhaps be taught some sense of women's worth through education and endow the girls with wise, open-minded fathers. For the time being there was no positive point to be made by giving women daughters; what had to be proved was that education improved women and that this was to the advantage of both women and men.

There are supportive links between women in these novels which are frequently true networks of survival, both materially and emotionally. Such friendship is more open and visible between the few professionals than between women of other groups because the former have a sense of themselves as individuals; they enjoy each other's company when times are good, and stand together against discrimination and oppression when necessary.

As we might expect given the social and cultural pressures, women went into the professions with a great sense of mission. The wonder is that many of them entered at all because the choice of a career was inevitably considered a selfish decision: a choice a woman made toward herself and therefore away from everyone else in her life. It was a denial of self-sacrifice of the usual kind and an almost certain refusal of love. It is true, of course, that more and more girls were being educated in the lycées, where they acquired more information and more encouragement to think for themselves than they would have had from most religious institutions, and as a result, they felt restricted in their traditional roles and began to question them.[21]

The novels of Gabrielle Reval and Colette Yver chart the struggle the new women teachers in lycées had in both their professional and personal lives as the state gradually took over much of the education of girls. The lycées had been established as a deliberate political campaign against the traditional conservatism and protectiveness of culture attributed to women, with the result that there was much bad feeling about their disruptive influence on community life and values in many parts of France. Women teachers were often trapped between abusively oppressive school inspectors who made their professional lives miserable and local people who refused even to lodge the "subverters of religion and the family." Under the constant scrutiny of everyone around them, the poor women lived as chastely as nuns while being blamed for all the evils of the age.

For the feminists, particularly the socialist feminists, marriage as currently practiced was the greatest evil. They attacked patriarchal attitudes, in the private and the public spheres, as abusive. Marriage was described as legalized prostitution: food and lodging in exchange for sexual and domestic service. As one of Colette Yver's characters remarked wryly, "Marriage is only good for men." Once this kind of economic analysis began to be made, however, and marriage to be seen as the commerce it was, the sacrosanct dichotomy between "ménagère et prostituée," homemaker and prostitute, could no longer be used to control and subdue women as before.

For the traditionalists the greatest evil was the spectre of free love. These people were certain that if women were educated they would be provided with information—facts and examples of a sort that would corrupt their weaker nature and lead them to practice all the ills they had learned about. Women fall inevitably into all temptation, so they must remain ignorant and dependent for the good of society. Men must harness women's desire.

As a result, perhaps, of the association of ideas between free love and the Fall on the one hand and between the Garden of Eden and a new society on the other an extraordinary number of books in this period have the name "Eve" in the title. One of them, *Eve victorieuse*, by Pierre de Coulevain,[22] is of interest here because of its ambiguities. The novel offers the example of a woman who withstands the ultimate temptation of love; she overcomes her suffering and remains a worthy wife who can ultimately feel at peace with herself and take pride in her strength and virtue. The example is curious, as the heroine of the novel is American and one of the aims of the book is to prove that Americans are less sensuous and less susceptible to love than women of the Latin races. Pierre de Coulevain sets Helen Ronald up to remain the incorruptible Eve, but scorns her slightly for being so. Not only does the novel give a double-edged description of the virtuous woman but it also carries a somewhat deprecatory view of modern, "new" women. Helen's niece Dora Carroll is the ultimate modern young woman—independent, outspoken, scandalous in her flirting—who gives up the New World for the old when she marries the son of an aristocratic Roman family. All the traditional values overcome Dora's autonomy: she becomes an obedient wife and loving mother of a son. She does remain outspoken, though, and given that she takes her husband to North America from time to time and makes one or two minor adjustments in the social behavior of the Roman nobility, we are perhaps to assume that she has not fallen totally into the traditional roles of European women.

Pierre de Coulevain does not seem sure of her views on the proper status of women. In contrast to her shifting attitudes are those of most of the novelists in this book. They stand firmly with the socialists and share their desire for reform. However, as is frequently the case, many socialists thought only in terms of the needs of men in society, whereas the feminists, male and female (there were a number of outspoken male feminists such as Léopold Lacour and Paul and Victor Margueritte at this time),[23] believed that a satisfactory future could be built only by a society in which women were free and equal citizens, in which "new" women and "new" men lived together in real love and mutual respect. As a result these novelists, many of whom were journalists and lecturers themselves, speak out to condemn the victimization of women. They chart the shifts and pitfalls as women seek autonomy inside and outside marriage, present the need for financial independence if women are to have true equality, and vindicate a woman's right to total control over her own body together with her right to love and affection.

The novels in this critical study have been selected to show as clearly as possible the position of women in 1900: the assumptions and social expectations; the values and customs that were being questioned; and the gradual move toward autonomy, both material and psychological. The organization of the study follows its own peculiar logic. In chapter 2 I examine three lesbian novels because the issues which will be seen to be very important in the subsequent heterosexual novels can be seen much more clearly when love is separated from men. In the lesbian novels the component parts of the relationship loosely called "love" become apparent in their specificity; emotional support and affection can be distinguished from sexual payment for material support, parenting and professional work become androgynous, and women are allowed their creative muse. A chapter on Marcelle Tinayre comes next because her work is structured around a refusal of the usual choices forced on women by love. Colette serves as a counterweight because Tinayre writes as a woman about women in their own terms, whereas Colette usually writes as a woman about women for men.

The opening chapters establish the relationship between love and choice; the subsequent chapters deal with the various effects of love. As maternity frequently predates marriage, and as it is the prime experience, it is discussed first. Parenthood leads to relations between son and mother, father and daughter, so the chapter on daughterhood comes next, followed by the chapter on professional women. The choice of a profession is a choice against marriage, so the chapter on marriage follows. The Colette chapter takes up the question of love as choice once again, but here sensuality is the focus. That sensuality prepares the way for the decadence in chapter 9 while, at the same time, the way in which the "perversions" are presented allows them to be interpreted as deliberate social criticism such as exists in the lesbian novels with which the study began.

All the novels discussed are interesting in terms of social history, and many of them hold their own as novels to this day. Certainly Tinayre, Yver, and Rachilde deserve to stand alongside Colette as representatives of a period when the whole perception of woman was changing and when many of the views we still hold today were being stated in French literature for the first time. The fact that must never be forgotten throughout the study is that whatever is or appears to be happening in each of the novels discussed, the heart of the matter is always love. Although this may seem to be a well-used cliché it is important to stress that French women have always been brought up to believe that love is the core of their existence. The novelists in this book had also been brought up in a society where adults of both sexes were always together. There is no tradition in France of men's clubs and women's societies, of couples who rarely meet because each is happily engaged in some single-sex occupation with friends who play as important a role in their lives as their spouse does. Concomitantly there is no place in French society for single women to live with dignity, autonomy, and a sense of themselves, so the issues of feminism and the position of women have to be considered within a context where men and obvious heterosexuality always prevail. A choice against men is a choice for solitude in a culture where lesbianism, if recognized at all, has been seen as harmless because it is perforce an apprenticeship into heterosexuality. Hence it is significant that in all the novels considered in this book, the wholehearted lesbians and the only woman who not only refuses to succumb to sensuality and passion, but also actually overcomes it happily, are all Americans. The concept of a woman living without a man is profoundly alien to French culture.

It is important to bear this in mind when studying French feminists of any period; it is particularly important as we consider those writing at the end of the nineteenth century.

In the novels examined in this book there is a constant refusal of roles that would be considered normal in this period, because these roles are normal only when seen from a male perspective. The first premise established by these works is the fundamental rejection by most men of any suggestion of women's equality. Time and time again we see that the normal state of affairs is that women should be there to satisfy male desires and masculine needs, but should make no demands that are not financial. A man is expected to pay for sexual and material services but not to understand or support, to commune or communicate with a woman, and certainly not to justify his actions or share responsibility with her. To take but three examples, Liane de Pougy makes this abundantly clear in *Idylle saphique* (The Sapphic Idyll), as do Jeanne Marni in *Pierre Tisserand* and *Souffrir* (Suffering), and indeed Colette in *La Vagabonde* (The Vagabond).[24]

Most men make selfish and self-protective decisions while women still tend to make selfless ones, or at least to make choices that are good for as many people as possible in the circumstances. (Harlor's *Tu es femme* [You Are a Woman] is an excellent example of such behavior.)[25] The men who make the effort to comprehend the values of their womenfolk and who painfully learn to respect these values in their daily life are few: Noël Delysle in *La Rebelle* (The Rebel), Henri Deborda in *L'Un vers l'autre* (One Toward the Other), and Stéphane Etcheverry in *Sibylle femme* (Sibylle as Woman.)[26] Even feminist writers, it seems, cannot suggest that such a phenomenon is anything but rare.

It is interesting to note in this context that the novelists most clearly identified with Nietzschean thought are the ones who create strong women, but instead of freeing them from the old practice of self-sacrifice, they endow them with a grandiose idea of martyrdom: the heroines in Camille Marbo's *Christine Rodis*, Daniel Lesueur's *La Nietzschéenne* (The Nietzschean Woman), and Valentine de Saint-Point's *Un Inceste* (An Incest)[27] change their own lives radically for the good of the man they love, be he husband, lover, or son.

Rachilde's *La Jongleuse* (The Juggler)[28] is a parody of such self-sacrifice, as indeed it is of a mother's need to get her daughter married at all costs, of the eternal mystery of woman, and of the nature of men's "love." By her nightmare explorations of the real structures that support the relations between men and women in society, Rachilde reveals a situation the nature of which is inescapable and unacceptable. She shows that women are taught to become beautiful dolls by means of whom men satisfy their lusts and fantasies, that all exchanges are sexual and commercial, that women are exploited, that society condones the abuse of women in power relationships called love and marriage.

A sacrifice made through love may be sublime, but a sacrifice demanded in the name of love is not on the same plane. Marcelle Tinayre struggles with the distinctions in *La Rebelle* as Josanne Valentin comes to terms with the inconsistency of her desire to serve and obey Noël Delysle through love and her long struggle against him to preserve the integrity of her sense of self in relation to her past. She concludes that as long as a man believes sincerely that his companion is his real equal as a human being, a woman can be submissive in the privacy of their intimate relations without their fundamental equality being threatened. Louise-Marie Compain arrives at the same conclusion from a different direction in *L'Un vers l'autre* (One Toward the Other): Laure leaves Henri when she realizes that he is using their lovemaking to force her submission in other realms; Henri realizes why Laure left him when he visits a prostitute and recognizes the distinction between a master-slave relation in love and the joy of free and mutual giving.

There is no need for a woman to have to choose between her independence and the expression of love unless her partner abuses the gift of self that she offers him. Colette Yver describes and analyzes examples of such abuse in *Les Cervelines* (Brainy Women), *Princesses de science* (Princesses of Science), and *Les Dames du palais* (Ladies of the Law Courts), then returns to the question many years later in an essay entitled *Dans le jardin du féminisme* (In the Garden of Feminism),[29] in which she tries hard to distinguish between needed reforms concerning the status and circumstances of women and unnecessarily excessive demands that destroy the possibility of loving relationships between men and women, to justify change and defend the sanctity of marriage, and, above all, not to sound like a feminist. The essay is a tour de force of accommodation and supports to a certain extent my belief that Yver is a closet feminist. I think she wanted to persuade her readers of the justice of women's demands for change without frightening them. Not all women could have a fascinating career, as did Marceline Rhonans in *Les Cervelines*, so most women would opt for marriage. Yver shows the best that a woman might expect in the social climate of the period and does not hesitate to depict the injustice of the situation.

In the Belle Epoque a woman had to choose between love and autonomy, and because few women had as fulfilling a life as Marceline, few would have made a choice such as hers. Yver uses the term "cerveline" to mean a heartless woman and is very careful to make a distinction between Jeanne Boerk, the doctor who is not interested in marriage at all, and Marceline Rhonans, who refuses a particular man for a specific reason. Yver does not condemn intelligence, competence, and independence in women; she describes a context in which such women are refused a natural life by the men around them, men who are ambitious, vain, and selfish. Marriage is shown to be a compromise at best; at worst, total tyranny.

The making of careful distinctions in their questioning of society is one of the interesting traits of these novelists. What is the reasoning of a society in which a good wife may be unacceptable to her neighbors because she is not legally married and an unmarried mother is anathema whatever her qualities as an individual, while a neglectful or vicious woman, properly wed, is considered a pillar of the community? Renée d'Ulmès and Louise-Marie Compain in particular treat the whole question of the status of women. They challenge the logic of a culture in which maternity is said to be of primary importance and yet there is persistently abusive treatment of all poor women with children, illegitimate children suffer lifelong discrimination, and in no way is it expected that a man whose pleasure provokes a pregnancy should take any further responsibility for either mother or child unless he happens to be both rich and married to the woman in question. Tinayre and Delarue-Mardrus discuss these issues, but only d'Ulmès offers a radical solution to them; in *Sibylle femme* and *Sibylle mère* (Sibylle as Mother) she creates a heroine who chooses to remain unmarried in order to try to give some dignity and self-respect to the unmarried mothers around her. Sibylle refuses to be a bourgeois wife and stands firmly by her principles.

Marriage on unacceptable terms, forced self-sacrifice, the obligation to choose between the people one loves, the passive acceptance of imposed views on social inequalities and injustices, and automatic and inevitable male dominance are all refused by "new" women.

What is particularly interesting about the group of novels discussed here is that they offer a fresh perspective on women's lives and aspirations. Marriage was still the future and aim of most women, and love was still the focus of women's lives, but by 1913 the possibilities open to them had multiplied and some of the worst abuses were being discussed. Because these novels present a variety of strong and enterprising women, from Berthe Robin, the snake charmer in *Pierre Tisserand*, to Mademoiselle Miracle, the Christian spinster, and Mademoiselle Bon, the universal feminist in *La Rebelle*, they give dignity and support to the single woman and validate a woman's right to choose a life for herself. Most of these women are presented with a certain humor, but none of them is undermined by mockery, and all of them command respect in unexpected ways. These novels are a testimony to the importance of women's integrity, women's power, and women's work within society, and an argument for women's rights and women's values. They include a multitude of unusual roles and many opinions that should be heard.

All traditional roles are shown from a woman's perspective. We are accustomed to marriage being presented as a curb to men's liberty, a restriction on their desires, an inconvenient weight on conscience and pocket; but male authors tend not to consider the possibility that their wives might share their attitude toward a mutual yoke. Here we have a generation of women writers criticizing the central tenets of both culture and society—love and marriage—and, as is the way with women, applying themselves to a search for solutions that will be good for everybody, rather than joining in a power struggle with men in order to displace them from the dominant and most comfortable position in private and public life. One cannot help but speculate that perhaps Gide's Marceline in *L'Immoraliste* and the pastor's wife in *La Symphonie pastorale* found their husbands to be every bit as much of a trial and impediment to their happiness as Michel and the pastor described their wives to be. And how different a novel would Proust's *Un Amour de Swann* have been if Swann had struggled, as Noël Delysle did, to overcome his jealousy instead of reveling in the exquisite pain he felt. The men write to maintain the status quo for others and allow every individual to avoid its discomforts for himself as he may. The women write in search of better relations between men and women in an improved world.

The First World War cut off all hope of the particular improved world imagined by the novelists of the Belle Epoque. Then, in devastated France after 1918, the male-dominated machine of critics, publishers, and literary histories gradually silenced all the interesting women writers except Colette. She survived because she wrote for men. All her heroines have affinities with the siren figure annihilated by Rachilde in *La Jongleuse.* Colette continually created versions of the eternal feminine victim, the only exception being Renée Néré of *La Vagabonde* (cf. chapter 8); not for her the emancipated and therefore emancipating "new" women of her feminist peers.

In sum, we may well smile when we hear Gilbert and Sullivan's Lord High Executioner sing:

> And that singular anomaly the lady novelist
> I don't think she'd be missed,
> I'm sure she'd not be missed

but our smile should be a wry and rueful one, because it does not seem that conditions for French women have improved very much since the first night of *The Mikado* in 1885. These forgotten writers bear witness to an age of concern for women, a period of feminist effort for social reform that had no parallel until very recently. In my view Gilbert was wrong, and the voices of the women novelists have been sorely missed indeed. As I shall endeavor to show, there is still a great deal we can learn from them today.

Men and the Issues

The lesbian is the antithesis of the figure of the bourgeois wife, who was the measure against which all women were judged at the beginning of the twentieth century. For contemporary male writers the lesbian was the symbol of the "new" woman. Considered half-man, half-woman and thought to love only a reflection of herself, she was the fashionable allegory of emancipated womanhood and of sexless and therefore purified love. This was, of course, true only in the realm of metaphor, where the lesbian was swiftly adopted into masculine symbolism and then became an androgynous figure, a sublimation of all that is sensitive and female in men. She was co-opted as being the least female of women, the one that was, therefore, the most acceptable for incorporation into a description of the male psyche. In reality, however, lesbians were shunned as unhealthy manifestations of antibourgeois decadence.

It is a fact that the very possibility of true female homosexuality is profoundly subversive in a society in which the lives of all women are controlled by male desires. Were she wife, courtesan, or prostitute in the nineteenth century, a woman's livelihood depended on the exchange of sexual services for emotional and physical protection. All other women also earned their living in some sort of material service to men, the only difference being that these jobs did not include "love." Thus women who were the objects of desire had a different range of professions from those who were not. Until the opening of the medical and teaching professions there was no concept of any occupation for women that did not concern men, and there was, of course, no such stated concept of love. In the rare references to lesbianism before this period, we find that it is classified as a prelude to heterosexuality, a harmless exercise in sensitivity and covert sensuality in which women might indulge while waiting to find the right husbands.

At the turn of the century, groups of young women in Paris gathered around Natalie Barney and around Gertrude Stein.[1] Rich and foreign, these two were free to break social taboos and to create centers for those French women who had tastes similar to their own. Many of these women were writers, and three novels were written specifically about love affairs with Natalie Barney herself: *Idylle saphique* (Sapphic Idyll) by Liane de Pougy; *Une Femme m'apparut* (A Woman Appeared to Me) by Renée Vivien; *L'Ange et les pervers* (The Angel and the Perverts) by Lucie Delarue-Mardrus.[2] I am putting a discussion of these novels at the beginning of this study of the period; not only are they the ultimate examples of love as a lifestyle, but also excellent examples of subversive texts, novels in which the major preoccupations of the period can be seen very clearly because of the distinctions drawn between the relationships possible between men and women on the one hand and, on the other, women's attitudes toward love, motherhood, and work. Such a separation is almost impossible to make in the usual heterosexual circumstances, and the resulting confusions go a long way toward maintaining women's continued state of inequality and continued loss of power.

Idylle saphique is a curious book, based as it is on the values of Liane de Pougy's own life as one of the great courtesans of the Belle Epoque.[3] It tells a story similar to that of a number of famous French novels, such as *Adolphe* by Benjamin Constant, *Dominique* by Eugène Fromentin, Gide's *La Porte étroite*, and Radiguet's *Le Diable au corps*, where in each case a young man falls in love with an older woman who subsequently dies—the difference being that here the love is between women. A text in which every chapter contains an explicit scene of sensuous pleasure of one kind or another, de Pougy's novel is nonetheless, by its own standards, a very proper book. This odd combination of immorality of context and morality of precept produces a novel which is revelatory and critical of the relationships between men and women that are found in more usual circumstances without challenging any of the hierarchical structures of class, money, and sexual commerce accepted at the turn of the century. De Pougy has no awareness of any abuse of women in general, no social conscience. *Idylle saphique* is a blatantly autobiographical

novel whose interest lies in the acute sensitivity attributed to the narrator. From this comes a perspicacity of analysis born of the not-unusual
mixture of profound narcissism, frustrated desire, and irritated conscience. Indeed the more famous male-centered novels referred to above
have much the same tone. What is unusual is first to find this combination in a woman and then to find it directed toward another woman. The
result throws light on social interactions from a peculiar and revelatory
angle, especially when we consider that Annhine de Lys, de Pougy's protagonist, lives a life similar to that of Odette de Crécy in Proust's *Un
Amour de Swann*.

Annhine de Lys has a permanent lover, Henri, who pays her bills and
generally plays the discreet "husband." The stability he provides is complemented by passionate encounters with her current "sin"—some
young man she finds attractive—and by occasional men she picks up for
an evening's entertainment. Her friend, Altesse, has a similar lifestyle,
though she is older, more businesslike, and less sensitive than Annhine.
Ernesta is the faithful maid. Into this household comes Florence (Flossie) Temple-Bradfford, a rich young American who throws herself at
Annhine's feet, declares her love, and begs to be allowed to serve as
Annhine's page. Annhine accepts Flossie's presence, and becomes fond
of her but will not make love with her, and the resultant nervous tension
between refusal and desire kills Annhine (as it killed Alyssa in *La Porte
étroite*). Twice Annhine agrees to let Flossie make love to her. The first
time, having reached a pitch of acute desire, they are about to dash off
together when the woman Flossie left for Annhine stabs herself before
their eyes. Annhine collapses and is thereafter taken away from Paris by
Altesse and Henri. The second time they get as far as the bedroom, but
Annhine cannot bring herself to go through with it, much as she now
loves and wants Flossie.

Annhine is inhibited for two paradoxically opposed reasons: (1) that lesbian love is a vice; (2) because of her commerce with men her body is
unclean and not worthy of Flossie. In a bourgeois novel the husband
might well take mistresses but would not go to a prostitute because of
the danger of moral and physical contagion; Annhine's code is parallel.
Sexual commerce with men is normal and right—moral, one might say—
but similar relations with women are dangerous to one's health, vicious,
and addictive. Altesse talks about lesbian lovemaking in the same terms
as those used to discuss masturbation in other books of the period: those

who practice such a vice get old before their time, risk being paralyzed, losing their hair, going mad. Annhine is therefore afraid of succumbing to Flossie's "perverse embraces" even while finding her friend ever more enticing and desirable.

The ambiguous treatment of the subject lies in the contrast between the tone of the descriptions of intimate moments between Annhine and Flossie and the judgmental vocabulary used at other times. As this novel is autobiographical, it would seem that de Pougy's own memories and reticences have marked her style very clearly. The sensuous nature of the physical intimacy between Annhine and Flossie is immediately established and shown to be a source of pleasure to both of them. Flossie helps Annhine to dress, shares her bath, kisses and caresses her at all times. Such behavior is quite acceptable to Annhine as long as the sensuality of the embrace remains polymorphous, because if the contact is not genital she can deny its sexual nature and remain free of vice.

Whenever there is any discussion of lesbianism it is referred to as perversion—even by Flossie, who is trying to convince Annhine of its charms. It appears that de Pougy enjoyed her escapade with Natalie Barney to the full, but in retrospect she either does not think she should have or, being prudent, does not think that her friends and admirers will approve of the episode. The result is a rather eighteenth-century mixture of licentiousness and prudery which manages to be suggestive and proper at the same time—the story of a courtesan who has her moral standards.

The novel is neatly constructed, plausible, and well written. It does not suffer from the excesses of self-indulgence that spoil de Pougy's other novels, and it does give some insight into the period—the quantities of jewels that pass through Annhine de Lys's hands, for example, are quite breathtaking—although, that is not, of course, where its main interest lies. It is certainly curious to see the real relationships between the various characters when all the circumstantial details and decorations have been stripped away.

Annhine is surrounded by five men and three women—four, if we count Jane d'Espant, the woman who kills herself at the ball. Henri, the man who keeps her and claims to love her, is thoughtful and generous. He seems to provide support and stability until she is pregnant, but all he wants then is that she should have an abortion. Willy, Florence's finacé, is also supposed to be kind, selfless, and loving, prepared to accept Flossie's lovers as long as she will marry him. When he thinks Florence is getting too involved with Annhine, he arranges in secret, through a procuress, to pay Annhine a fabulous sum of money if she will meet him in a brothel. For her it is business, and she does not know who the foreigner is who wants to see her so desperately. When she arrives he makes her undress and then drags Florence into the room in an attempt to expose Annhine as a courtesan. He buys her in order to humiliate her. Luis, the Spaniard she invites to her room one day, uses her and leaves money. Max, the doctor with whom she falls in love and who is supposed to be passionately in love with her, merely sends a laconic note and a brooch when she leaves him. Maurice, the young lover who is desperate when sent away by his family, never contacts her after his farewell note. All the men desire her, use her body, and claim to love her, yet they provide nothing but money and occasional pleasure. They offer no emotional support, no understanding of her needs or desires. The relationships, however romantic they may appear to be at first, are all crass and commercial. The men hold the economic power and therefore believe they have the right to use the woman and dominate her life. She is a commodity for them all.

The women are quite different. They all provide support. Altesse is a true friend. She provides advice when necessary; she gives up her time to take care of Annhine, takes her away when she is ill even though Altesse loses the man she loves—he marries while she is away. Altesse is a tower of strength and common sense. She cheers Annhine up when the latter is depressed—in fact, the only real fun in the novel is had by these two when they dress up as working girls and go to Montmartre for an evening. Altesse provides moral support; Ernesta provides physical support, looking after Annhine's daily needs cheerfully and without question. Ernesta is faithful to Annhine, Altesse is fond of her, and Florence loves her. It is clear that the love that Flossie feels is every bit as violent as the men's passion, but it is not expressed in the same way. Flossie restrains her desire when Annhine refuses her demands, and instead gives comfort, affection, and pleasure.

The parallels in the structure of the novel make the comparisons quite evident. Henri refuses to buy some jewelry, which Flossie gives to Annhine instead. Henri wants nothing to do with Annhine's pregnancy, as a baby costs too much; yet when Ahhnine is ill Flossie is prepared to marry Willy to get the money to look after her. Henri cannot leave his affairs to take Annhine away from Paris for long enough for her to get well, but Altesse does, though she loses love and livelihood in the process. The parallel between Flossie and Maurice is developed at greater length: both are very young, and Flossie had first appeared dressed as a page boy; both have to escape from their families; both meet Annhine in the theater and in the Bois de Boulogne; both are allowed into her bed; yet Maurice, who is responsible for the apparent pregnancy, leaves her without a word, whereas Flossie loves Annhine devotedly throughout their long separations and endures her bitter frustrations without complaint.

Whether or not de Pougy intended it to be so, the message transmitted by *Idylle saphique* is that men cause women pain because they are crass and undependable. Any dealings with them should be very well paid in consequence—and as Henri is spoken of as Annhine's "husband," this is a message for wives as well as mistresses. For real affection and support women must turn to each other. Annhine died not from the vice of lesbianism, frustrated or otherwise, but from being taught that she was wrong to love Flossie, such an autonomous relationship being forbidden by society because it interferes with the fulfillment of men's desire. Annhine can have Altesse as a friend because Altesse is a professional: to her the job comes first, so men come first, and her care of Annhine is in men's interests. She does not recognize Annhine's desire for Flossie (even when in a nervous crisis Annhine clutches Altesse's hand to her breast and falls down in a fit), but assumes that Annhine is better when she is attracted by Luis and goes out to find him. Altesse is the woman who plays by the rules, who keeps society stable. She is who separates Annhine from Flossie the first time, who destroys Flossie's letters. She means well, but is in great measure responsible for curtailing Annhine's freedom and therefore helps to cause her death. On the other hand, the doctor also declared that her lesbianism would kill Annhine and that she must be separated from Flossie at all costs.

Here again the text presents us with a paradoxical truth. Women can get real support only from other women, yet all women are dangerous. Living within a male-dominated system, they must perforce either support it or struggle against it, neither of which provides the opportunity for a satisfactory life. There are those strong, dependable women who do not question the social system, who are survivors and do not see themselves as victims because they are being well rewarded in some way, who work to maintain the status quo and keep other women within it. They are rigid and stifling. There are others who subvert the rules of society by insisting upon their own autonomy and who tempt other women to join them. Because of the difficulties they and those with them must face in a male-centered society, they are dangerous too.

Who killed Annhine de Lys? Henri, Luis, Max, and Maurice? Was she exhausted by her life as a courtesan, and did she die in the service of men? ("Pas de saletés . . . oh! non! je ne veux pas! j'en ai assez . . . 'en meurs . . . j'en vis aussi, hélas!" [p. 43] "No nasty tricks . . . oh! no! I don't want to! I've had enough . . . I'm dying from it . . . I make my living from it too, alas!"). Altesse? Did she die of her frustrations when faced with a social taboo? Flossie? Did she die of fear and desire of another kind of life?

If we accept the surface of the novel, Annhine died a martyr to her virtue. If we look at the underlying structures, we see that she is caught in a network of financial and sexual exchange from which she cannot escape as long as she has to earn a living. Most women are in a similar situation; even Flossie is not rich enough to offer her a home without having Willy there to pay for it.

The various attitudes toward love underlying the commerce are obvious also. The men pay to satisfy their desire for a woman, or they accept the financial contract their family makes with another family, as in the case of Raoul, Altesse's lover, who is obliged to marry a girl from a list of appropriate candidates. There are different attitudes among the women. For Altesse, love is her business, and that is how she maintains a luxurious lifestyle. She does her job well and keeps all sentiment aside. For Flossie and for Jane, love is an all-absorbing, total passion. Jane kills herself from unrequited love, whereas Flossie lives her life to the fullest as a matter of sentiment and pleasure whenever possible, or of selflessness, devotion, and restraint. Either way it is life itself and yet has no connection with the business of living; for that Flossie is prepared to take a rich husband as long as he allows her the freedom to love elsewhere. Annhine is caught between the positions of the other two. She works as a professional lover but is not satisfied with that, as Altesse is. She yearns to be in love with Henri; wants tenderness, affection, and thoughtfulness from her men; and suffers from the lack of it. She likes the comforts provided by love as a profession but wants the emotion of all-absorbing love, and she dies of the tension between them.

These issues are not particular to this novel, although they are easier to see and analyze here because the problems caused by love are isolated so that the commercial nature of the usual relationship between men and women is not hidden or confused, as usually is the case. Rachilde is one of the rare authors who also shows the economic values underlying most "love" relationships (cf. chapter 9). Love is a lifestyle for all the women in de Pougy's novel. It can be a business arrangement or a total obsession. The difficulty arises in trying to combine the two attitudes, and yet that is exactly what most women in novels of the period expect to be able to do in marriage. No wonder they suffer.

In terms of its date of publication *L'Ange et les pervers* by Lucie Delarue-Mardrus has no place in this chapter because it did not appear until 1930. I have included it nonetheless for several compelling reasons: (1) it is also an autobiographical novel based on a love affair between the author and Natalie Barney which took place before 1914; (2) Delarue-Mardrus is a notable author in the period under study, and the novel presents a number of her major preoccupations very clearly,[4] (3) it is interesting for the way Delarue-Mardrus presents her protagonist and thus throws light on problems pertaining to motherhood and to work. The protagonist is an androgynous figure who lives a double life as Marion de Valdeclare, an apparently eternally adolescent male who earns a living publishing, and Marion Hervin, a woman who is about thirty at the time of the novel and who is not known to work (p. 32).

The question of androgyny haunted many male writers around 1900, those who were in the modernist movement in particular, but here there is no question of the bisexual (therefore sexless) woman being the feminizing spirit of male culture. The question is dealt with on a practical plane. Marion de Valdeclare is a hermaphrodite brought up as a boy until the death of his parents and legally transformed into a girl by his guardians when he leaves school. How is s/he to live? He earns his living as a ghost writer of plays and has a social life among people in art and literature. She is a friend of Laurette Wells, who is fond of her, accepts her periodic disappearances, and above all respects her strangeness and her privacy. Marion de Valdeclare is adored by a young man; Laurette and her ex-lover, Aimée de Langres, find Marion Hervin attractive. S/he tells Laurette that s/he has never felt desire for anyone, that s/he is one of the "oeufs clairs" of the world—unfertilized eggs which will never produce anything (p. 29). S/he suffers from intense solitude and wants desperately to be normal. To this end s/he is very much tempted by the idea of becoming a monk, but instead adopts the illegitimate son of Aimée de Langres. She is a working mother untouched by the exigencies of male sexual demands.

The surface structures of the work provide a series of oppositions between male and female, dream and reality, the church and motherhood, aestheticism and charity (in the theological sense of *caritas*). On the one hand lies a secure, self-contained sterility which offers a certain stark beauty and certain spiritual satisfaction for those who have faith; on the other are the need for love and motherhood, totally divorced in this case from any concept of nature and fertility, and therefore of biological fate. Hence Delarue-Mardrus removes her protagonist from the context, usual at the time of her love for Natalie Barney and still prevalent in the 1930s, that whether the reason be love or fear, "real" women are totally occupied by the attentions demanded of them by their lovers/husbands. She suggests further that the result is that they are not good mothers, whereas the androgyne can be the total parent.

Why the androgynous figure? Perhaps self-parody on the part of Delarue-Mardrus, who did not succumb to Natalie Barney or have a child by her husband, Dr. Mardrus (so as not to mar her smooth body, it is claimed), but also, it seems to me, because Marion provides a symbolic description of the "new woman." S/he says: "J'ai eu la chance dans mon malheur de naître à l'époque de la confusion des sexes" (p. 63: "In my misfortune, I was fortunate enough to be born in the era when the sexes are confused"). Marion Hervin was thus able to study law in her youth and intends (at the end of the novel) to continue with the contract writing she had done as Marion de Valdeclare—all she had to do was to avoid meeting her clients. This gives us an insight into the work world. Men work, so in that context Marion had to be perceived to be a masculine figure, albeit a sexless, beardless one. An incomplete man passes more easily than a woman, hence the job as a ghost writer: Marion can work as long as s/he remains invisible.

In the Belle Epoque the working woman is autonomous, but she must remain free of the snares of love and will suffer somewhat from her solitude. In this case Marion has a young man at her feet, but this is because he needs her assistance for his career and so adores her from a distance. We see that older and more suitable men find her strange, as do society women. Like Delarue-Mardrus, Marion de Valdeclare is a curiosity on the social scene. Again, when we analyze the relationships in the novel we see that her only real friend is a woman who is interested in women. Laurette accepts her as she is and asks no questions. She shows affection and support, and calls on Marion in her turn when she needs her.

This novel is not in itself important, but it makes an interesting and very important symbolic statement. The modern working woman before 1914 may be regarded as unnatural by the people around her, but working does not make her unfit for her natural and traditional role, which, indeed, she fulfills better than do "normal" "feminine" women. Delarue-Mardrus's comment is useful to help us set in perspective the conflicts among marriage, motherhood, and a profession, which are central concerns for women in the early years of the twentieth century, although her novel appears far too late to be of use to the early feminist analysis of the situation.

Renée Vivien's novel *Une Femme m'apparut* is also an autobiographical work in which all the characters can be named and in which Natalie Barney plays a key role. This time, however, she is neither the ardent lover nor the faithful friend but, rather, the narrator's destiny. The realities of the relationship between Vivien and Barney have been transformed into a meditation on the nature of love at one level and an allegory describing Vivien's apprenticeship into poetry on another.[5]

There is no hint of the material or of the corporeal world in this text. Because both muse and love are female figures in a female world, the narrator's search for love and her desire to become a poet are transformed also into a search for self—for love of self and for self as another whom one can love. Thus in a curious way this long, allegorical prose poem full of art nouveau decoration, irises, lilies, and violets is one of the first French female *Bildungsromanen* to be written, for it is a recounting of how one must suffer, be consumed, and then be reborn into a higher plane, which is that of art, in order to survive. The narrator is following her destiny and discovering her metaphysics of existence, the first step of which is to abandon hope—hope that she will ever gain the love of the beloved. Yet the beloved remains her soul sister, the only one who understands both what she is and what she is seeking.

Vivien has taken the standard male concepts of woman as muse, of woman as body, of woman as death, and of woman as impossible love, and has transformed them into concepts in a women's world. In this world physical love is shown to be unsatisfactory and true love unattainable. Lorély is transformed into both impossible love and muse, the perverse archangel against whom is Eva, the archangel of redemption, the narrator's other muse. Death comes in the form of a friend, Ione, who leaves the narrator to suffer and find herself rather than be destroyed. In this text Vivien has not only defined a female psychology of love, but she also has claimed for women the right to a spiritual quest, to a muse, and to a poetics of their own. Her own feeling for Barney has been transformed into a study of the apprenticeship of a female poet.

The three novels show that the lesbian is indeed one clear example of the "new woman" of the twentieth century, though perhaps she is not exactly what the male writers of the time had in mind when they used the figure of the androgyne to symbolize the female in themselves. Certainly it is in women's conception and depiction of women and their environment that the real obstacles to women's autonomy can be seen without ambiguity. The central issue is love, be it on the material or on the metaphysical plane: women want partners who will show affection, tenderness, thoughtfulness, even desire, but emotional closeness is more important than the sexual expression of physical proximity. Relationships with men are power relationships in which the women are bought and dominated. They do not seem to provide emotional support, though they sometimes offer pleasure and a measure of security. The demands of men create further complications at this time, as our analysis shows that a relationship with a man and love for a child are not compatible; a woman must choose to be lover/wife or mother.

Most women must also earn their living, and this has to be done through men or as men. Either way, there has to be an identification with the values of male-dominated society, and this necessarily brings a loss of individuality and of sense of self. Yet a woman who is not economically independent has no real power in either the private or public sphere. She cannot make for herself the choices on which her life is based and so has no status as an adult human being.

The way to the discovery and expression of self is long and hard. Annhine de Lys dies of the tensions created between what she does and what she would like to be, between financial and emotional self-sufficiency, work and love. Marion de Valdeclare/Hervin goes through a parallel struggle expressed in different terms—monastic solitude or maternity—as does the narrator of *Une Femme m'apparut*, though her struggle is between ordinary joys and those that are produced by the sufferings of the creative artist. Each in her way is searching for self-expression, the right to material autonomy and to emotional satisfactions defined and chosen by and for herself. The way to fulfilling these perfectly reasonable needs is difficult enough even for the heroines who are surrounded by overtly loving and supportive women. Let us see how the issues recur in the most usual context, that of heterosexual society, and how other women writers perceive them.

Love and the Choices 3
MARCELLE TINAYRE

Marcelle Tinayre, journalist and *femme de lettres*,[1] is the writer of the period who has most comprehensively explored and understood love as a phenomenon. She makes it clear that until the status of women changes radically so that women have economic independence and the right to make for themselves the choices that shape their lives, they are trapped. Love is the only emotion the culture allows them to show; marriage is their only recognized goal. Love is therefore the major preoccupation for women and the pivot of male-female relations. It is the key to the structures of personal power and hence to the interrelation of the private and public spheres, the politics of domination and strategies of equality.

What, then, is love? How is it defined at the turn of the century, at a time when social values are shifting and opportunities for women are changing somewhat? For the most part, in novels of this period "love" is the word used whenever a woman states feeling for her husband, whatever that feeling may be: passion, affection, indifference, dislike, or hatred. The word itself is therefore totally useless as anything but the marker of a relationship, yet the concept of love is the essential factor that underlies the thought and behavior of women of all classes. Most women need to be married to survive economically; most women make the decision to marry or not in terms of a choice for or against "love," even though for most of them the decision is an economic one only. Language is a cover; commerce is presented in terms of emotion.

Tinayre offers a variety of perspectives on love and marriage. In her various novels she strips off many of the ambiguities that hide the realities of the social context of women's lives and the nature of the choices women must make within that context. In her work there are three loves that come under consideration: marital love, desire, and maternal love. They are very different in kind. We are still at a time when marriage is the major career for women of all classes and the choice of marriage partner is essentially a commercial transaction upon the success of which the livelihood of the woman depends. Once the marriage is settled, a woman has a certain number of duties to fulfill within the explicit and implicit terms of the contract she has accepted. She must be a fastidious housekeeper; must dress as well as possible within the limits of a prudent budget; must provide teas, dinners, and balls with a regularity that will be calculated upon her husband's real or potential status, festive meals in working-class households filling the same role within the contract as social functions do for the bourgeoisie; and must bear children. Only if the husband fulfills his part of the contract will she be expected to remain faithful to him; otherwise, as long as she is discreet, she will be forgiven for seeking comfort elsewhere. Affection and desire are not necessarily part of the arrangement. La Tourette, in *La Rebelle*[2] (The Rebel), describes a good working-class husband as one who does not get very drunk, brings most of his pay home, is kind to his wife, and beats her only if she fails to fulfill her duties. Tinayre describes her own concept of a good bourgeois man in *Madeleine au miroir* (Madeleine at Her Mirror), a book of reminiscences in which she writes:

> Mes parents m'ont tendrement élevée; j'ai fait un mariage raisonnable, un vrai mariage à la française, que tout le monde appela "un mariage d'inclination." Mon mari que j'ai perdu il y a six ans, fut un compagnon brusque, autoritaire et affectueux, assez jaloux de ses droits et très convaincu de ses devoirs. Il me fit pleurer quelquefois, mais il employa son énergie et son intelligence pour les seuls intérêts de la famille. Loin de me traiter en maîtresse ou en servante de son bon plaisir, il m'initia à ses affaires, il m'associa à ses projets, il me mit en contact avec toutes les réalités que certaines pécores veulent ignorer—par élégance!

> [I was lovingly brought up by my parents; I made a sensible marriage, a real "French" marriage that everyone called "a love match." My husband, whom I lost six years ago, was a blunt, authoritative and affectionate companion, jealous of his rights and very sure of where his duties lay. He sometimes made me cry, but he used his energy and his intelligence solely in the family interests. Far from treating me as a mistress or a servant for his own convenience, he acquainted me with his business, included me in his

plans, put me in touch with all the realities that certain stupidly preten-
tious women refuse to recognize—thinking it elegant to do so!]

She concludes:

> Je fus sans amour, une amie dévouée; notre amitié conjugale me donna le
> courage de résister et de vaincre quand vint l'heure de la tentation
> inévitable—car je fus tentée, moi aussi. Si je ne l'avais jamais été pourrais-
> je me dire vertueuse et saurais-je excuser mes soeurs plus faibles que moi?
> (p. 4)[3]

> [Without loving him I was his devoted friend; our marital friendship gave
> me the courage to resist and overcome when the moment of inevitable
> temptation came—for I too was tempted. If I had not been, would I have
> been able to call myself virtuous and would I have known how to excuse
> my weaker sisters?]

A woman who marries young in this period is lucky to find this "amitié
conjugale." Once she does life remains stable until or unless the woman
meets someone with whom she falls in love. At that point, she must
make the serious choices that will determine her life. Passion is a hazard,
an irresistible, overwhelming force which upsets the stability of a well-
organized society. It can be an even greater trap for women than marriage
is, or it can be a liberation.

Tinayre's major works provide a dispassionate analysis of the situation
as it exists for most women, and illustrate various possible pitfalls and
successful decisions. Here they are in chronological order. Her first novel,
Avant l'amour (Before Love),[4] explores the way in which young girls are
given a romantic idea of love and how they become disillusioned. *La
Rançon* (The Ransom)[5] is the story of a serious, moral man and a good
woman who fall in love. The woman is married, the man is the husband's
friend, and their love is presented as profound and overwhelming. The
novel charts the growth and realization of love, their struggles, brief liaison, and scruples, and withdrawal from the expression of passion back
into deep friendship. The psychology of a banal but frequent happening
is treated in all its social complexity. *Hellé*[6] offers Tinayre's ideals of
woman and marriage. *La Maison du péché* (The House of Sin),[7] the most
admired of Tinayre's novels at the time, is the story of a young man who
has been brought up as a Jansenist by a mother who wanted to be a nun.
He falls in love with a sensible, wholesome woman artist; first he wants
to save her soul, then feels passion and finally guilt. His family wants to

separate him from her; he allows it to do so and dies of his emotional struggle. The real theme of this novel is not, as was thought in 1902, the beauty and purity of Jansenist celibacy, but rather the all-pervading misogyny of the Catholic church and the power of the life-destroying force the Christian religion represents. *La Rebelle* (The Rebel) deals with the double standard that men and women are taught to accept in matters of love and marriage, and depicts a couple's struggle to achieve equality in their relationship. Finally *L'Ombre de l'amour* (The Shadow of Love)[8] develops a neat parallel between two kinds of pity that are mistaken for love. Denise Cayrol, daughter of a free-thinking doctor, has been brought up with no false modesties, no pruderies, to understand the importance of healthy parents for the procreation of children. Nonetheless, aged twenty-seven, she cares for a young man who is brought into the household in an advanced state of tuberculosis. Gradually she comes to think she loves him and gives herself to him just before he dies. Denise's seamstress, Fortunade, is the innkeeper's daughter who desperately wants to be a nun, but everyone tells her she is a dreamer and just needs to marry a good man to be set to rights. She starts looking after the local poacher because she feels sorry for him and wants to save his soul. Ultimately she commits suicide and is found to have been pregnant. Unhealthy soul or unhealthy body, women are tempted by weakness and the result is disaster.

The messages that emerge from the structure, tone, and symbolism of Tinayre's novels are very clear. Hellé's marriage is best; Josanne Valentin's relationship with Noël Delysle *(La Rebelle)* improves with effort; both women find their way in the teeth of society and the church, and succeed only because they are strong and thoughtful. A critical reading of any of the works shows that for Tinayre, there is no question but that women have the right to autonomy, equality, and love, no matter what social obstacles might be in their way.

Let us look more closely at *Avant l'amour, Hellé,* and *La Rebelle* to see the development of the case Tinayre is making for a pragmatic, practical feminism, and the analysis she is offering of the kind of choices women should be making for themselves.

Avant l'amour is the story of an orphan, Marianne, who is brought up by her godfather and his wife. She falls in love with a musician and, as a result, learns that she is poor, illegitimate, and therefore unmarriageable. She also learns that a woman cannot reveal her feelings to a man and be considered virtuous. Maxime Gannerault, her godfather's son, falls in love with her; however, he is tied to a mistress who has lent him money, and Marianne is still in love with the composer. Things do not run smoothly: Maxime seems to be the ideal of the handsome young man who loves his orphan "little sister," but his image degenerates progressively throughout the novel. Marianne has no respect for him because of his lack of moral standards, whereas Maxime declares that Marianne is no better than he is because on several occasions she comes very close to losing her virtue. A man slips in business; a woman slips in love. The result is a relationship between them that is by far inferior to the one Marianne imagined when she met the composer. She has abandoned her ideals and will live a life of shoddy compromise.

We see from an analysis of Tinayre's novel that compromise is unsatisfactory to Marianne because she was taught to seek an unrealistic goal, an ideal and romanticized love relationship. She learned to scorn the standard commercial transactions of the marriage market, but was not provided with any capacity for judgment which would permit her to select a partner who might be worthy of her ideal, nor indeed with any moral sense and fortitude to make her worthy of it herself. She was brought up instead to desire love. This is made very clear in the early scenes of First Communion, where the emotional relationship of the little girls to God represents the first stage of their dreams of human union. It is an unrealistic and idealized relationship. Marianne may well wait for her dream husband, but without a dowry, she will certainly have no choice but to take a *"pauvre diable"* (poor wretch) as husband because, given the class structure of society, the proud and poor intelligent men who would interest her do not mix in her circles; the company there bores them. As a poor woman she has no status and few possibilities for the future. Her only hope would be to use her youth and charm, the only power she has to get a rich husband; but the idealized view of marriage she has been brought up on precludes such an action totally. As she becomes disillusioned, realizing how empty are the declarations of love her musician made to her, she becomes cynical, recognizing the hopelessness of her position. She is trapped by social requirements that she appear virtuous:

> Et depuis mon enfance, on m'a tenue agenouillée devant le dieu. . . . Il faut être considérée. Il faut être estimée. Il faut accepter les usages, les tra-

ditions, les moeurs—ou se déclasser, mal tourner, comme dit ma
marraine. . . . Va! ma fille, demeure la demoiselle "comme il faut." Etouffe
les révoltes de ton coeur et de la chair mais garde ta situation sociale. Le
monde te verra vieillir, vierge et morose; il ridiculisera le célibat que tu
auras supporté par pusillanimité, par lâcheté d'âme, par stérile et vaine
vertu.
   "Non! Cela ne sera pas!" crièrent des voix dans mon âme. (p. 40)[9]

[Ever since my childhood, I have been kept kneeling before the god. . . .
You must be respected. You must be thought highly of. You must accept
the practices, traditions, customs—or come down in the world, go to the
bad as my godmother says. . . . Come along, my girl, remain the "proper"
young lady that you are. Stifle the revolt in your heart and your flesh but
keep your social position. The world will watch you grow old, a gloomy
virgin; it will ridicule the celibacy you have endured through faint-
heartedness, through spiritual cowardice, through sterile, vain virtue.
   "No! That will not be!" exclaim the voices of my soul.]

Her desire for love makes her recognize the hollowness of the appearance
of love for what it is. Having no inner strength to fall back on, however,
her only response is fear of solitude, fear of an empty future—hence the
ease with which she succumbs to the appearance of love when Maxime
kisses and caresses her. The illusion of love and the physical reality of
desire overcome the scruples she has about the man himself in the clear
light of day. We see clearly that without any education, any moral support, or any real alternative to marriage, a woman has no hope of with-
standing the assault of her senses and her own fears. She accepts the
attentions of any man who seems to offer love, and she is forever
unsatisfied. By this upbringing, bourgeois women are set up to be victims:
victims of social pressure, of the weakness inculcated into them by their
situation, and ultimately of male desire and dominance.

   Tinayre lays bare the abuse inherent in the ideal fostered in young girls
and the insufficiencies of their moral judgment. She proposes one answer
to this unhappy situation in *Hellé*. In this novel the heroine is educated
to have good judgment, a sense of her own worth, and mental and emotional resources within herself on which to fall back. Also, Tinayre has
the male authority figure state without equivocation that it is better not
to marry than to make an unsatisfactory and inferior arrangement. Hellé
is therefore provided with the possibilities of making a good marriage and
of not making one at all, although she is not offered economically realistic alternatives to marriage. Tinayre is dealing with the major issues of

the period one at a time. Hellé's uncle has an ideal view of marriage (rather than an idealized one), and his statement offers a radical shift in the advice usually given to a young woman:

> Je ne prétends pas que tu fasses un sacrifice, reprit mon oncle. Je souhaite, au contraire, que tu accomplisses ta destinée. Toutes les femmes ne sont point nées pour les soins du ménage. De même qu'il y a des hommes de génie, il y a des femmes élues par la nature pour s'apparier à eux. Rarement ils se rencontrent: ils s'attendent, s'espèrent, se cherchent toujours, et, de déception en déception, ils traînent jusqu'à la mort leur désir et leur nostalgie. Mais quelquefois, passant l'un près de l'autre, ils se devinent, ils se reconnaissent, amants prédestinés; ils s'unissent, et la beauté de leur amour demeure comme un exemple aux hommes. Crois-moi, Hellé, un mariage vulgaire, pourvu qu'il réunisse ce que le monde appelle des conditions de bonheur,—c'est-à-dire la fortune, la beauté, les titres,—pourra t'offrir quelque appât: garde-toi de te prendre à ce piège. Ce serait trahir à l'avance ton légitime possesseur. Le jour où tu seras en sa présence, tu sentiras une force irrésistible te pousser vers lui. Rappelle-toi mes paroles, petite fille, tu n'arriveras à l'amour que par l'admiration. (p. 27)[10]

> ["I don't require you to make a sacrifice," my uncle continued. "On the contrary, I hope that you fulfil your destiny. Not every woman is born to look after a household. Just as there are men of genius, there are women chosen by nature to match them. Rarely do they meet: they wait, hope search for each other, and, from disappointment to disappointment drag their desire and longing after them till death. But sometimes, passing close to each other, they sense, recognize each other as their predestined love; they unite and the beauty of their love endures as an example for humanity. Believe me, Hellé, an ordinary marriage, provided that it combines what the world calls "conditions for happiness"—that is, wealth, beauty, titles—could be somewhat tempting for you: take care not to get caught in that trap. That would be a future betrayal of your true possessor. The day you are in his presence, you will feel an irresistible force pushing you toward him. Mark my words, little girl, you will arrive at love only through admiration.]

Tinayre changes all the lines of power in male-female relations by the fact that Hellé has been educated to be a superior being, "la récompense des héros" (p. 26: "a hero's reward") and has been taught not to undervalue herself. She is the pure example of Tinayre's dream: an active, autonomous woman who finds her equal and joins her life to his so that they can work together for a better future. It is true that her uncle states that she should find her "legitimate owner"; however, we see that this idea may fit his concept of marriage but is certainly not an accurate description of Hellé's attitude to either of the men she considers marrying. *Hellé* is a feminist and socialist utopia in many ways; in it Tinayre sets a standard against which all her other novels should be measured if they are to be fully understood. It puts into perspective the false kind of ideal love Marianne dreamed of, the various romanticized versions that we find in the secondary works: *La Vie amoureuse de François Barbazanges* (The Love Life of François Barbazanges, 1904), and *La Douceur de vivre* (The Good Life, 1911) in particular, and the stories of male vanity in love in *L'Oiseau d'orage* (The Storm Bird, 1900).[11] All these slight texts take on more weight and interest as examples of the insufficiencies that can occur in relationships between men and women, and the entire body of work from 1897 to 1914 takes on a coherence of theme and interest that gives it a substantial place in any social and psychological study of women and the politics of love and marriage.

Hellé depicts a true ideal of deep affection between equals. It is not achieved, however, without error of judgment, pain, and struggles against heavy opposition. Tinayre's descriptions of Hellé in society, a swan in a barnyard, are perspicacious, ironic, and frequently very funny. There is not a façade that emerges without crack or chip at the end of this description.

Hellé meets two men simultaneously, and these men are friends: Maurice Clairmont, a charming young poet who is believed to have talent and potential, and Antoine Genesvrier, a somber philanthropist who has given up his title and spent his fortune in an attempt to help the poor gain skills and basic education. He is a writer on social reform and a recluse from society. Hellé is attracted by Maurice, whereas her uncle, Sylvain de Riveyrac, who brought her up, develops a deep friendship for Antoine. The first evening, Maurice presents himself as a hero who is off to Greece to fight the Turks, and within a few days he has gone, leaving his brave words and handsome face in Hellé's memory. During his absence Hellé grows to appreciate Antoine's virtues and to feel a deep affection for him. He has just brought himself to propose to her, and she has agreed to give the matter careful thought and respond within three months, when Maurice returns. In the meantime Uncle Sylvain has died and Hellé is living alone in her own house in Paris, looking after her own affairs and seeing whomsoever she wishes. Maurice charms her more and more, she agrees to marry him, and suddenly her autonomy is at an end.

He and his family demand the right to control her life; she is expected to spend her days at idle social events; her books are of no importance (and should be sent to the country because the library is ugly); she has no time for reflection or good works—all the things she appreciated with Antoine. It seems that she is trapped, and she begins to suffer, hoping nonetheless that after the wedding Maurice will spend time on issues more important than whether he will be awarded the *légion d'honneur*. However, we see clearly that the shape of the relationship between Hellé and Maurice has changed. His concept of love is a possessive one that expresses itself through dominance: Hellé is now his to use as he sees fit, and she is supposed to act and react only in his interests, whatever she may think or feel herself. Maurice is behaving like a traditionally oppressive and self-centered husband who is sure of his power. Everything comes to a head at the dinner given for their engagement by the Baronne de Nébriant, Maurice's cousin. There is a politician present who has influence and can help Maurice's climb through the levels of polite society. This man bears an old grudge against Antoine Genesvrier. During the course of the evening, the conversation is turned in such a direction that the politician vents his spleen in slanderous suggestions against Antoine; Maurice, careful of his future, disclaims his friend. Hellé is outraged by such opportunism and moral cowardice. She defends Antoine, leaves the dinner, breaks the engagement, and retires to the country to think. Of course she returns to Antoine, having recognized at last that heroism lies in the heart and mind of a man, and not in the beauty of his face and voice.

Antoine, meanwhile, has been faithful to his love. He sees in Hellé the only woman he had ever considered as a possible partner. His concept of marriage is that of equality of value and of effort. Tinayre shows us that Hellé has a harmony of mind and body, a finesse of judgment that delight Antoine. He is somewhat afraid that she might be a perfect "statue," however, so he tests her by taking her to a hospital to visit an unhappy poor woman and her baby, and discovers that she also has a heart. Antoine is seeing Hellé as a independent human being and not as an extension of his own interests. Hence when she turns to Maurice, he is true to his own code and puts no pressure on Hellé, makes no display of his pain, and affirms the friendship upon which she can count. His is quite the opposite of the increasingly shallow and shrill behavior of Maurice, and the dynamics of his relationship are quite different also. Hellé finally separates appearance from reality. She then appreciates Antoine's true worth and its effects on her own life.

It is interesting to note that the only other person in the novel who seems able to do likewise is Mademoiselle Frémant, "une femme de lettres, très laide, très intelligente, pétrie de fiel et de vinaigre, recherchée et redoutée de tous" (p. 234) ["Miss Frémant, a literary woman, very ugly, highly intelligent, full of piss and vinegar, sought after and feared by all"]. It is she who continues the conversation about Antoine Genesvrier, when social manners would suggest a change of subject; and she does not let the matter drop until it has become impossible for Hellé not to see what is happening, not to understand Maurice's selfish attitude. Then she checks to make sure that Hellé knows what she has done by her outburst:

> —Ma chère enfant, me dit-elle à mi-voix, savez-vous ce que c'est qu'une gaffe?
> —Une maladresse involontaire . . . juste le contraire de ce que j'ai fait.
> —Vous êtes brave. C'est très bien, mais savez-vous que votre bravoure peut coûter cher à Monsieur Clairmont? . . .
> —Un bout de ruban serait trop payé par une lâcheté. (p. 245)

> ["My dear child," she murmured, "do you know what a gaffe is?"
> "A piece of unintentional tactlessness . . . just the opposite of what I did."
> "You're a courageous girl. That's very good, but do you know that your bravura can cost Monsieur Clairmont dearly?"
> "The cost of a piece of ribbon would be too high if paid for by an act of cowardliness."]

And only then does she give her approval, adding that Hellé is a fit wife for Don Quixote but not for an ambitious socialite. She is indeed repeating, in another mode, a conversation Hellé had a little earlier with Madame Marboy, the disapproving aunt of Antoine and adoring godmother of Maurice, who is a "good" woman in traditional terms. Madame Marboy preaches the submissiveness of dutiful wives. She views Hellé as ill-prepared for marriage and asks her whether she is ready to eliminate her personality and become invisible for love, to which Hellé responds by a passionate declaration of equality in marriage:

> —Mais à quoi bon? m'écriai-je. Et quel étrange idéal d'amour propose-t-on à la femme? Pourquoi doit-elle plutôt que l'homme se briser, se sacri-fier? Pourquoi effacerais-je ma personnalité dans l'amour? Celui qui

méconnaîtrait la justice au point de m'imposer un suicide intellectuel serait un tyran ou un imbécile: en aucun cas, je ne saurais l'aimer. Je ne veux ni me sacrifier, ni sacrifier mon mari. Nous devons nous efforcer de réaliser ensemble une vie harmonieuse en nous respectant, en nous aidant, en nous complétant. Je hais l'effroyable égoïsme qui se cache sous la galanterie hyperbolique de certains hommes, et je plains les femmes qui le subissent par vanité ou par lâcheté. (pp. 230–31)

["But what's the good of it?" I exclaimed. "And what sort of strange ideal of love is being proposed to women? Why must they, rather than men, be broken and sacrificed? Why should I efface my personality for love? The man who would repudiate justice to the point of forcing me to intellectual suicide would be a tyrant or an idiot: in neither case, could I love him. I don't want to sacrifice myself or my husband either. We must both make an effort to create a harmonious life by respecting, helping and fulfilling each other. I hate the appalling selfishness that is hidden beneath the exaggerated gallantry of certain men and I pity the women who submit to it out of vanity or cowardliness."]

The old lady remarks sadly that she is a woman of the new era, which indeed she is intended to be.

Analysis of the novel shows that Hellé is proof of the need for equality in marriage. Equality does not imply identity, however. A man and wife complete each other, and may well work together to the same end, but their roles and attitudes are not the same. To a certain extent the division remains traditional: man dispenses order, woman nurtures the weak. Antoine sees his work among the poor as an attempt to establish social justice and Hellé's role as social angel dispensing emotional comfort.

La justice n'est que la loi d'ordre et d'équilibre; la charité, c'est le miracle de l'amour. Et si l'oeuvre de justice appartient à l'homme, à la femme surtout appartient l'amour. (p. 137)

[Justice is only the law of order and balance; charity is the miracle of love. And if the work of justice belongs to men, love belongs, above all, to women.]

Love becomes universal love expressed through social work. Hellé is supposedly better equipped to help unmarried mothers than Antoine is, and here she joins Mademoiselle Bon and Mademoiselle Miracle in *La Rebelle* in doing works of "charity," in Antoine Genesvrier's sense of the word.

Tinayre is extending her interpretation of "love" and offering the possibility of public love—social work—as well as of private love. Every

woman's life is built around one or the other; those who are in the public
realm have a much greater sense of themselves and of their power and
place in the world: Mademoiselle Bon and Mademoiselle Miracle refused
marriage because "they had their own ideas," and both play an important
role in the network of support for women in society. The ideal Tinayre
offers in *Hellé* and develops in *La Rebelle* is that women who are happy
manage to combine public and private love in their lives; they recognize
the differences between appearances and reality, and are able to choose
reality.

In *La Rebelle* public love is represented by a women's newspaper and
by the church. At the newspaper, where Josanne Valentin works, there
are visible and false "feminists," such as Madeleine Foucart, the publisher, and Flory, the theatre critic—women who have no real understanding of and give no real support to other women, though the rhetoric
of feminism is firmly in place. There is also Mademoiselle Bon, a dowdy,
aging spinster with grapes on her hat whom they hide in a back office.
She is a "heroine of charity" (in terms taken from *Hellé*). She reports on
social needs; does good works; supports weak, poor, lost women; attends
feminist meetings and works for feminist causes. Mademoiselle Bon's
love for female humanity is total and inexhaustible. Throughout the
book she is mocked gently and defended vehemently. Her parallel is Mademoiselle Miracle, a pious, elderly spinster who is Josanne's aunt by marriage. She loves and understands each individual who comes into her
sphere: Josanne, Claude, the canon, and, more surprisingly perhaps, Rosa,
the thirty-year-old unmarried daughter of one of her friends, a modest,
well-brought-up young lady who is discovered to be pregnant. Everyone
is shocked and horrified except Mademoiselle Miracle, who recognizes
that thirty is the age of real temptation for unmarried women. In her attitude toward Rosa there is not the larger vision that is found in Mademoiselle Bon's attitude toward the unmarried mothers she visits, but compassion for other women is in both of them. They understand the effects
of love better than all the married women who mock or pity their single
state, and they see the pitfalls. That is why each of them refused a suitor
who was less than they had hoped for.

The way in which Tinayre's choice of names for these characters prevents any misreading of their qualities is both allegorical and ironic. Interestingly, the irony is directed more at Tinayre herself and her readers
than against the admirable women she depicts. Her society had no digni-

fied place for single women who were not nuns, no established ways of treating them seriously, so in order to create such characters at all, Tinayre has to make it appear as though she is mocking them while she gives us time to appreciate their worth. Every time someone is lacking in respect to one or other, Josanne defends her. We note also that Tinayre makes each of the women state that she had the opportunity to marry and refused it because the husband was not suitable to her concept of the life she wanted for herself. This is a revolutionary social attitude in women who are depicted as elderly in 1905; to show them as happy, independent, useful, and respected members of society is just as revolutionary in literary terms.

The lines of strength and criticism do not run through *La Rebelle* in ways that might be expected. To begin with, as I have said, it is very unusual to find two nonstereotypical spinsters in a novel; it is even more unusual to find them strong and well-respected characters who display and maintain the most important values in the book. Mademoiselle Bon and Mademoiselle Miracle represent true understanding of social conditions and psychology expressed in real charity and love of humanity. One is a feminist, the other a traditional Christian; and yet their fundamental attitudes toward the world are very similar. Each has the life she has by her own active choice; neither of them is in any way a victim; no one has power over them. They are outside the sphere of male power and domination, two examples of serene solitude and useful independence, of autonomous womanhood.

The contrast between them is expressed in the geography of the novel, where Paris is opposed to Chartres, the bustling capital and the little town in the shadow of the cathedral, avant-garde and traditional values. Josanne travels from one to the other as she changes her way of life. Indeed, every time there is a shift in the relations between Josanne and the men in her life, Tinayre writes a scene where Josanne is in a vehicle of some kind: carriage, riverboat, train, or metro. Similarly, Tinayre uses the choice of public or private sphere for Josanne's meetings with Maurice Nattier, her neglectful lover and the father of her child; Pierre, her dying husband; and Noël, her new friend and lover, to guide and transform the reader's attitudes toward the various relationships. She does not use topography in a blatantly symbolic way or structure her novel formally according to shifts of décor in the way Gide does in *L'Immoraliste*, for example.[12] Nonetheless, the reader's recognition of her use of Paris and the surrounding area to create a subtle social and emotional geography is crucial to full appreciation of the power structures between men and women in the novel.

The focus of pain is the Odéon. There Josanne waits for Maurice, a critical victim of his lack of love. Noël Delysle goes there in his turn when, his belief in Josanne shaken, he is anxiously preparing to hear her story. In a sense each is waiting for the manifestation of Josanne's past. Flory, the theatre critic, goes to the Odéon also. As she is a constant victim of turbulent and unhappy love, her presence there strengthens the symbolic role of the location within the novel. In contrast to the Odéon is the Valley of the Chevreuse, where Noël and Josanne go at the romantic and ideal stage of their relationship. Pain finds its expression at night in the city; desire grows in the countryside. Passion as untrammeled as the vegetation around them causes problems for the controlled and reasoning people Josanne and Noël are shown to be. Clearly they are not children of nature to give in to their desire and forget all other considerations. Their solid, stable, true, and everyday love is finally expressed in Delysle's apartment, where they find a harmony between culture and nature. It is in the Place des Vosges, where the trees and birds in the middle of the square and the ancient arcades around the edge form a nice topographical compromise between the values of Chartres, the modern city, and the Valley of the Chevreuse—family, feminism, and desire. Josanne's own apartment is always the symbol of her integrity and refusal to deny any element of her complex emotional makeup.

The story of *La Rebelle* is simple. Josanne Valentin is married to an engineer, Pierre, who is too ill to work and who has become very difficult to live with. She works for a women's newspaper to earn their living and takes care of her husband devotedly, enduring his rage and his caresses. She believes, however, that she has a right to happiness, and so when she falls in love with Maurice Nattier she does not hesitate to take him as her lover. Maurice leaves the country when she tells him she is pregnant, but returns to her later. The novel starts when the child, Claude, is three years old. While waiting for Maurice at the Odéon one evening Josanne leafs through a book called *The Working Woman* by Noël Delysle, finds reflections of her own thought in it, and buys the book; then, by a fluke, she is asked to produce some emergency copy for the paper, a review of this book.

At about this time Maurice leaves her and marries a rich young girl,

Pierre dies, and Josanne finds herself in Chartres staying with Mademoiselle Miracle. She is wondering whether to try to return to her old job when Delysle writes to her. They continue to exchange letters. She subsequently goes back to work, and one day Delysle walks into her office. Their friendship grows and turns to love, but perhaps unfortunately, their love declares itself before they have told each other their past. Delysle accepts that Josanne had a lover but is very jealous of the presence of that lover in the child. Gradually he works through his rage and suffering, and Josanne detaches herself from the past. Meanwhile Maurice's wife has lost a child and cannot have any more, so Maurice starts trying to take an interest in Claude. However, after two nights when Noël and Josanne nurse Claude through suspected meningitis, Josanne does not even recognize Maurice when he comes to the door, and when she does she tells him, "Your place is not here." All problems are over, and she can marry Delysle.

The main theme, which dominates the pattern of interwoven varieties of love and the multifarious examples of real and false feminism in the novel, and which is the pivot on which the whole novel turns, is the problem of the double standard; this is why Mlles Bon and Miracle chose not to marry, this is why Noël Delysle suffers. As we study Josanne's actions we see that she has claimed her right to the enjoyment of her emotions and her body, and her right to establish and live by her own moral values. She has claimed the autonomy that every man takes without question. And contrary to all taught behavior and social pressure, she has no sense of wrongdoing. Tinayre has created an extraordinary modern woman who recognizes that she has a right to meet those needs. Josanne feels and expresses love, desire, and happiness. She also maintains the traditional wifely virtue of devotion and sees no conflict between these elements. When Noël is in great emotional pain because of events in Josanne's past, she is sad that he is hurt, but gives nothing more than a passing thought to the idea of repentance before rejecting it out of hand. She has done nothing of which she should repent: she cared for her husband, loved Maurice, loves her child. Each action is a right action, and she refuses to choose between them. She has done nobody wrong, and she too has a right to self-expression and happiness. We see this in the way she moves through the world of the novel, and the fact that such an attitude is normal to most women today should in no way allow us to underestimate the importance of such behavior in the Belle Epoque. In Josanne Valentin,

Tinayre has created a new woman who has a strong sense of self and is not self-conscious about her independence and autonomy. Indeed, in the novel there is no sense that she is conscious of any difference between her way of being and that of other women.

There is a great difference, however, between the dynamics of Josanne's relations with the men in her life and those of the "typical" wife of the period. Tinayre has loaded the dice for Josanne to allow her the autonomy necessary to the theme of the novel; she causes the reader to have such sympathy for Josanne in the early chapters that the fact that there are actually advantages for Josanne in the miserable situation with her husband tends to pass unremarked. It would be normal at this period for a woman such as Josanne to be dominated by her husband and for her to sacrifice herself for her lover. This appears to be true of Josanne also. Pierre Valentin is a demanding husband in respects concerning his physical needs, health care, and marital rights; Maurice Nattier is a romantic yet careless, insentive lover. However, if we look closely at the two men we discover that the power lines of the relationships rest in Josanne's hands and that in both cases the expected male-female relations have been subtly reversed. Pierre is dependent on Josanne in all the ways a wife is usually dependent on her husband: economic, emotional, and sexual. She is who earns their living, moves in the public sphere, accepts or rejects his desire for her—his "love"—and who deceives him with a lover while he is trapped at home with the child and the servant.

Similarly Maurice is given a somewhat "feminine" role to play in both its main lines and its superficialities. He is the one who is late, delayed by his mother or his letters; he is the person who is urged to make a "good" (that is, commercially and socially successful) marriage and who clings to the memory of their relationship nonetheless, coming to Josanne for approbation, forgiveness, and support. He importunes her; she makes all the real decisions that affect their lives. The transitory nature of their dealings with each other is made obvious by the fact that they meet only outside and in transit. He is peripheral to Josanne's working life and home life; like a mistress, he provides secret pleasure, some mystery and romance, a little happiness, and some inconvenience. There is no evidence in the novel that Josanne would have it otherwise.[13]

It is when Josanne begins to explain her attitudes to Noël Delysle that she becomes conscious of them. As the work advances, she moves from practice to justification of the rights she has claimed for herself, whereas

Noël travels in the opposite direction, from the theory of equality to the experience of it. Their relationship starts with an exchange of ideas, moves on to friendship and then to desire and love. Throughout its development the most important element in it is open and sincere communication. This is quite unlike the deceits practiced between husband and wife, lover and mistress, and it is in the continuous attempt at truth and honesty in the exchange that much of the interest lies for the reader.

It is true that Noël defines the relationship in his writing, but it is also true that Josanne recognizes in his book the theory of the way she is trying to live:

> Rêver la liberté de l'amour, en conservant le mariage sous des formes nouvelles, moins rigoureuses, délivrer les hommes et les femmes de l'obligatoire hypocrisie, reconnaître leur droit d'arranger leur vie comme il leur plaît en acceptant toutes les responsabilités de leurs actions, mettre dans les relations des sexes plus de loyauté, plus d'indulgence, est-ce donc encourager la débauche? Est-ce détruire la pudeur de la femme? Non. Qu'une femme connaisse le prix de sa personne, la gravité du don qu'elle fait, qu'elle ait de l'amour et des conséquences de l'amour une idée claire, haute, grave, si cette femme a l'esprit et le corps sains, elle sera bien armée contre les tentations de débauche. . . . Et, si elle se trompe dans son choix, elle saura que son erreur n'est pas infamante, qu'elle ne la traînera pas, toute sa vie, comme un boulet, et qu'elle pourra mériter l'estime et l'amour d'un honnête homme. (pp. 16–17)

> [Dreaming of freedom in love, while preserving marriage in less rigorous forms, by liberating men and women from obligatory hypocrisy, recognizing their right to arrange their lives as they wish while accepting total responsibility for their actions, creating more loyal, more generous relations between the sexes, does this really encourage dissolute living? Does it destroy women's modesty? No. As long as a woman knows the value of her person and the seriousness of the gift she is giving, as long as she has a clear, noble and serious idea of love and the consequences of love, and if this woman has a healthy mind and body, she will be well armed against the temptations of debauchery. . . . And, if she makes the wrong choice, she will know that her mistake is not an ignominious one, that she will be able to win the respect and love of a decent man.]

Delysle seemed to understand that women have the same needs and rights as men, and has postulated a new marriage formed by equality in love:

> Les termes du contrat conjugal seront changés par cela même que la femme pourra vivre sans le secours de l'homme, élever seule ses enfants. Elle ne

demandera plus la protection et ne promettra plus l'obéissance. Et
l'homme devra traiter avec elle d'égal à égal—disons mieux: de compagnon
à compagne, d'ami à amie.—Leur union ne subsistera que par la tendresse
réciproque, l'accord toujours renouvelé des pensées et des sentiments, la
fidélité libre et volontaire, et cette parfaite sincérité qui permet l'entière
confiance. (pp. 14–15)

[The terms of the marriage contract will be changed by the very fact that
women will be able to live without the assistance of men and bring up their
children alone. They will no longer ask for protection and will no longer
promise obedience. And men will have to deal with them as equals—better still, as one companion to another.—Their relationship will continue
to exist only through mutual tenderness, an ever-renewed harmony of
thought and feeling, faithfulness freely and voluntarily given and that kind
of perfect sincerity that permits complete trust.]

To underscore the importance of Delysle's writing as key to the structure
and development of Tinayre's novel, the title *La Rebelle* is defined within
the passage Josanne reads:

Trop tard! . . . Si toutes les travailleuses ne sont pas des affranchies, toutes,
déjà, sont des rebelles. . . . Rebelles à la loi que les hommes ont faite, aux
préjugés qu'ils entretiennent, à l'idéal suranné qu'ils imposent à leurs
compagnes. . . . Elles ne pensent plus qu'il suffise d'être une femme chaste
pour être une honnête femme, et elles ne se croient pas déchues parce
qu'elles ont aimé plusieurs fois. (p. 14)

[It is too late! . . . Even if every working woman is not liberated, all are
already rebels . . . rebelling against man-made laws, against the prejudices
men support, against the antiquated ideal they impose on their companions. . . . Women no longer think that it is enough to be chaste in order
to be decent and they do not feel that they are fallen because they have
loved more than once.]

Noël Delysle, the social theorist, envisages a morality for women
which is not different from the one men have already. Noël Delysle, in
love with Josanne Valentin, who has a child by a previous lover, finds it
impossible to live according to his own theory without considerable
struggle and pain. Tinayre shows her readers an honest man working to
bring together the diverse reactions of his reason and his emotion. It is
a fascinating study in its own right of a deliberate changing of attitude
by strength of will, a transformation for the sake of love. Once again in
La Rebelle Tinayre reverses the expected male-female relations. In
French literature one frequently finds women who make a supreme effort

to alter their attitudes to the men they love; it is rare indeed to find a male character doing likewise, especially when the ultimate aim is to marry the woman he loves and live well with her in the future. Tinayre postulates a radical shift in relations between the sexes here. It is also a particularly noticeable one in terms of literary history because it offers a reversal of the situation depicted in Proust's *Un amour de Swann*.[14] Whereas Swann settles into his jealousy and revels in his sensitivity, Delysle fights his jealousy in order to live a normal married life. The contrast between the books raises a major question about the values explored in women's writing and those found in books by male authors, their relative sense of the real and of the social role of literature.

The interest here lies in the struggle between learned attitudes and chosen responses. Delysle is a self-styled feminist, he has learned to appreciate Josanne for all her strengths and virtues, and he loves her; yet even with this solid basis for understanding, the old lessons that woman is man's possession and that a man should never accept secondhand merchandise rise to the surface. Delysle manages to avoid the traditional patterns of superiority and contempt for women only by diverting his emotion into jealousy of his predecessor. For Josanne this jealousy expresses itself in extreme posessiveness and exclusivity, a need to know her very thoughts and to question the quality of her feeling for Claude. Does she love the child for himself or as a manifestation of his father?

Tinayre, in one of the many thought-provoking echoes which structure the novel, raises the same question in a different form in the scenes at the home for unmarried mothers. The women who look after the pregnant girls try very hard to give them a sense of the importance of their babies, of their role as mothers, but all too often a girl abandons her child in order to return to its father or to another lover. Delysle has too much integrity to ask Josanne to choose between him and Claude, but she understands what is at stake, and the reader is encouraged to compare the parallel situations. Josanne has a sense of herself and of the child that the destitute girls have not. They have no defense when their young men declare that they do not want any children, and also, having no personal strength or resources, they feel they have nothing to give to the baby. Brought up to dream of being loved, they are the victims both of society and of love, whereas Josanne is free to make her own choice. It is clear, however, that the problem of the unmarried mothers is the public side of the situation in which Josanne finds herself in private. They are all victims of a double standard in society, though Josanne is in a position to understand this and refuses to accept what is happening to her.

It is manifest in the oppositions and reflections in the structure of *La Rebelle* that Tinayre holds men responsible for women's suffering while recognizing that they incur no social opprobrium, no scorn, no poverty. Her novel criticizes the state of society in which men have status, income, and access to another woman, should the one they "love" become pregnant or otherwise inconvenient. We see that in the early twentieth century most women cling to men because, having neither skills nor sense of self, they have no means of physical or emotional survival other than life with someone who will support them. It also seems to be true, however, as Mademoiselle Bon remarks to Josanne one day, that women are incapable of shaking off the idea that they should be someone's servant. Josanne reflects on the remark while watching the unmarried mothers:

> Ah! Mademoiselle Bon disait vrai: nous gardons toutes le pli de la servitude, le besoin d'aimer, de souffrir pour celui que nous aimons; le besoin d'obéir; le besoin de pardonner.... Nous avons toutes, tant que nous aimons, la même lâche indulgence. (p. 103)

> [Oh yes! Mademoiselle Bon spoke the truth: we are all marked by servitude, the need to love and to suffer for the person we love; the need to obey, the need to forgive.... Whenever we love someone, we all show the same weak indulgence.]

This is, of course, in one form at least the sense of sacrifice taught to women in Christian cultures. The novel raises the question of whether Josanne herself is caught in a pattern of traditional behavior when she gives herself totally to Noël and whether there are in fact different standards for women according to whether or not they are in love. Does a statement of this kind mean that as soon as a woman falls in love, she gives up her rights both public and private? That the fact of being in love with and submissive to one man makes a woman the victim of all of them? Does a woman who respects her rights and those of others have to be dowdy, single, and a bit fanatical, like Mademoiselle Bon? What is Tinayre suggesting? Josanne certainly does not submit to Noël when he wants her to dissociate herself from her own past. She stoutly defends her marital love for Pierre Valentin and her passionate love for Maurice

Nattier: these loves are the justification of her nonstandard behavior. They may be in the past, but their existence is not to be denied just because Josanne has moved on into another life. Josanne is an autonomous being. How can she reconcile her life with the statement she has made?

The question returns later in the novel, and Josanne's reflections are again provoked by a remark made by Mademoiselle Bon: that she should beware the master in the lover as well as in the husband. These are Josanne's thoughts:

> Mon maître! mon maître chéri! . . . Je n'ai pas d'autre volonté que la vôtre. . . . Je ne suis qu'une chose, une très petite chose, dans vos chères mains. Que je sois votre égale respectée, devant le monde, devant votre raison et votre amitié, c'est notre désir à tous deux. Mais la rebelle s'est rebellée contre la société injuste, et non pas contre la nature; elle ne s'est pas rebellée contre la loi éternelle de l'amour. . . . Elle ne repousse point la tendre, joyeuse et noble servitude volontaire, qui n'humilie point, puisqu'elle est consentie. Vraiment, il me plaît de vous appeler "mon maître," parce que vous êtes fort, et clairvoyant, et bon; parce que, si je peux vivre seule, sans votre secours, il m'est beaucoup plus agréable de vivre près de vous, avec votre aide. . . . Et même—je ne l'avouerai jamais!— il me plaît d'avoir peur de vous,—un peu, très peu!—et de vous tenir quelquefois sous mon pied, si faible, comme une belle bête fauve que j'ai domptée, mais qui saurait rugir et qui me dévorerait, si j'étais méchante. . . .
>
> Et cela ne m'empêche pas d'être féministe, et de revendiquer mes droits à la liberté, à la justice, au bonheur. . . . Vous savez bien mon chéri, que si j'ai voulu m'appartenir à moi-même—c'était pour mieux me donner à vous! (pp. 305–6)

> [My master, my dearest master! . . . I have no will but yours. . . . I am nothing but an object, a very small thing, in your dear hands. That I may be your respected equal in the eyes of the world, in your mind and in your friendship, is what we both desire. But the rebel has rebelled against the unjust society and not against nature; she has not rebelled against the eternal laws of love. . . . She does not reject tender, joyful, noble, voluntary servitude, which cannot humiliate her since she has accepted it. It is true. I enjoy calling you "my master" because you are strong and clearsighted and good: because, even if I can live alone without your aid, it is much more pleasant for me to live by your side, with your help. . . . And even—I shall never admit it—I like to be afraid of you,—a little, a very little!—and sometimes to keep you beneath my feet, so weak, like a beautiful wild animal I've tamed, but one that could roar and that would devour me if I were bad. . . .

And that does not stop me from being a feminist and claiming my right
to freedom, justice and happiness. . . . You well know, my dearest, that if
I wanted to belong to myself—it was to better give myself to you!]

The rebel rebelled against social injustice and not against nature, we
are told. What, then, is nature? It seems to me that Marcelle Tinayre is
trying to make a very careful distinction here between the different
realms of a woman's life. She is allowing her heroine to claim rights in
the public domain while leaving her tenderly submissive, and thus play-
ing the traditional role, in love. She is letting her remain to all appearances the equal of her spouse in public, and indeed believes herself to be
his equal in his mind and in his heart, while she relinquishes voluntarily
anything that might prevent him from being her master in love. Tinayre
allows Josanne the desire to serve Noël on the grounds that she has
proved that she can live without him, and so has nothing to fear from
such subservience, that in age-old ways a woman can make man her slave
from time to time if she so wishes. The little irony in the image of the
man "si faible, comme une bête fauve que j'ai domptée" ("so weak, like
a wild animal I've tamed") is supposed to make a game of inequality and
show how such an attitude can be maintained within the greater equality. Unfortunately, it seems to me, it also brings back to mind the greater
strength and violence of men, and their ability to destroy anything that
women might acquire. The delicate balance among power and love, dominance, subservience, and equality that Tinayre presents for our analysis
remains clearly dependent on the goodwill of the man in the relationship,
whom the woman must trust not to abuse her voluntary servitude. Is this
the best situation that can be envisaged during the period under study?
    Tinayre is writing to encourage women with inadequate education, no
money, no legal rights, and no supportive networks to try to improve
their lot within marriage. If she presents a change that is too extreme,
she will scare and discourage her readers or find her books censured by
irate husbands. Her book is a subversive attempt to teach autonomy to
women in both the public and private spheres. She challenges a vast number of preconceived attitudes and values in the novel, structured as it is
by the tensions between a certain number of opposing forces: public and
private attitudes toward women, reality and appearance in love, a
woman's love for her man and for her child, the public and private nature
of women's equality with men, the difference between the life of a

woman working outside the home and one working within it, life in the city and in the provinces. (The expected opposition between the secular and the religious is one in appearance only. Christianity teaches women to be submissive and sacrifice themselves, yet Chartres produced Mademoiselle Miracle, who refused to sacrifice herself to a husband she did not want; she is in no way less sure of herself and of the value of her life, no less understanding than Mademoiselle Bon, her secular counterpart.)

Given that *Hellé* has been created as a superhuman wife against whom Tinayre's heroines must be measured and to whom her readers cannot compare themselves, I offer the hypothesis that Tinayre leaves inviolate the accepted roles apparently played between a loving man and wife in the bedroom as a gesture of reassurance to her readers. It is a statement that a "natural" woman can also be an autonomous one, and Tinayre's choice of characters shows that autonomy can take many forms even within one society. The essential element at all times is the ability of any woman to make for herself the important choices upon which her life will be built. Love of men, love of children, appreciation of women, independence, integrity, and feminism are not mutually exclusive concepts. They are, however, very difficult to combine in any woman if the man in her life does not show proper respect for her needs and desires. Equality is hard to maintain unilaterally.

Marcelle Tinayre is not the only author to deal with the need for love and the issue of the difficult choices that women have to make, but she is the author who deals most comprehensively and coherently with these themes. She has the best grasp on the complexity of the assumption that underlies the whole period, namely that a woman's ultimate aim is to love deeply and be loved well. Any exploration of this central idea requires an awareness of the power structures in male and female relations, and an assessment of the social context in which these relationships are situated. Tinayre's work attempts a systematic description of the pitfalls and traps that surround love, and shows the many ambiguities inherent in both the concept and the use of the word itself.

Maternity
THE PITFALLS AND THE PLEASURES

The problem with love as a lifestyle in 1900 is that eventually and inevitably it is complicated by pregnancy. The issues that ensue have been touched on already. First, in *Idylle saphique* (chapter 2) we see the consternation of the courtesan, her attempt to give herself and the child security by persuading the richest and most permanent of her admirers that the child is his, and the man's solutions: an abortion or his departure. A pregnant mistress ceases to exist as an individual who is loved and cherished, becoming instead a potentially costly object that can no longer be used. The same pattern is evident in *La Rebelle* (chapter 3), where Maurice abandons Josanne until after the birth of Claude. What happens to the woman is clearly of no consequence whatever to the man. He does not care whether she dies at the hand of an abortionist or loses her job and starves trying to bring up his child, as long as he is not inconvenienced. Hence the institution for unmarried mothers in *La Rebelle* and the story of Madame Nine, who abandons her baby because her lover does not want his life disturbed by children. Rich women can go away to have the child and then put it in the care of a nurse, as happens in *L'Ange et les pervers*, but the child does not usually live long in those conditions. The most fortunate are those who, like Josanne Valentin, can make everyone believe that their husband is the father of the child. Motherhood is a continual danger, and few are the children who are truly welcome in the novels of this period.

The aim of the authors in dealing with the topic is quite complex. They want to show the pitfalls for a girl who is ignorant of the facts of life, yet brought up to be avid for love (as in *Avant l'amour*, chapter 3) and the tremendous difficulties that confront a girl who is pregnant. They denounce the cruelty and injustice perpetuated by society because of the double standard applied to the actions of women and men. And they juxtapose to the negative side, which is the pregnancy itself, a declaration of the value of motherhood and the joy that comes from the child's love (an important political issue of the period). This love is frequently opposed to the relations between a man and a woman, especially when these are described as dominated by jealousy or voluptuousness. Indeed, we see that a woman who loves her child draws personal power from that relationship and as a result is less available as a total slave to her husband's desires.

All of this has been sketched briefly in previous chapters. I propose to discuss the issues more fully in relation to five novels: *Le Roman de six petites filles* (The Story of Six Little Girls) and *Marie, fille-mère* (Mary the Unmarried Mother) by Lucie Delarue-Mardrus; *Sibylle femme* (Sibylle as Woman) and *Sibylle mère* (Sibylle as Mother) by Renée d'Ulmès; and *Un Inceste* (An Incest) by Valentine de Saint Point.[1] In these we may compare normal motherhood, instinctive mother love, a reasoned feminist perspective on maternity, and the exaltation of a supermother.

Let us start with the *Roman de six petites filles*, because it is the only novel I have found in which there is a description of an ordinary bourgeois mother surrounded by her children, and it therefore suggests a possible definition of normality against which we can measure attitudes depicted in the other books under discussion. Madame Teriel lives in the country with her six daughters and their governess. Monsieur Teriel spends much of his time in Paris both because he needs to be there for his work and because he has an apartment there and can pursue his amorous adventures in comfort. When they married, the couple had a feeling for each other "qui, peut-être, était de l'amour" (p. 12, "which was perhaps love"), but "dès le premier enfant, le volage mari de vingt-deux ans a cessé de considérer sa femme comme une maîtresse" (p. 12, "from the arrival of the first child, the flighty twenty-two-year-old husband stopped treating his wife like a mistress").

The structures of the novel make a clear separation between sexual and maternal love. Madame Teriel is portrayed as a jealous wife who is not perspicacious and as a result notices little—mainly, we realize, because she does not know what she is looking for. She is described as a frigid and silent wife. "Elle ne connaît, de la féminité, ni la coquetterie, ni la sensualité, mais, seul, le sentiment maternel (p. 10, "She knows neither flirting nor sensuality only the maternal feelings that belong to femininity"). She likes looking after the house: she likes supervising the maids and the children—piano, catechism—making clothes, and above all looking after her children when they are ill. We are told that she has all she dreamed of: that the girls speak excellent English, that they all learn music, and that they are always dressed alike. These are simple and traditional ambitions for a family with money, and they show clearly how girls are not perceived as individuals. Most of the novel deals with the daily routines of the house, and with the actions and thoughts of the children. This unusual perspective and the significance it gives to women's daily domestic concerns are what makes it interesting.

The drama inevitably comes from a misplaced love affair. Monsieur Teriel is attracted by the governess, an innocent English girl who falls in love with him. Madame Teriel might not see what is going on, but her daughters do, and the eldest brings the situation to her mother's attention. After a scene among Madame Teriel, her husband, and Miss Olive—with the little girls glued to the other side of the door, as usual—the governess leaves. Presumably Paul Teriel will be more careful to restrict his flights of fancy to Paris in the future, his wife will suffer a little more from jealousy and suspicion, and the family will remain intact.

The division of womanhood into the mutually exclusive roles of mistress and mother is a frequent theme in the work of Lucie Delarue-Mardrus and indeed of other writers of the period. Madame Teriel can survive because she is clearly described as experiencing motherly love only. She might be vexed that her husband takes mistresses, but her vexation is a matter of pride. She does not suffer physically from unassuaged sensuality or memories of lost pleasure: her mind is jealous, but her body is not. She is free of desire.

Such is not the case for Marie Avenel in *Marie, fille-mère*. She is both voluptuous and maternal; it is the struggle created by the opposing passions which destroys her.

In her life are two men, Budin's boy (le fils Budin), the son of a rich farmer who fancies the attractive daughter of a poor neighbor, and Natale

Fanella, a Sicilian workman who falls in love with her. The novel is divided into two parts, the better to oppose the blond, down-to-earth Norman to the dark, violently emotional Italian. Marie loves the former with all the dreams and idealism of an innocent seventeen-year-old, and he refuses to marry her when she becomes pregnant. She does not love the second, but he insists on marrying her and awakens all her voluptuousness. The first destroys her life, and the other kills her.

Budin's son (he is never given a name of his own) courts Marie slowly, charms her patiently for several months, and then rapes her. The violence over, his desire satisfied, he runs away, leaving Marie, who "d'un geste vaincu, rabaissa sa robe sur son corps blessé" (p. 35, "with a defeated gesture, pulled her dress down over her wounded body"). She then tries to gather her wits and goes home. When the young man returns, penitent, ashamed of his actions, Marie accepts him, primarily because he is the only person who knows her secret and can protect her:

> L'homme, maître brutal mais bon, qui fait si mal mais qui console si bien. Elle sent que celui qui l'a maltraitée est pourtant son seul ami sur la terre, lui qui *sait*, et qui cependant pardonne, puisqu'il est la cause de tout. (p. 46)
>
> [Man, a brutal but good master, who hurts you so much but comforts so well. She feels that the one who has ill treated her is nevertheless her only friend on earth, the one who *knows* but forgives even so, since he is the cause of it all.]

This is a nice statement of the double standard: he who knows and who pardons *nevertheless, since* he is the cause, is pardoned because the girl has nowhere else to turn in her sense of guilt and shame. All the power is on his side. Marie is the total victim of her aggressor, the innocent, ignorant, and passive woman. Marie does not enjoy their sexual relations, but accepts them "because they make her friend happy" and she loves him. Inevitably, she becomes pregnant. Because she is loving, loyal, and innocent herself, she is quite certain of her lover and thinks all she has to do is tell him they are going to get married. She does this, but even as she is doing so his thoughts are elsewhere—on his engagement and wedding to a rich wife. Marie was only a fleeting pleasure, a temporary amusement, and she has no value for him at all as a human being. He knows that her father might well kill her, but he has no thought of giving her any support. The situation she is in, *because of him*, is now her problem and hers only. He has moved into the economic and public sphere of the commerce of marriage.

Marie, already the victim of Budin's son's desire, is left as the potential victim of her father's rage. One of his possessions has been devalued, and this must be hidden from him if Marie is to survive. As in previous novels, we see that she is now dependent on other women for support: her mother and Aunt Maltide. Because of the dominant role of the man within the family, the view of woman as object and possession, and the total lack of autonomy of wives and daughters, Marie's mother has no power to do anything but hide her daughter's condition and conspire with her to subvert the father's "right" to punish her for the actions of another man. So just at the time when Marie needs emotional support she is packed off to Paris to Aunt Maltide and her brother Alexandre.

It is interesting to note that before Marie leaves the village she claims the only power she has—that of telling her story. She tells it to Marie Legrix, Budin's son's fiancée. Marie Legrix then uses the only power she has—that of refusal. Disgusted by such behavior in her future husband (though not supportive of Marie in her poverty and misery), she throws away her engagement ring. Neither she nor Budin's son is married at the end of the novel.

This is not a direct act of alliance between women in the face of male abuse, but it is symbolic of a growing refusal of the status of victim and possession that the women share and a challenge to the double standard in "love." Budin's son is no more marriageable than Marie is once Marie breaks the traditional silence created by the cultural inculcation of shame in women for being victims. (Given that Budin's son has no name of his own, he becomes the symbol of every man in such circumstances.) Marie will thwart Natale also by speaking out against him, though it will cost her her life. Marie survives as well as she does because she claims her right to speech, her right to tell her own story, to own her actions and reactions. This makes her a very interesting character: instead of being, as she seems at first, the stereotypic fallen country virgin, we realize as we analyze her behavior that she is poor and downtrodden, but she is shown to be instinctively aware of what power she does have and is not afraid to use it when sufficiently threatened. Here is still a fairly primitive response to danger, but for a woman in her condition—poor and "fallen"—to use the right to break her silence is a profoundly subversive act at the turn of the century, even though Delarue-Mardrus does have her collapse and die from the emotional effort she has made.

The description of Marie's life in Paris is an indictment of the living conditions and inhumane treatment of all serving girls. Marie lives in squalor, is treated badly, is constantly humiliated. Above all, she must not let her pregnancy show if she is to keep her job, and so is in constant discomfort because of the corset she must lace ever tighter. When her employer finds out about Marie's condition, she first intends to throw her out, but then decides to pay her less and work her harder. For this Marie is supposed to be grateful.

The structure of the novel opposes country and city, fertility and death. The only place where Marie can find a little quiet, space, and greenery which remind her of home is the local cemetery, and it is there—in an ironic opposition to the forest and the hay where she made love with Budin's son and a prefiguration of the eventual result of the birth of her child—that she feels the first birth pangs and that her waters break. She has nowhere to go, struggles desperately through the darkness until, in ironic imitation of her namesake, the Virgin Mary, she comes to rest in the goat pen of a neighbor. That is where she spends the night, worn out and full of rage and hatred for Budin's son, her father, and the child (all male) for causing her so much pain, and even for her mother, who is not there when Marie needs her. Next morning the neighbor finds her, treats her kindly, and sends for Marie's Aunt Maltide, who takes her to the hospital, where Marie is surrounded by women suffering as she is.

The description of labor from Marie's awareness of the first contractions to the final birth of the baby is long, graphic, and quintessentially female. To my knowledge there is no such description that predates it in French literature, nor have I found one in more recent writing. For this alone *Marie, fille-mère* deserves a place in the annals of women's recorded experience.

The birth scene itself is also important in both literary and social terms. Delarue-Mardrus creates a direct critical and ironic opposition between the roles of men and women in the birthing process. In the middle of the description of the women's physical labor, emotion, and ultimate powerlessness in a hospital context she inserts the pompous self-importance and power of a teaching gynecologist:

Elle est là, la femme, cet être pâmé. Sa face ruisselle de sueur, ses narines
sont pincées, sa bouche ouverte; et tout son être crie: "à l'aide!"

Et elle ne sait pas que, dans l'hôpital, plein des victimes de la nature,
se trouve une salle de cours, où un maître aux yeux profonds, tout possédé
par le génie du mâle ordonnateur, développe, devant des jeunes gens
attentifs assis en amphithéâtre, ses magnifiques pensées sur la maternité,
leur enseigne, avec des gestes frémissants d'éloquence, cette sorte de grand
poème physiologique qu'il a conçu à force d'avoir assisté, pendant les
longues années de sa jeunesse, l'agonie de celles qui accouchent. Il exalte.
Il souligne d'un geste péremptoire les paroles qu'il prononce. Sa voix
scande presque religieusement le mot qu'il a trouvé, le *Rythme*.

Il dit: "La nature est admirable, messieurs!"

Il dit: "Sachez que la femme n'est vraiment épanouie qu'après le
troisième allaitement."

Il dit: "La femme qui n'enfante pas n'est qu'un bel écrin vide; elle est
une manière de monstre."

Marie, écartelée, sanglante, comme les autres, avait senti que l'effort
naturel qu'elle faisait pour chasser d'elle cette tête d'enfant plus dure
qu'une énorme pierre, lui molestait tout le dedans du corps. Elle avait senti
s'introduire en elle les mains qui l'aidaient et qui, positivement, sem-
blaient lui tordre les tripes. (pp. 156–57)

[There is the woman, this swooning being, Her face is running with
sweat, her nostrils are pinched, her mouth open; and her whole being cries
out: "Help me!"

And she does not know that, in the hospital full of nature's victims,
there is a classroom where a teacher with deep-set eyes, totally absorbed
by the genius of the organising male, is developing his magnificent
thoughts about maternity in front of a lecture theatre full of attentive
young men. With gestures quivering with eloquence, he is teaching them
that sort of great physiological poem that he conceived by dint of watching
the agony of women giving birth throughout the long years of his youth.
He becomes impassioned. He emphasizes with decisive gestures the words
he is pronouncing. With almost religious fervour, his voice stresses the
word he has found: Rhythm.

He says: "Nature is wonderful, gentlemen!"

He says: "I realize that a woman is only in full bloom after nursing her
third child."

He says: "The woman who does not bear children is a beautiful, but
empty jewel-case; she is a sort of monster."

Marie, spreadeagled and bloody like the others, had felt that the natural
effort she was making to drive out that child's head that was harder than
an enormous stone, was molesting the whole inside of her body. She had
felt the hands that were helping enter her and it seemed to her that they
were actually twisting her guts.]

That the long night of pain and fear should end with such a transposition of a woman as subject of her own primary experience into woman as object of men's observation and redefinition is both extraordinary in its impact and timely in its comment. The technique of juxtaposition is immediately reminiscent of the famous scene in *Madame Bovary* in which Emma's love is in counterpoint to the voices at the agricultural fair. Likewise here, male and female worlds are out of joint. Marie and Emma are both victims of "love." Here also the introduction of the teaching gynecologist is a reminder that it is not until the twentieth century that male doctors gain control of the process of birth from midwives, and that the number of women dying of puerperal fever increases dramatically as rhetoric and technological manipulation replace wisdom and experience. Before then, only the rich had doctors; women of all other classes could not afford their services.

All the way through the novel we see the man using the woman for his own ends, controlling her life by his definition of it. Budin's son's values, Marie's father's sense of honor, and now the professor's interpretation of birth transpose Marie's reality into a world which is not hers. This male-defined world denies the existence of Marie's experience and causes her great suffering, both mental and physical. This will continue as she accepts her brother Alexandre's idea that he and his wife take her son, Alexandre, as their child and when she decides to marry Natale: in both cases her existence as a mother is refused, though in different ways. In neither case is she free to love her son openly. In the first instance she is not allowed to claim him as her own. In the second she no longer belongs to herself, having become the object of Natale's desire.

Delarue-Mardrus depicts maternal feeling as an instinct which women cannot and do not analyze, and which overrides everything else in their lives. She suggests that the bonding between mother and child is such that a child will prefer his natural mother at all times: in *Marie, fille-mère* Alexandre always turns to Aunt Marie. He likes her to cuddle him and put him to bed, and as he gets older states his preference quite clearly. This maternal love comports a great sense of responsibility for the child's future, his behavior, and his education.

All the writers in this chapter create in various ways single-parent families in which the mother is alone with her son, and each puts the son in a different relationship with the absent father. For Marie, her son replaces her lover, and gives her the love and joy she found in the early stages of her relationship with Budin's son. (Her husband, Natale, will see the child as a rival.) In Valentine de Saint-Point's *Un Inceste* the son is a reincarnation of the father and, as such, the object of a double love. Renée d'Ulmès creates in Sibylle Heursay a thoughtful mother who loves and appreciates her child for himself. Hers is the least complex of the maternal relationships, as we shall see later.

The first part of *Marie, fille-mère* ends with Marie's delight in her newborn son, the news of the death of her father, and Marie's realization that she cannot return home, even now, because her shame would still harm the reputation of the family, and social judgments do not include the needs of the individual, especially if she is female. Alexandre is all Marie has. The second part begins five years later, when Natale begins his courtship. The structure of the two sections is parallel. Just as Budin's son courted her, initiated her into lovemaking, took her virginity, and wrecked her future, so Natale courts her, initiates her into sensuality, tries to separate her from her son, and kills them both. In each case the man's desire changes the woman's life; in each case the man uses violence against the woman, and thus destroys both her peace of mind and the love that made her life happy.

The parallel structures are developed on various levels: Marie is as anguished before her wedding as she was before the birth. Again she runs terrified through the night, dragging the child with her. The first time, the pain is physical and the child is inside her body; the second time, the pain is mental and the child is enfolded within her mental space. The first night, she went from a cemetery to an animal's shelter; the second time, she circles around Notre Dame Cathedral and contemplates suicide in the river. The symbolism of death and motherhood is clear, even in the choice of a goat shed, with its metaphorical overtones of the stable at Bethlehem, biblical distinction between the legitimate and the illegitimate and the whole concept of the scapegoat. The first time, however, Marie moves from death to life as a mother; the second time, the move is from happy motherhood to death in marriage.

It is abundantly clear that desire and power are male prerogatives by which the female is abused constantly. Marie suffers violence by physical and emotional means from every man in her life. Natale is as violent in his way as was Marie's father. This time, however, she claims her right to her own actions and declares her situation: Alexandre is her child. Natale accepts the child in order to obtain the mother, but he and the child are violently jealous of each other because each wants to have her as his own. On their wedding night Natale declares it openly: "Senti, Maria! . . . Bientôt, tu m'aimeras mieux que ton petit!" (p. 264, "Soon you will love me more than the child"). Marie defies him: "Oh! mais ça, n'y comptez pas, vous savez! . . . dit-elle" (p. 265, "Oh, don't count on that, you know! . . . she said"). And he rapes her, reviving in Marie all the fear and rage she felt the first time. The opposition is evident; the sensation is compared directly with the pain of childbirth, and at the height of her pleasure she denies her child.

Sexual violence is the instinctive way in which the male maintains dominance over the female. It is brutal, unsubtle, and effective. Delarue-Mardrus's characters are uneducated, unreflective people. In them the basic power relations are totally undisguised. The men take Marie by force, and in a reaction of self-defense she strikes back in speech. The woman's position is not uncomplicated, however. Delarue-Mardrus presents the traditional view of woman as a sensual, carnal being. The first time, Marie was enjoying Budin's son's caresses until she realized where they were leading—to copulation like that between bull and cow. The second time, Natale being an accomplished lover, Marie is overcome by her own sensations of pleasure. Her body betrays her, and she is portrayed as encouraging the first rape and enjoying the second—a depiction that undermines the reality of the abuse of "love" and power of which she was object.

Her feelings after the second experience are parallel to those she had after the first. She no longer feels innocent. She has been separated from her world by guilt. She is torn between two loves and two value systems. Delarue-Mardrus suggests that this is because her pleasures came in inverse order—she should have been a lover before loving her child. Her allegiances could then have been successive, as were those of Madame Teriel in the *Roman de six petites filles*, or she could have remained attached to her man, as did Madame Nine in *La Rebelle*; but this way she is divided between the child, who delights her heart, and the man, who delights her body. We note that there is never any suggestion that a man might be capable of doing both. Emotional love is for women and children; desire and sensuality, for men.

The solidarity Marie had established with the child against the foreigner has been damaged by her voluptuousness. But she does not live her passion easily. She understands that Natale is the enemy of both her and her child, and that his weapon is his control of her sensuality. Again, there is no suggestion that a woman is able to refuse a man's advances. Her body will let her down because of its muscular or sensual weakness; she will therefore "fall" and will see herself as guilty.

Delarue-Mardrus does not free her heroine from any of the biological imperatives that imprison her, but she does allow her to use the one power offered by these very imperatives which is the other aspect of motherhood: the power to name the father.

Once again, she, the person in the weakest position, is able to take her revenge by speaking out. When Budin's son would not marry her, she prevented him from marrying someone else. Now, when Natale will not let her love her son, she takes away all joy he can ever have in a child of his own by suggesting that any child she has might not be his. Unfortunately, the taking of revenge does not cure the original hurt. Marie's life was ruined the first time, and this time she dies. Natale stabs Alexandre, and Marie collapses, just as her father collapsed and died at the end of the first section of the book, "parce que les sangs lui ont tourné d'une émotion pas endurable" (p. 356, "because an unbearable emotion curdled his blood").

This novel takes a particular angle on motherhood because the subject is a poor, unmarried girl. There is no reason to suppose, however, that her experience is uncommon, certainly among the working classes. Lucie Delarue-Mardrus shows clearly the humiliation and suffering that Marie goes through during pregnancy, and juxtaposes that pain with the joy that Marie feels for her child. Maternal love is shown as a happy, deep emotion, whereas love between lovers is shown rather as sensuality, pleasure, and desire not based on any sort of mutual trust, tenderness, or fellow feeling. Lucky indeed is the woman who is given pleasure by her partner. The events of Marie's life show clearly that women have great power over men because of their ability to bear children but that they rarely know how to profit from that power or are in a position to do so. The men in society have defined the rules of women's fertility in order to be able to avoid the very doubt that Marie plants in Natale's mind. They must know who is the father of each child, and so women must bear children only within prescribed bounds. Any woman who choses to use her power outside the defined limits must be destroyed. Hence Budin's son can abandon Marie, her father can repudiate her, her brother can take her child, and Natale can expect to possess her totally. Marie has committed a crime against society. She feels this shame until she has Alexandre, and then her loyalty changes. When she has spent the night with Natale, instead of feeling that she has taken her proper place at last, she feels rather that she has committed a crime against her son. Man is woman's enemy and by the traditions of society manages to transform his violence against her into her guilt before him; thus she becomes a double victim. A mother will not accept the role of victim when her child is at stake. Delarue-Mardrus writes: "Aussi, dans l'amour maternel, pas de déviation. La femme s'y rue avec la même violence que la bête. C'est le seul instinct qui n'ait pas été dépravé par des défenses et des damnations" (p. 333). [Hence, there are no deviations in maternal love. Women throw themselves into it with the same violence as do animals. It is the only instinct that has not been depraved by strictures and taboos.] But she has no way of defending herself against either the individual or social violence that will be used against her. She has neither status nor strength. She does, however, have two avenues to power: her right to tell her experience and her right to name her child's father.

Marie Avenal is humble and uneducated, and her story is one of bodily pain and emotional trouble. She is a victim whom her menfolk follow their instincts to dominate. The strength of Delarue-Mardrus's novel lies in the physical immediacy of Marie's experiences. The traditional power structures are very clear; the analysis of the situation emerges to a great extent through the organization of the events, the mode of description, and the juxtaposition of elements of the story. Marie herself is presented as incapable of abstract thought.

In total contrast to Marie Avenal is Sibylle Heursay in Renée-Tony d'Ulmès' two novels *Sibylle femme* and *Sibylle mère*.[2] Sibylle is a rational, autonomous feminist who makes her personal choices deliberately to be in accord with her understanding of her social context and her desire to help improve the status of women. She decides to live with the man she loves and bear children outside marriage in order to fight the social taboo against unmarried mothers. The outline of the plot is very simple. In the first volume Sibylle meets Dr. Stéphane Etcheverry at the house of Vera Norsoff, a feminist doctor friend; they fall in love, and he wants to marry her but feels that his mother and grandmother will be against it. Sibylle decides to give herself to him simply because she loves him. Marriage is not important to her, and she does not want to force her way into an unwilling family, although just before he leaves for a holiday with his family she does agree to marry him if he so wishes. He then spends some time in very traditional circumstances, and tells his mother about Sibylle, but his mother refuses to meet her. When he returns from the visit home, he finds that Sibylle has decided that she will live with him but will not marry him. When the second volume begins, four years later, Stéphane has just died; and his mother, who has never seen Stéphane since her refusal to meet Sibylle, has nonetheless come to Paris for the funeral. She meets Sibylle and the baby, Francis, and stays with them for a year; but, unable to break the habit of a lifetime, she cannot express her affection even to her grandson. Eventually she returns home, a lonely old woman still. During the year Sibylle gradually recovers from her grief and, at the end of *Sibylle mère*, agrees to live with Mourovkine, Stéphane's collaborator in his medical research.

The two novels are clearly constructed for the purpose of providing a careful examination of a variety of attitudes surrounding motherhood at the turn of the century. They contain a series of episodes which allow Sibylle and Stéphane to observe a number of different women and provide a commentary on the values of the different characters. Part 1 of *Sibylle femme* is set in a feminist context in Paris; and part 2, in an ultratraditional setting in the provinces. *Sibylle mère* shows the same contrast on a personal level, this time between Sibylle and Stéphane's mother.

The most outrageous example of destructive morality is the behavior of Mr. Kerven, a magistrate with an only daughter, Marthe. In flagrant abuse of his economic control of her life, he had given the girl no education that could enable her to provide for herself in any way, had lost the money her mother left her as a dowry, and had refused an offer of marriage made by an honest young man because he considered him to be their social inferior. Marthe went to work as a governess and companion. Not unexpectedly, she fell in love with the son of the house where she was employed; he seduced her and left her. When she told her father she was pregnant, he threw her out. Alone in a hotel, she miscarried. Sibylle finds her in a hospital and on the verge of death.

Despite the many ways in which her father has ruined her life, Marthe still loves and respects him. Sibylle goes, therefore, to ask Mr. Kerven to visit his daughter. Full of righteousness, he refuses and Sibylle explodes. I quote her outrage in full. As an indictment of traditional male attitudes, it needs no further comment:

La jeune fille, vouée au célibat malgré elle, rencontrait un jeune homme qui lui parlait d'amour et elle l'écoutait. Fallait-il l'accuser? Le père était plus coupable qu'elle. Il avait élevé sa fille dans l'idée de la suprématie du mâle. Donc il la préparait à croire et à admirer aveuglément celui qui la courtiserait. Il la considérait comme incapable de gérer sa fortune, de décider un mariage, de choisir une situation. Tenue pour irresponsable en toute autre circonstance, pourquoi aujourd'hui était-elle seule responsable? Et le séducteur? Depuis des siècles, la société tolère cette monstrueuse injustice, une morale pour l'homme, une morale pour la femme. Toutes les indulgences pour celui-ci, toutes les sévérités pour celle-là.

Si la femme se donne, non seulement elle a tous les risques et toutes les souffrances matérielles et morales de la maternité, mais elle est marquée d'une honte ineffaçable.

Si l'homme séduit, on dit que c'est une folie de jeunesse, une bêtise. S'il abandonne maîtresse et enfant, esquive tout devoir, il conserve quand même l'estime générale.

Il faudrait savoir ceci:

L'acte d'amour ne déshonore pas plus la femme que l'homme, mais la méconnaissance des obligations que crée cet acte les déshonore également tous deux. (pp. 180–81)

[The girl, pledged to celibacy in spite of herself, met a young man who spoke to her of love and she listened to him. Should she have been blamed? The father was guiltier than she. He had brought up his daughter with the concept of male supremacy. So, he prepared her to believe and to admire blindly the man who would court her. He considered her incapable of managing her fortune, of deciding on a marriage or of choosing an employment. Held irresponsible in all other circumstances, why, now, was she alone responsible? And the seducer? For centuries society has tolerated the monstrous injustice of one moral standard for men, another for women. Every indulgence for the former, nothing but severity for the latter.

If a woman gives herself, not only has she all the risks and all the material and moral suffering of motherhood, but she is branded with indelible shame.

If a man seduces a woman, it is called youthful folly, silliness. If he abandons her mistress and child, evades every duty, he nevertheless remains generally well thought of.

Here is what should be made known:

The act of love dishonors a woman no more than a man, but failure to recognize the obligations created by this act dishonors both of them in equal measure.]

This from a young woman to a man respected by society is in itself an extraordinary statement, but it is to no avail—the councillor was asleep.

Quand Sibylle se tut, il eut le réveil professionnel immédiat, et, son
calme et froid regard fixé sur la jeune femme, prononça:
Cela suffit, mademoiselle. Je vous l'ai dit, et je vous le répète: Cette créa-
ture n'est plus de ma famille. Je la renie!
L'arrêt tomba, net et irrévocable comme une sentence de mort. (pp.
181–82)

[When Sibylle fell silent, his professional reflex woke him instantly and,
fixing his calm, cold eyes on the young woman he pronounced:
"That will do, Mademoiselle, I have already told you, and I repeat: This
creature no longer belongs to my family. I disown her!"
The judgment fell, clear and irrevocable as a death sentence.]

This man of justice has no concern at all for his daughter. His behavior
is dictated by the importance of appearances—the caretaker of the build-
ing must not discover the truth. Marthe dies without seeing her lover or
her father again, a victim of bourgeois morality.

It becomes ever clearer as we read and analyze novels of this period
that the linchpin of the entire system is the appearance of male respectability, and this must be maintained at all costs. To this women of all ages
and of all classes are sacrificed ruthlessly. In her manual on how to adjust
to marriage, Camille Pert gives a horrifying example of a wife infected
with venereal disease by her husband, who is not treated for syphilis by
her doctor. The reason given is that the pharmacist would recognize what
the treatment was for, and this would besmirch the husband's reputation.
This is sufficient cause for leaving the wife to die a dreadful death (cf.
chapter 7). Mr. Kerven's behavior is very similar in its egocentricity.

Families reject pregnant daughters on grounds of moral respectability.
Employers mistreat unmarried pregnant working women, as we have already seen in *Marie, fille-mère*. Renée d'Ulmès reveals the callous exploitation of such women in an ironic opposition between an unwillingly but
righteously pregnant bourgeois wife and her maid. Again the author uses
Sibylle's questions to make the situation obvious to her readers:

—Alors elle ne travaillait plus?
—Oh si! merveilleusement! Mais on ne peut garder une fille enceinte.
Sibylle interrogea encore:
—Qu'est-elle devenue?
—Ma foi! Je n'en sais rien! Quand j'ai découvert son état scandaleux, je
l'ai mise immédiatement à la porte. Ça me dégoûtait de voir ce ventre de
fille!
Et Yvonne reposa sa tasse sur son ventre de femme. (pp. 100–1)

["She wasn't doing her work any more, then?"
"Oh yes! wonderfully well! But you can't keep a pregnant girl on."
Sibylle went on to ask:
"What has become of her?"
"Goodness, I haven't the slightest idea! When I discovered her scandalous condition, I sent her packing immediately. I was disgusted at the sight of that unmarried belly!"
And Yvonne rested her cup on her married woman's belly.]

Here we see Sibylle's indignation at the social distinction made between the flagrant pregnancies of the rich and the necessarily surreptitious pregnancies of the poor. Later, when Yvonne's baby is born, Sibylle is present at the interview of a wet-nurse, a simple country girl who, unlike Yvonne, loves her baby. As soon as Yvonne Terier and her mother discover that she is not married, they offer her less money. This time Sibylle speaks her indignation at the injustice perpetrated on the poor by the rich and uncaring, again to no avail. Custom prevails.

Clearly Sibylle does not see the world from a bourgeois point of view, for she goes on to ask Yvonne why she does not nurse the baby herself, and Yvonne is scandalized:

—Nourrir moi-même!
La jeune femme ouvrit des yeux effarés.
Nourrir elle-même! Avoir toujours un enfant pendu au sein, comme une femme du peuple, être réveillée la nuit, ne plus pouvoir sortir. Ah! non, par exemple! C'était déjà bien assez, trop même, d'être immobilisée neuf mois et de souffrir les tortures de l'accouchement. Après, elle aurait besoin d'un peu de mouvement et de distraction, elle l'aurait bien mérité! (pp. 109–10)

["Nurse the baby myself!"
The young woman's eyes opened wide in dismay.
Nurse the baby herself! Always having an infant hanging at her breast, like a lower-class woman, being wakened at night, not being able to go out any more. Oh no, for heaven's sake! It was already quite enough, too much in fact, being immobilized for nine months and suffering the tortures of childbirth. Afterwards, she would need movement and amusement, she would certainly have deserved it!"]

Yvonne sees the baby as something that will upset her comfortable life. She has no thought at all about her responsibility to her baby, nor has she any sense of solidarity with other women less fortunate than herself. Her thoughtlessness is rendered both apparent and reprehensible by the presence of Sibylle. Renée d'Ulmès is using Sibylle as a mouthpiece for feminist views on motherhood. The novel is a piece of propaganda written to arouse the social awareness of the reader. As such, it has no literary value whatever but a good deal of sociological interest; also, I find that one becomes fond of Sibylle. She has a splendid line in outrage and is a thoughtful woman who commands respect. After the encounter with Yvonne the author sets her meditating on the whole issue of motherhood and brings her to the conclusion that, as a feminist, she certainly does not believe in reducing women to the state of broody hens, nor does she think that the fate of a woman who spends all her life looking after a house full of children is anything but hard and painful. She does, however, see dignity and beauty in the task of bringing up a child and thinks how much more than the empty-headed Yvonne she, a thinking woman, would enjoy her child. (Here we are being prepared for the second novel of the series.)

D'Ulmès then proceeds to have Sibylle serve as a model. Not only does Sibylle think differently from Yvonne, but she also acts differently. She looks after Berthe, her pregnant maid, and shares Berthe's pride in the baby. Indeed, it is in holding this child that she realizes how much she wants children herself. (D'Ulmès is very careful to deal with the various commonplace ideas which maintain that intellectual women have no use for children. Already, we have seen Sibylle thinking about the importance of a child's upbringing; now she feels maternal instinct too.) First comes an appreciation of a mother's moral duty and its recompense:

Cet être nouveau, tout à créer moralement, serait le devoir présent, l'occupation constante, et aussi le but nécessaire à son âme, avide d'inconnu, toujours prête à s'évader hors du temps, dans un lointain qu'elle façonnerait un peu à son gré. Elle n'aurait plus peur de vieillir, avec cette jeune existence près d'elle. Elle connaîtrait les joies puériles de soigner, de dorloter, d'embrasser un doux petit corps tiède, et les joies hautes de former un coeur et un esprit. Une femme ne sait qu'une partie de la vie bien incomplète, qui n'a pas été mère. (pp. 240–41)

[This new being, all ready to be created morally, would be the immediate duty, the constant occupation and also the goal necessary for her soul that was athirst for the unknown and always ready to escape outside the bounds of time to a distant place that she would invent more or less as she pleased. She would no longer be afraid to grow old with this young existence at her side. She would know the childish joys of caring for, pampering and hugging a sweet little warm body and the great joy of shaping a heart and a mind. A woman who has not been a mother knows only a very incomplete part of life.]

Then, finally, comes physical tenderness for the child.

To have a child, Sibylle is prepared to consider marriage, even though it is against her personal principles and values. She debates the whole question with her friend Vera Norsoff. Vera is a doctor who would very much like a child herself, but she is not interested in men and they do not find her attractive. In some ways she recalls Jeanne Boerk in Colette Yver's novel *Les Cervelines* (chapter 7). The author depicts her as a chaste and sexless woman who is a marvelous friend and who would be for that reason an excellent mother. As it is, she looks after other people's children. Because of her lack of illusions about men (work with them in a dissecting room reveals a lot, she says, and in this she agrees with some of the women doctors in Yver's *Princesses de science* [chapter 7]) and her desire for a child, she understands Sibylle's position and is able to challenge her on the subject of illegitimate children and the attitudes of society: she, of course, sees all the young girls who want an abortion and, as a result, has no use at all for bourgeois "morality," in which, as we have seen, love is encouraged, chastity is mocked, and yet the natural results of such attitudes are rejected with hypocritical shock and horror, the women involved then being treated as a source of public shame. Vera urges Sibylle to live her life according to her principles, to remain unmarried, and to bear children, and thus by her example help young women less fortunate than herself to hold up their heads in society.

This is a brave but somewhat idealistic solution, though it is the logical conclusion of the thought process the author is pursuing through her heroine. Sibylle remembers Marthe Kerven, who had said sadly that it was better for her child to be dead than illegitimate, and she thinks of all the infanticides she sees where she works. She decides that she will live freely with Stéphane.

Meanwhile Stéphane sees other disastrous effects of traditional morality. A friend of his mother tells him how her sister, who was pregnant, cut her own throat; she then adds, "Elle ne pouvait pas agir autrement. On ne survit pas au déshonneur" (p. 212, "She could not do otherwise. You cannot survive dishonor"). Then his own mother acts in similar fashion. She listens to his description of Sibylle, her qualities, her values, and his love for her with sympathy until she suspects that they have made love. Immediately all personal feeling is pushed aside, and she states, "Celle qui se donne en dehors du mariage n'est pas une honnête femme" (p. 223, "She who gives herself outside of marriage is not a decent woman"). There is nothing more to be said. She herself, as a young mother, resisted the temptation to join the man she loved for one night because she feared the effect it might have on her baby later in life, if he ever found out what she had done. She thinks no further than this memory of her own virtue and on this basis opposes her son's marriage. It is impossible for her to conceive of a woman's making the choice that Sibylle has made, let alone for her to approve of it. We see that the rules of traditional society are cruel and intransigent. As a result of her upbringing Madame Etcheverry gave up the man she loved for her son and is now going to lose that son because of the same strict moral code, yet she cannot bring herself in any way to modify her attitude and behavior. Madame Etcheverry's prospect of a loving life and joyful motherhood has been destroyed as effectively by her upbringing as Marthe Kerven was killed by hers.

D'Ulmès is alert to all the various ways in which women are oppressed by society and in particular how this oppression operates on them as mothers. We see clearly that all the women in *Sibylle femme* are deprived in some serious way of the satisfactions of motherhood. Rich or poor, city or country women, they all suffer from the dictates of society. The rich are bound by their upbringing; the poor, by necessity; and all suffer.

In *Sibylle mère* the emotional deprivation caused by Madame Etcheverry's upbringing and moral code of appearances is contrasted with the motherhood Sybille assumed freely and the joy she finds in her child.

Francis is the delight of Sibylle's life, and like Josanne Valentin (*La Rebelle*, chapter 3), she is prepared to give up the possibility of a new married life if the relationship is not good for the child. For her the mother-son bond is one of loving responsibility and responsiveness. Madame Etcheverry, on the other hand, is desperately lonely and has always been alone. Patriarchal requirements for the upbringing of a boy, and the accepted behavior for a mother, required that she remain distant from her son all his life. Now he is dead, and she wasted their last years because of what she had been brought up to believe. Those beliefs separated her from her own mother and are now keeping her distant from Sibylle and even from Francis, the grandchild who could take some of the place left by her son. The kind of motherly feeling that she represents is the absolute opposite of the flexibility, warmth, and careful thought for the child's well-being that is Sibylle's way of life. Mme Etcheverry sacrificed the man she loved for Stéphane, but neither she nor Stéphane profited from her decision, because she did it with the thought of what his opinion of her reputation would be rather than for a less superficial reason. Sibylle is about to make a similar sacrifice at the end of *Sibylle mère*, though for rather more substantial reasons, but Dr. Mourovkine convinces her of his affection for Francis and, in opposition to the split we have seen in Delarue-Mardrus's novels and indeed in Tinayre's *La Rebelle*, declares it inconceivable that he should cease to love the child just because he now loves the mother too. We are offered a perfectly reconstituted family. This is indeed propaganda.

Sibylle Heursay is the model of thoughtful love. She cares for all who need her and has a special compassion for other women in trouble. Again in *Sibylle mère* there are examples of unmarried women to whom she gives material assistance and emotional support, and never does she judge, for she knows how difficult a woman's situation is, and especially the situation of a pregnant woman. D'Ulmès shows even more clearly than most of her contemporaries the importance of supportive networks of women in the lives of women. She does tend to see this support as a class issue, however, where bourgeois women with developed social consciences use their money, education, and status to help women less fortunate than themselves. The support is somewhat patronizing in contrast to the peer support in some of the other novels. It is, however, representative of the situation at the turn of the century, and one the socialists protested about. Only women for whom survival was not a full-time occupation had the time and energy for feminist support and reform.

The fact that Sibylle should accept Mourovkine is, in fact, slightly ironic, because in her choice we hear a faint echo of Thérèse Darau, a friend who became the cossetted mistress of one of Mourovkine's colleagues in order to obtain some comfort and security for herself and her illegitimate daughter. It is true that Sibylle's comfort comes from mutual respect, love, and independence, whereas Thérèse accepts a more traditional role, but as she explains to Sibylle, she is a simple petite bourgeois who has not Sibylle's crusading spirit and who is making the best life she can. The difference between the two women lies in their attitudes about themselves: Thérèse is Dr. Lianés' mistress; Sibylle is Dr.

Mourovkine's equal. Thérèse is, like most women, making the best of a life that is out of her control; Sibylle has chosen her way in the world. She is autonomous, she is strong, and she is happy. Here the author is dealing with a different class of people from those Lucie Delarue-Mardrus depicted in *Marie fille-mère*, and already there are a few more solutions possible. Sibylle has control of her life, whereas Marie was continually the victim of fate and the men around her. Unexpectedly, they do share a number of attitudes: the joy they find in their child, the responsibility they feel toward his upbringing, and their awareness that the only way a woman can protect herself and others is by breaking the silence expected of women and making public the way in which they are abused in the name of love.

In *Marie, fille-mère* we analyzed motherhood as oppression and instinctive protection of the child. *Sibylle femme* and *Sibylle mère* offer a feminist critique of the attitudes toward maternity at that period and a model of reasoned motherhood for the benefit of the child. Now to complete the triptych we explore exalted motherhood and total control of the child.

Un Inceste (An Incest) by Valentine de Saint-Point is the second volume of *A Trilogy of Love and Death*.[3] The first volume, *Un Amour* (A Love), tells the love story of our heroine (she has no name). She selected a young man with whom she made love, intending never to see him again. He refuses to be abandoned in this cavalier fashion, declares his love for her, and they live a brief idyll. She becomes pregnant, joyfully writes the news to her lover, and says she will call the child Siegfried if it is a boy. Before the child is born the lover dies. *Un Inceste* begins eighteen years later. Siegfried is a handsome and talented musician, and his mother is as young and beautiful as ever. As remarks one guest at the gathering which opens the novel, "Sa chair est unique" (Her flesh is unique). Siegfried calls her "Unique."

Un Inceste is a novel written to create a Nietzschean superwoman. De Saint-Point writes with sustained lyricism to glorify Unique as a superb human being and a positive force. In the third volume of the triology, *Une Mort* (A Death), Siegfried depicts himself as the destructive counterforce that will destroy all that his mother brought into being because he has no will to create after her death. But never, in the terms of the novels themselves, is it suggested that Unique prevented her son from reaching his full potential, nor is there evidence to extrapolate such an interpretation, as there is no description of Siegfried's formative years in the novels. Unique is the mother in her life-giving function, and any temptation to transform her into an image of the devouring mother would be a deformation of the character as de Saint-Point presents her. She is an unambiguous manifestation of creation.

It is, however, true that Unique is such a strong character that she leaves her son very little space to develop his identity for himself; he has no physical space and, as we gather from the title, no sexual space either, because *Un Inceste* is the story of a mother-son incest and that inevitably raises a whole range of issues concerning power relations. However, if we analyze the novel in its own terms, we must accept the Nietzchean premises: Unique gives herself to Siegfried so that his energy and talents shall not be dispersed by lesser beings. Unfortunately, their love makes him so happy that he never writes the great work she intends he shall compose, with the result that she commits suicide in order to ensure that he will suffer and then express his emotion in music. Unfortunately, Siegfried is not made of the same stuff as his mother; in the third novel, *Une Mort* (A Death), he marries a mediocre wife, has an ordinary child, and writes only one composition: a symphony of his love for his mother. He is not the accomplishment of her pride and will, as he himself muses on reading her annotated volume of Nietzsche:

> —Tout ce qui exaltait, la domination de soi, la volonté, l'orgueil.
> Puis il répéta les deux dernières strophes.
> —Ceci n'est pas écrit pour moi.... Serait-il possible qu'avec moi l'orgueil d'Unique sombrât? Elle avait été la créatrice, et moi je serais le destructeur, sa déchéance, sa véritable mort. Serait-ce possible? (*Une Mort*, pp. 40–41)

> ["Everything that was exalting: self-discipline, willpower, pride."
> Then he repeated the last two verses.
> "This is not written for me.... Could it be possible that Unique's pride foundered on me? She had been the creator and I would be the destroyer, her downfall, her true death. Could that be possible?"]

This interpretation is borne out by the novels: Siegfried creates neither a masterpiece nor genius. His mother's intentions are dead. The question is, of course, whether any mother has the right to take over her child's life so totally as to force her intention upon him even from beyond the grave. It is certainly true of Unique that she saw herself as the creator. In *Un Inceste* we are offered an exalted vision of motherhood.

Durant dix-huit années, avec un courage joyeux et sans cesse renouvelé toute sa jeunesse, toute sa force, toute sa vie avaient dirigé leurs rayons ardents sur cette jeune âme. Ni regret, ni désir n'avait amoindri la volonté de celle, qui après avoir été la divine amante, était la sublime mère.

Toute l'ardeur qui avait magnifié son amour pour le père mort en exultant, faisait sa maternité unique, capable de parfaire un chef-d'oeuvre, et de tracer la route escarpée du génie. (p. 18)

[For eighteen years, with joyful and endlessly renewed courage, her whole youth, her whole strength, her whole life had directed their incandescent rays at that young soul. Neither regret nor desire had lessened her will, she who, after being the divine lover, was the sublime mother.

All the ardour that had glorified her love for the father who had died rejoicing, had made her motherhood unique, capable of perfecting a masterpiece and of mapping out the steep path of genius.]

The love for the child is a development of the passion for the lover. (Unique is the full expression of all that Noël Delysle fears when he thinks that Josanne loves the manifestation of Maurice in Claude [*La Rebelle*, chapter 3]). Siegfried has to be a genius, as he is the product of the perfect love, and his works must and will be the ultimate expression of their personal trinity. It is not for nothing that the book is punctuated with references to paintings and sculptures of the Virgin Mary and that in *Un Amour* her lover calls her Divine. Siegfried, like Christ, communicates with the universe; his mother is his only link with humanity, and through Siegfried's music his mother's power moves the world. At first this power appears innocent. Unique would give her lifeblood for her son; his pain is her despair. The first section closes with a slightly ironic image of the Virgin (ironic for the reader, but not for the author), in which the implication is that the Virgin Mary has never known the passion of love for the father of her child and so does not feel passion for the child either. It becomes clear as the novel continues that Unique sees her strength as superior. She, after all, was Divine as well as Unique.

We realize very quickly that Siegfried is struggling against carnal desire for his mother; he recoils more and more from her caresses, but she persists in trying to cure the pain she sees in him. Thus his struggle gets harder and his pain ever greater. Meanwhile she offers herself totally, though for the moment the vocabulary is metaphysical:

Viens, je t'étreindrai comme lorsque tu étais tout petit. Viens, je me pencherai sur ton âme comme lorsque tu n'étais qu'un petit bloc de chair inconscient. . . . Pour toi j'en ferai de la joie et par mes mains puissantes je soulagerai ton corps, et par mon sourire je guérirai ton âme.

Viens, je te ressusciterai. . . .

Viens, Siegfried. Je suis la terre, mais je ne suis pas comme le sol, inconsciente, et tu es toutes mes fleurs, tous mes arbres, tous me fruits.

Je n'ai pas l'impassibilité de l'éternité. Je n'ai ni passé, ni avenir. Et toute ma puissance et toute ma force sont à toi. Prends. (p. 26)

[Come, I shall embrace you as I did when you were small. Come, I shall study your soul as I did when you were nothing but a little lump of flesh all unaware. . . . For you, I shall draw joy from it and with my powerful hands shall ease your body and with my smile, cure your spirit.

Come, I shall revive you. . . .

Come, Siegfried. I am the earth but I am not unfeeling like the soil and you are all my flowers, all my trees and all my fruits.

I do not have eternity's impassiveness. I have neither past nor future. And all my power, all my strength, are yours. Take them.]

The vocabulary may be metaphysical, but the body language is not: Unique digs her nails into her suffering flesh. She lives entirely for and through her son, and the idea that he will leave her for other women is not one that she can accept. In her pride she thinks that only she can focus his future. Meanwhile, Siegfried is fading before her eyes, and as he does so he looks more and more like his father: Unique begins to see the one as a reincarnation of the other. As a result, she begins to superimpose her lover's death and her physical passion on to Siegfried. This time she intends to conquer death by her strength and her will. When Siegfried rejects her maternal comfort, she throws herself on him, as she had thrown herself on her lover's body eighteen years before to give her all to save him:

Je suis la force, je suis le soleil. Etreins-les. Etreins-les.

Tout est pour toi.

Tout mon être arde en un feu qui est le soleil, qui est la vie. Et ma bouche est le coeur de la vie.

Je vaincrai, je vaincrai.

Accueille la vie. (p. 42)

[I am the power, I am the sun. Embrace them. Embrace them.

They are all for you.

My whole being burns in a fire that is the sun, that is life. And my mouth is life's heart.

I shall conquer, I shall conquer.

Welcome life.]

The incest is consummated, and Siegfried's struggles are over.

There is no indication in the novel that Unique's "rape" of her son is seen as traumatic for either of them. They settle into an apparently happy relationship and travel around Europe and North Africa so that Siegfried will understand as much as possible of the world around him: the glory of nature, the nature of chaos, power, death. The succession of cities they visit become more and more symbolic of death. Meanwhile, however, Unique glories in her creation of the child and of the man—double motherhood, double happiness—but she does not realize that she has created so much of Siegfried and so much for Siegfried that when she says, "Nous sommes seuls et un" (p. 106, we are alone and one), she is too right. Siegfried is not capable of finding his own inspiration. He is aware of this, but his mother is not. He attributes no blame to his mother, although we can see that in his sublime way he is no more prepared to survive alone than was Marthe Kerven in *Sibylle mère*, whose father has kept her to himself and brought her up to fit his view of the world, nor indeed than Charlotte Bugeot in *Ma petite Lotte*, who is raped by her father (chapter 5). Unique may be a sublime mother for her creator, but we might feel that she destroys her son. The image she contemplates of Michelangelo's *Pietà* again becomes ironic for us:

> L'esprit alangui et serein, les yeux clos, elle contempla la face douloureuse que la Vierge-Mère penche sur le visage éteint du Christ son fils, dans la Pietà de Michelangelo. Elle s'émut de la volupté des doigts maternels dans les cheveux souples où s'attarde encore la vie.
> Puis elle s'aima d'avoir encore défié et enfin vaincu la mort par l'infini, l'illimité et l'amoralité de son amour. (p. 76)
>
> [With her mind calm and relaxed and her eyes closed, she contemplated the grief-stricken expression of the Virgin Mary bent over the lifeless face of Christ, her son, in the Michelangelo *Pietà*. She was moved by the voluptuous touch of the maternal fingers in the flowing locks, where life yet lingered.
> Then she felt delight in herself for having again challenged and finally conquered death through the infiniteness, boundlessness and amorality of her love.]

For her it is the sign that she had the courage to challenge death and that she won: Siegfried was reborn in her love. It is, of course, possible to have another view of the situation: the mother is alive but the son is dead. Only under the mother's caress is there a little life.

Despite all his mother's encouragement, Siegfried writes no music; Unique begins to suffer from the thought that she might have failed in her life's work, and she begins to wonder whether Siegfried must choose: "Peut-être est-ce l'Oeuvre *ou* moi" (p. 216, "perhaps it is the Work *or* me"). As a result, she tries to force Siegfried's hand by making him promise to write his compositions down, then she goes away to die, leaving him a long letter explaining her aims and her actions. Siegfried has lived perfection; now suffering should mature him and his Work will come into being.

> Comprends mon supplice et mon courage, car ma vie est finie, mon oeuvre est terminée, et pour te laisser à la tienne, emportant ma beauté encore sans déchéance, je vais au néant. (p. 227)
>
> [Understand my torment and my courage, for my life is finished, my work is over, and in order to leave you to yours, I am taking away my still flawless beauty and am going toward nothingness.]

(I find it curious that Valentine de Saint-Point should choose to attribute to a woman with such a sublime philosophy this last reference to her beauty. Unique seems to be suggesting that she would find it easier to die if she were showing signs of aging. Presumably it is a final reminder of her perfection. And we must suppose that as the book did open on the theme of her beauty and her "unique flesh," Saint-Point wishes to achieve a balance by ending on the same theme. To my mind it makes this superwoman disconcertingly and uncharacteristically mortal.)

The work that Unique leaves for Siegfried to do is twofold: he must compose music and have a child. He fulfills the minimum requirements of her request: one symphony, one pleasant and healthy daughter.

Valentine de Saint-Point suggests that bringing the child successfully to maturity is the dream of all mothers: "L'arbre ne rejette point la fleur, il la mûrit jusqu'au fruit" (p. 1, "The tree does not reject the blossom but ripens it into fruit"). Whether this be the general case or not, Unique is certainly such a tree. She is a strong, proud, and beautiful woman who controls not only her own life, but also that of everything around her. She is identified with the Virgin Mary by the iconography of the novel, with Mélisande by the quotations that punctuate the opening scene, and with Sieglinde by the choice of the name of Siegfried for her son/lover. Thus she becomes the ideal mother, the mysterious ideal lover, and both mother and incestuous lover all in one. Siegfried identifies her with the sun so that for him she is all light, all warmth, the great creative force without whom he has no life.

In the works by the three authors we have seen three strong women, each bringing up her child alone and each very different in her source of strength. Marie Avenal has an animal power when her child needs protection, and a low cunning and cruelty in revenge when she has been hurt. Sibylle Heursay is an intelligent, educated, and thoughtful woman whose strength lies in her clear-sightedness, flexibility, sense of social injustice, and courage to gainsay prejudice. Sibylle acts on her principles, Marie reacts by instinct, both on a daily basis in the real world. Unique is not on the same plane. She is a superwoman of Nietzschean proportions and, although perhaps rather exalted and full of hubris for today's taste, she is a marvelously uplifting creation. That the men around her should be weak merely enhances her strength and will. There is nothing she does not dare, nothing she cannot do. Such bravura is rare in the female imagination.

It is interesting to note that in all three cases the situations are parallel. In each case we watch a mother bringing up her son without his father. Each mother loves her son dearly and cares about his future. The differences between the lives of the characters are very clearly differences of class and money. Those between the various styles of writing come from the ideologies of the authors. Delarue-Mardrus has produced a realistic novel centered on women's experience as seen by a woman, where the major events are Marie's experience of love and rape, childbirth, and sexual desire—in sum, a description of the life of many a country girl, but one in which the focus is Marie's relationship with her body. Renée d'Ulmès has used the excuse of fiction to write a social tract. She has created an intelligent, educated, and articulate heroine to serve as a critic of society and an exemplary model of female solidarity and modernity; the body of her novels provides a series of examples for commentary. *Sibylle femme* and *Sibylle mère* are unabashedly didactic works preaching socialism and feminism. Valentine de Saint-Point's heroine, on the other hand, gives the impression of springing fully clothed from the brow of Nietzsche. Saint-Point's ideas are derivative and fashionably poetic, and the novel is not really to modern taste, but her heroine remains marvelously exhilarating. She is a female modeled on Nietzsche's superman, in the full knowledge of her power and her glory, with all the desirable strengths translated into female form.

We should take note that only Sibylle, the thoughtful mother, is able to combine happily her love for her child and her sensual delight in a man. Marie responds instinctively and physically to Alexandre and Natale without being able to deal with the emotional complexities of the relationships involved; but for her, as for Sibylle, there is a clear distinction between mother love and sexual love. The unresolved tension between the two kills Marie. Unique feels no such taboo and, although the mother-son relationship is explained, if not justified, in the novel by Unique's exaltation and superhuman view of her role, nonetheless, through the symbolic lyricism, appears a happy and prolonged incest that is utterly devoid of guilt and shame. It is the combination of the two modes of love that is presented as sublime motherhood. Natural mothering, social principles, and divine passion—the range of possible models is wide indeed, and always the love for her child is the most important thing in each mother's life. Marriage is shown as an obstacle to true mothering.

At least marriage is shown symbolically by its absence to be an obstacle to the mothering of sons. The novels studied in this chapter are three of the major illustrations of motherhood in novels of the period, and except for *Le Roman de six petites filles*, I did not find any extended discussion at all of a mother bringing up a daughter, although Jeanne Marni's *Pierre Tisserand* (1907) and *Souffrir* (1909) are concerned with the relationship between a stepmother and daughter. The most important relationship for daughters is the one they have with their father, as we shall see in the next chapter.

Why, then, the importance of heterosexual parenting at this period? The details may well vary from novel to novel, but the basic reasons are, first, the relative status of men and women in society, and, second, the values held by the persons of each sex. We must remember that we are dealing here with writers who are pragmatic and realistic for the most part, as well as being more or less feminist in their perspective. Consciously or unconsciously, they are aware of how much they can change the views of their readers, how far they can lead them along the way toward support of improvement in the status of women, how subversive they can be, and when they must perforce accept the prevalent codes of belief and behavior if they want to be read. This is not literature written to obtain a place in literary history; these are books written to produce immediate social effects. As such, their aims and techniques are very different from those of a Proust or a Gide.

It is my hypothesis that these socially conscious authors give their heroines sons because most of their readers attribute more importance to sons and thus are more likely to attribute more importance to the mothers of sons. Hence the heroine is permitted to step outside accepted behavior as long as her independence and autonomy can be seen to be for the good of her son. Such nonconformity would be seen as unjustifiable for a daughter or far too threatening to social norms. Two generations of strong women could not be allowed to exist unpunished, whereas one of the sources of strength, interest, and pleasure in these novels is that autonomous women, minor characters as well as heroines, survive and survive well quite regularly, certainly in numbers far surpassing the survival figures for strong women in the "great" novels of the male canon.

I suggest, however, that the heroines also have sons because in practical terms, the mother alone cannot give a daughter sufficient support in this period for the daughter to claim the opportunity of an independent future. And as we shall see in chapter 6, a woman with a husband is ipso facto not autonomous. Hence an author who wants to create a strong woman character has to choose the generations she wants to describe and arrange the sex of her other characters accordingly.

Also important is the education a mother can give her son when there is no husband present to enforce the inculcation of patriarchal values, as opposed to the extinction of affection or respect for women created by traditional schooling as illustrated in Louise Compain's *L'Un vers l'autre* (chapter 7).

Perhaps, alas, we must consider that however feminist our authors may be, the pains of motherhood and marriage as they represent and analyze them are such that they have difficulty in creating girls who will have to face the oppressions, obstacles, impotence, and frustration that most of them are struggling against. It is easier to create an optimistic future for sons. It is also self-protective in a society in which a reader's husband might check her reading material and forbid authors thought to be too seditious. These novels are full of compromises that cloak advances toward autonomy. This might well be one of them. Mothers and sons, fathers and daughters is an arrangement which both upholds and subverts the all-pervasive heterosexuality of patriarchal society.

Daughterhood
CREATION AND DESTRUCTION

Contemporary women writers, and feminists in particular, tend to concentrate on the relationship between mother and daughter, the way in which this bond has been weakened or twisted by patriarchal institutions, and the need for it to be reestablished in order for generations of women to profit from each other's strength and support. As we saw in chapter 4, mothers and daughters are not portrayed together in any important way in the novels of the Belle Epoque. Thoughtful exploration of motherhood tends to be done almost in a vacuum. The child is a minimal presence (Francis in *Sibylle mère* being the only one who remains in our minds as having any trace of personality), a token object of his mother's maternal subjectivity, and this token tends to be a son, for some of the reasons I have postulated. There is no shortage of daughters in literature, however. Daughters become a source of interest as they grow, and the way they grow is directly connected to the relationship they have with their fathers.

These novels are written in a period in which women have virtually no legal rights at all, education of any length and quality is very much a privilege, and few professions allow a women real economic independence. In this context a daughter's life is made or ruined according to her father's attitude. As we have seen already the two paths to a sense of self and a certain sense of freedom for women are created by knowledge—knowledge and acceptance of love in both its moral and physical manifestations, and the knowledge that comes from education.

It is evident that a father's support or, conversely, his abuse will create or destroy his daughter either economically or emotionally. The father holds all the power, his daughter has what he chooses to give; his character and behavior shape his daughter's future.

The novels in this chapter offer a variety of power structures, from parental self-sacrifice to sexual abuse, but every one of them, even the most idyllic, stunts the girl's development in some way. Every young woman's future is a compromise constructed on a foundation laid by her father, be it with love, lack of awareness of his daughter's needs, or thoughtless indulgence of his own. None of the fathers is deliberately destructive or cruel, but they are for the most part patriarchal: self-important, self-centered, and self-indulgent. It is their daughters who pay the price.

Once again *Hellé* by Marcelle Tinayre is exemplary.[1] Hellé is an ideal. She is given an education designed to strengthen her judgment, to provide her with a moral code and an appreciation of what is valuable because it is good and beautiful. Then, once she is prepared to think for herself, she is introduced into society and shown the pitfalls created by sentimentality, hypocrisy, and falsehood while learning about her own feelings. Yet even Hellé is deceived for a time by the appearance of worth because she has not learned that beauty of form is not necessarily an indication of inner beauty. She realizes her mistake in time, however, marries the right man, and sets off for a life of true love and social usefulness. Hellé has been brought up to make choices and makes them by herself in a context that simplifies the central issue for the daughters in this chapter. First, the father figure is actually an uncle, so the ties between the man and the girl are not complicated by learned expectations of father-daughter relations nor by the real complexities of family bondings and rivalries. Second, M de Riveyrac dies before Hellé selects her fiancé, with the result that she is free to choose the young man without any suggestion of refusal or abandonment of the older one. Hellé's situation is ideal; she has money, education, a sense of self, and autonomy. Her love for Antoine Genesvrier and his for her are based on awareness of the real qualities of their chosen partners; they should indeed live happily ever after.

Such is not the case for most girls, not because they are less intrinsically wise than Hellé, but because they rarely receive an education that prepares them to make their own decisions, are rarely free to make their own choices, and the choices, when there are any to be made, are not so straightforward. Hellé was autonomous, economically independent, and free of family ties. She could direct her life as she thought fit.

Tinayre provides us with a different situation in *L'Ombre de l'amour* (1910).[2] In this novel she opposes two modes of upbringing, scientific and religious; two kinds of father, educated and rough; two potential lovers with different weaknesses, physical and moral; and two young women of different class and outlook. She reaches a single conclusion: when a father is unaware of his daughter's needs, and the daughter is therefore obliged to make her choice and fulfill her desire as best she may in secret and against her father's will, disaster will occur. No matter how well-meaning the father may be, his lack of understanding can wreck his daughter's life.

Denise Cayrol is nearing thirty and lives with her father, the freethinking village doctor. After the death of Denise's mother, her father taught her to use and trust her own judgment; he also taught her hygiene and genetics, and his belief that unhealthy people should not have children. Before this, she spent some years at a convent school and despite her robust common sense has a lingering nostalgia for the notions of religion, love, and duty that were inculcated in her childhood. She would, moreover, like to have a child and sees that time is running short. Into the household comes a young man, Jean Favières, who is dying of tuberculosis. Denise cares for him daily; inevitably he falls in love with her (she is beautiful, gentle, thoughtful), and she comes to believe that she loves him. When he is sent away to die, she goes to join him and becomes pregnant. He dies. Denise finally confesses her state to her father and goes away to have the baby. It dies, and she returns home to her father.

Denise has a parallel in Fortunade Brandou, the innkeeper's daughter, who sews for her. Fortunade received the religious education Denise avoided. She is totally immersed in simplistic mystical piety and dreams only of returning to the convent to become a nun, but her family is opposed to her choice, as is the village priest, who thinks that a cheerful young man and a couple of children will cure her fantasies. When Martial Veydrenne, the local ne'er-do-well, has an accident, Fortunade goes to help him and his father; she returns to visit them because she feels some need to struggle against their moral weakness. Suddenly she refuses to go either to confession or to Mass, even at Easter, and one day is found drowned in the local waterfall. She was pregnant.

The novel is structured to reveal that both young women have needs

that their fathers (and Fortunade has two: her own father and the priest)
do not recognize and that cannot be met within the father's code of behavior for himself and his expectations for his daughter. Both young
women feel a love that they must express and that is denied in their normal daily lives: Denise, motherly care and affection; Fortunade, her love
of God as expressed in help to suffering humanity. In each case, to achieve
fulfillment the daughter is obliged to choose what she wants against her
father's beliefs, thus depriving herself of his support and protection. The
results are unhappy for them both. Because Dr. Cayrol is a good man and
Denise trusts her father, she is able at least to tell him of her action and
its result. He suffers pain but shows love in his support of his daughter,
so that Denise survives. Fortunade, on the other hand, cannot bring herself to tell either her real or her spiritual father what has happened to
her (she fears punishment from each) and in her desperation kills herself.

For her survival the woman depends, yet again, on her father. If he is
a kind, open-minded, thoughtful man who loves his daughter, he may be
able to revise his behavior and save her. If he is caught in ignorance and
prejudice, like Fortunade's father, or within a fixed code, like the priest,
the girl who transgresses has no hope of forgiveness and rehabilitation.
The fathers in this novel do not abuse their daughters deliberately; Dr.
Cayrol, happy in his comforts, makes no attempt to help his daughter
find a suitable husband. He would certainly have opposed her relationship
with Jean if he had known how it was developing, and his opposition
would have been wise in light of his medical opinion; he did not have
the psychological skill to see the need for other advice. Likewise the
priest, drawing on previous experience, thought that Fortunade's piety
was a passing adolescent whim and, with the best of intentions, treated
it lightly. Mr. Brandou, like Dr. Cayrol, though on a different level,
wanted his daughter's help and thought no further about her. Marriage
and children were offered to the girl who did not want them and not
to the one who did, and that decision was made by the father in each
case.

Both young women received unbalanced educations. Denise was
given reason and information, but no spiritual or emotional comfort;
Fortunade received spiritual and emotional comfort, but no knowledge
and no training of her reason. When prevented from taking control of her
life openly, each tried to fulfill her desire and fell into the trap of the

weakness in her education. Once her father had opposed her real choice, be it directly or indirectly, she made the best decision she could in the circumstances, and inevitably suffered for her disobedience.

L'Ombre de l'amour is a well-made novel in which the parallels between Denise and Fortunade are set up subtly and interestingly, as are those between the physical weakness of Jean Favières and the moral weakness of Martial Veyrenne. The moving force within the novel is the need women have for emotional satisfaction; the major theme is pity, which is shown to have the power to make women commit extraordinary sacrifices in a mode of love that often is categorized as Christian charity. As in her other works, Tinayre is exploring the phenomenon of love, the forms it takes, and the choices it imposes on women in particular.

Denise has a solid relationship with her father, individual to individual, and so, although she may have chosen against the knowledge he had given her, she was not accused of ceasing to love her father, even though her decision took her away from him and toward her love for Jean. In Gabrielle Reval's *La Bachelière*,[3] however, Gaude Malvos suffers such an accusation unjustly when in fact she is sacrificing her future for her father. As a result of the symbiotic nature of the father-daughter relationship, the pattern of her whole life is altered.

Malvos is a brilliant and obsessive archaeologist who has educated his eldest child in order to associate her with his work, his thoughts, and his passion. He sees himself in his daughter, and Gaude identifies with him entirely. The wife, Rachel, and the other children are shadows in their lives. But Malvos has spent all his money searching for the lost cities of Gaul and can do no more without funds, so his daughter decides to marry the richest of Malvos's students and to persuade him to pay for her father's research. She tells nobody about her decision, and when all the students are assembled for the presentation of a decoration to Malvos, she looks them over coldly, searching for the combination of devotion to her father and money. We are led to believe that all the young men love her, but that she is known to be so chaste and so involved with her father's fame that "chacun l'admirait comme une vestale" ("they each admired her as if she were a vestal"). She selects Tarette, a mediocre, pleasant young man, and, in an imitation of a Gaulish ceremony, asks him publicly to take her as his wife. She is quite confident of her superiority and the importance of her name; that she might be refused is not a possibility. Nor does she consider her action unkind or in any way base. Any action that will help her father fulfill his genius is good in her eyes. What she does not expect is her father's reaction. Everybody is astounded, but Malvos also is enraged. Seeing his daughter only as an extension of himself, he does not understand her enough to recognize the incongruity of her action, or to accept her individuality enough to conceive of the possibility of her marriage in the normal course of events. He feels that she has abandoned him, and reacts with pain and selfish anger, refusing to have any contact with either her or the young man. Gaude is devastated:

> —Les âmes sont-elles donc si fermées les unes aux autres, songeait Gaude, que mon père qui connaît toute ma vie, toutes mes pensées, tous mes instincts, n'a pas eu une seconde l'intuition que ces fiançailles me déchirent le coeur.
> Moi une rebelle! moi une fille désobéissante! O mon père, jamais je ne t'ai plus aimé qu'à la minute où je semblais me détacher de toi. (p. 31)

> [Are souls, then, so closed to each other, mused Gaude, that my father, who knows my whole life, all my thoughts and all my instincts, has not had for a moment the intuitive sense that this engagement rends my heart?
> I, a rebel! I, a disobedient daughter! O Father, never have I loved you more than at the moment I seemed to be breaking away from you.]

She is even more disturbed when the young man expects her to love him and proves to be recalcitrant when she explains her real aim in proposing to him. To her horror Tarette agrees to subsidize her father on condition that she live with him somewhere else and have nothing to do with the work. She never imagined being separated from her father and has given no thought at all to her fiancé as a human being.

Reval tells us that the education Malvos gave his daughter left her with no precise moral code, so she was able to justify whatever she chose, and, fortunately, being naturally generous and pure "elle devenait l'incarnation d'un type rare par la beauté du caractère et la force de l'esprit" (p. 65, "She became the incarnation of a rare type, through the beauty of her character and the strength of her mind"). She actually appears to the reader as being the blind, proud, and willing extension of her father's monstrous ego, in much the same relation to her father as Siegfried is to Unique. The poor girl wants to rise to superhuman heights and never admits her great sacrifice, yet she is disappointed when her father does not even suspect the nobility of her action. The decision she made for love of her father is going badly wrong; it has separated her from her father and imposed upon her the need to deal with the demands of another man. She is being torn in two.

Malvos collapses and dies as a result of his emotion. Gaude breaks her engagement, makes an unsuccessful suicide attempt, and finally sets off for Paris to complete her father's work, publish his notes, write the history of Gaul that he had outlined, and prevent him from being forgotten.

The rest of the novel treats her life in Paris, first lodging with a cousin, then hiding from a man who loves her. She lives as a recluse and teaches in a very bad school in order to write her manuscript, about which very little is said in the second and third sections of *La Bachelière*. There is one scene with her father's publisher in which he advises her to write a biography of her father rather than the history, which no firm will publish if it knows that she wrote it, and a brief mention of a jealous colleague trying to burn the trunk of papers. The papers survive, but we know nothing of their future.

La Bachelière is an unsatisfactory piece of work. If Gaude was supposed to live as a continuation of her father, the development of the theme is feeble; if her sacrifice was an excuse to get her to Paris, it was melodramatic. If the aim of the novel is to show her subsequent development of a real moral sense and awareness of other people, the chain of events could have been made clearer. Whatever Reval's overall aim, the novel does provide a very clear example of the domination of a father over his daughter's life. In giving Gaude an education Malvos seemed to be opening her future (and she was able to earn a reasonable living after his death), but as long as he was not prepared to allow her to live her own life as a woman, she had no freedom. That situation would have been the same whether she had decided to marry for good reasons or bad ones. The added poignancy is provided by Gaude's total devotion to her father and her resulting inability to see anyone else as a real human being with needs of his or her own; that includes herself. Gaude may have knowledge, but she has no sense of self and no concept of love between individuals. She has been brought up to satisfy her father's intellectual and emotional needs, and thus has been abused by him and seen her life ruined. There is no indication that in turn she will gain recognition for the history of Gaul or that she expects it. She sees herself as all-sacrificing. Her only comment is, "Je veux être murée dans ce vivant devoir, comme un chartreux dans sa cellule étroite" (p. 263, "I want to be shut away within this living duty, like a Carthusian monk in his narrow cell"). Nothing leads toward the future; in that sense her education has been wasted.

The education given to Catherine Aubier in Yvette Prost's novel *Catherine Aubier* (1912),[4] comes to a premature conclusion also, though under very different conditions. Catherine is the daughter of a hard-working peasant farmer; the novel tells her story from the day she starts school at six years old until she leaves at twenty, abandoning her scholarly aspirations just a few days before the date of the entrance examination to the Sèvres Normal School. At first the book is fun; the young Catherine is lively and nonstandard in her responses to her lessons and to the world. During her first days at school, for example, she decides that because the piano smells good and sounds good, it must be good to eat. So she tried: "Je passai dévotement ma langue sur le joli bois odorant et sonore" (p. 8, "I devoutly licked the beautiful, sweet-smelling, resonant wood"). Catherine is pert and poetic, and compares very favorably with Colette's Claudine until she is an adolescent. There are some funny scenes caused in particular by her passion for reading. One day, when she is minding both the cow and her little brother, she is so deep in her book (a Fenimore Cooper) that she does not notice that Pierre is cutting her hair with her embroidery scissors, and appropriately, he half-scalps her. Another day, as she is rocking the baby, he slips gradually out of the shawl, and Catherine's mother comes home to find her daughter solemnly rocking an empty bundle while the baby is asleep in the warm ashes by the fire. (It was a Sir Walter Scott that time.)

This is a hard-working and happy household as long as the mother is alive. The children are well loved and have a solid sense of themselves as individuals. There is a particular warmth in the relationship between Catherine and her father.

Unfortunately, after Catherine's mother dies, Aunt Françoise moves in, and life is not so cheerful. Aunt Françoise is a criticizer and a complainer with no sense of any future for Catherine except the traditional work of domestic service. Catherine's father believes in education, however, and also listens to his children's desires. When he learns that Catherine dreams of being a teacher, opening children's minds and imaginations the way Mme Lhombre opened hers, he makes the necessary sacrifice to continue to send her to school: "Les vieux papas sont sur terre pour faire le bonheur de leurs enfants, non pour murer leur avenir" (pp. 212–13, "Old papas are here on earth to bring happiness to their children, not to cut off their future"). Knowing that he is committing himself to a lonely old age because he will never leave his land, whereas Catherine will now move on, he supports Catherine and rejoices in her success. The day she passes the "brevet" he is at the station to meet her, dressed in his best clothes, clearly as proud as she is.

Catherine works harder and harder, and while defending her peasant origins to a snobbish classmate with aristocratic roots, she nonetheless changes her patterns of behavior, becoming less attentive to her natural surroundings, her family, and their friends. Her new friends see exciting futures ahead and have abandoned the traditional role of caring, nurturing women. When she does likewise, however, Catherine's father reproaches her for it: "J'ai peur Catherine qu'en devenant si savante tu ne deviennes bien différente de tes parents" (p. 247, "I'm afraid Catherine that in becoming so learned you are becoming very different from your parents").

Here begin the obstacles to Catherine's future and freedom. From this point on the author creates oppositions which devalue education for women. Catherine's new "hardness," born of her intellectual interests, is contrasted to the kind and thoughtful sacrifices made by her father and their neighbor Jeanne Lebrec. Not only that, Catherine is provided with a parallel character, Jeanne's own son, Etienne, a gentle poet who abandons his success in Paris to live an honest, hard-working life in the country. Beside him Catherine appears sharper, thoughtless, even cruel. She thinks he has failed and is determined to succeed. But her success, which was a positive thing early in the novel, has become a sign of her loss of humanity, and she must be deprived of it in order to become an acceptable women in the eyes of those around her. Catherine overhears a conversation between Françoise and Claude in which her father admits that he would have liked to marry Jeanne Lebrec but had sacrificed his desire, knowing that adolescent girls suffer from seeing someone take their mother's place. (Aunt Françoise is not considered to have done that, presumably, as she did not marry Claude and was not his partner in love.) He hopes that Catherine and Etienne will marry instead. However, he declares magnaminously that he regrets nothing, as he wanted his children to have wider horizons than he had in his youth. Society needed more educated people.

Catherine is, of course, touched by such devotion and denounces all her aspirations:

> Cet amour fervent de l'étude, cette ardente curiosité de la pensée humaine, cette ivresse de l'accroissement illimité de mes facultés intellectuelles, tout cela, n'est-ce pas un égoïsme très délicat, mais un égoïsme enfin? (p. 270)

> [That fervent love of studying, that burning curiosity of human thought, that feeling of intoxication at the boundless growth of my intellectual faculties, is not all that very subtle selfishness, but selfishness nevertheless?]

Despite her negative reaction to Etienne's return home, she realizes she had always admired him and felt him to be her superior. Now enlightened by her own change of heart, she appreciates his true worth once more.

It is the tale of the rustic sage. Claude Aubier is utterly beyond reproach; Catherine renounces her future independence but returns to live with four remarkably enlightened people. Jeanne, Etienne, Pierre, and her father are all intelligent, thoughtful, selfless folk—perfect companions for a pastoral idyll. So good are they that the reader never questions Catherine's decision. The way in which Prost undermines her heroine and the whole question of education and increasing freedom for women slides by, concealed by the wisdom of the other characters. *Catherine Aubier* is an exemplary tale but not, perhaps, the one it appears to be. This is reverse subversion in terms of female emancipation. It is interesting for its depiction of a happy childhood, an enlightened schoolteacher, loving parents, and an appreciation of peasant life. It is pernicious in its denouncement of personal growth as egoism, although such statements are not unusual in this period, in which all women's love is expected to manifest itself in sacrifice so that a choice for the self is necessarily a choice against anyone else. *Catherine Aubier* gradually falls into the usual mold. The novel is disappointing, however, as it begins in a original way only to lose the spirit that makes the early chapters a delight to read.

It would be hard to find a greater contrast to Catherine Aubier than *La Petite Lotte* (1908), by Simone Bodève.[5] Whether we agree with the moral of the novel or not, Catherine does receive a sense of self, an education, and a model of behavior from her father, whereas Charlotte is demoralized and deprived by Charles Bugeot. Charles is weak and selfish, as abusive and destructive physically toward his daughter as Malvos was mentally toward Gaude. The only thing he does give Charlotte is more education than is usual for a working girl. Unfortunately, she does not have enough to save her from unnecessary tragedy.

This is a novel of unhappiness and violence in working-class Paris. The child spends all her time in a corner of her mother's workshop, is beaten regularly and deprived successively of everything she loves dearly. Fortunately, her father believes in education, and Lotte is clever at school even though she is not liked and has no friends. The one happy period in her life comes when she goes to Neuilly with her father and they go for walks together on a Sunday morning:

> Tout le long du chemin, on causait des études de Lotte, on discutait de la solution des problèmes de son arithmétique. L'enfant les faisait tous les uns après les autres, tout ce qui était calcul la passionnait. On rappelait les faits de l'Histoire de France, de la Révolution, Lotte croyait la connaître dans ses moindres détails, papa l'avait abonnée à un cabinet de lecture, lui-même allait lui chercher des livres, ainsi elle avait lu, dévoré, les Révolutions de Michelet, d'Edgar Quinet, d'Henri Martin. (p. 46)

> [All along the way, they chatted about Lotte's school work, they discussed how to solve her arithmetic problems. The child went through them one after the other as everything about computation fascinated her. They recalled facts about the History of France, about the Revolution. Lotte thought she knew it down to the last detail as Papa had subscribed to a lending-library for her and he himself went to get books for her. This is how she had read, even devoured, the Revolutions of Michelet, Edgar Quinet and Henri Martin.]

Lotte loves this encouragement from her father, and Charles remembers the enjoyment he got from reading in his youth. Unfortunately, the nostalgia leads him to thoughts of how his life has been ruined because his wife, Lise, did not fulfill his dreams of love and enjoyment (she refuses to do anything but work and save money). Charles is a sensuous man deprived of affection and sexual comforts, and when he drinks he becomes both violent and sentimental. The result is predictable. One Sunday he feels sorrier for himself than usual. Charles rapes his daughter.

> Il éclata en sanglots violents. Il pleurait sur lui, convaincu qu'il était l'être le plus abandonné de tout l'univers, un être généreux que tout sans cesse avait desservi.
> L'enfant atterrée, le prenant par le cou, essayait de le consoler:
> —Papa, je suis là, ta petite fille qui t'aime bien.
> —Ma petite fille, ma petite fille chérie, toi, tu es affectueuse déjà, tu sais

les mots qui apaisent, toi tu m'aimes, tu m'embrasses.
—Papa, je t'aime bien, pas ainsi, laisse-moi.
—Charlotte.
La voix sonna étrangement, à la fois comme une menace et comme une
prière. L'enfant eut peur, se recula. L'homme les yeux injectés de sang, la
face écarlate, essayait de la renverser au fond du bateau, tandis qu'elle se
cramponnait désespérément à l'un des bords, affolée, voyant la barque
osciller au milieu des herbes, appelant d'une voix lamentable:
—Papa! Papa! (p. 49)

[He broke into violent sobs. He was weeping for himself, convinced that
he was the most abandoned being in the whole universe, a generous soul
for whom everything always turned out badly.
The child was upset and flinging her arms around his neck and tried to
comfort him.
"Papa, I'm here, your little girl who loves you dearly."
"My little girl, my dear little girl, you're already loving, you know the
words that soothe, *you* love me, you kiss me."
"Papa, I love you dearly, not that way, let me go."
"Charlotte."
His voice had a strange timbre to it, both threatening and begging. The
child was frightened and backed away. Eyes bloodshot, face scarlet, the man
tried to push her down onto the bottom of the boat, while she clung desperately to one of its edges, terrified, saw the boat rocking in the midst of the
reeds and wailing:
"Papa, Papa!"]

The trauma gives Charlotte brain fever, and her mother discovers what
happened from her feverish ravings. As is frequent in such situations silence is imposed on Charlotte because "cela nous gênerait pour plus
tard" (p. 88, "that would embarrass us later on"). She obeys her mother's
injunction but vows an implacable hatred toward her father. From then
on she is haunted by distrust of men, terror of love, and a total lack of
self-worth. Charles realizes what he has done and sees the change in
Charlotte. He is upset because in his way, he does love his daughter, but
he is inadequate to deal with the situation:

Qu'éprouvait-il devant elle? Un sentiment de gêne insupportable. Pour s'en
délivrer, il aurait voulu lui demander pardon, lui dire qu'il regrettait, lui
expliquer. Il ne trouvait pas les mots, dès qu'il tentait une démarche, il
sentait son insuffisance, bien plus son action néfaste qui avait pour effet
d'éloigner l'enfant davantage. Alors, il voulait se persuader, ainsi qu'il
affectait de le croire vis-à-vis de Lise, qu'il n'avait rien fait de tellement
blâmable et essayait de la brusquerie maladroitement. Il aimait sa fille,

mais il n'était pas profond psychologue, il ne voyait pas qu'entre elle et lui, plus rien n'était possible que la haine, sinon l'oubli, que son crime était d'avoir profondément troublé, bouleversé une jeune âme, fière, naïve et tendre, en répondant par l'infamie à une effusion charmante. Et en méconnaissant la pureté, il lui avait appris la méfiance d'elle-même et la petite surveillait ses gestes et ses paroles, toujours renfermée en une réserve plus que prudente. (p. 70)

[What did he feel in her presence? A sensation of unbearable discomfort. To rid himself of this, he would have liked to beg her pardon, tell her that he was sorry, explain to her. He could not find the words and as soon as he attempted to do something, he felt how inadequate he was and how disastrous his behavior, which had the effect of driving the child farther away. Then, he wanted to convince himself, as he pretended to think to Lise, that he had done nothing as blameworthy as all that and he would awkwardly try to seem brusque. He loved his daughter but as he was no psychologist, he did not see that between her and himself, nothing was possible, except hatred or forgetting, that his crime consisted of having deeply troubled, distressed a young, proud, naive, tender heart by responding dishonorably to a charming outpouring of feeling. In failing to recognize her purity, he had taught her to distrust herself and the little girl kept watch on her gestures and words, always withdrawn into a reserve that was more than prudent.]

The family is unable to deal with the sexual abuse. The mother locks herself into silence, complicity with the father, and the need to keep up appearances. Lise's attitude is that a child should love her parents because they are her parents; that Charles loves her because she is his wife; that her place and that of the children is with him. (This is a perfect example of the ambiguous usage of the word "love" in novels of this period. It is the word used for whatever emotion people locked into an intimate relationship might have for each other.) Lise maintains her position even when Charles has neglected her for other women and then tried to shoot the whole family. Lotte is amazed at this until she hears her teacher explain that parents always want the best for their children:

Qu'on doit aimer ses parents au-dessus de tout, que les petites filles ignorantes doivent se garder de juger sur les apparences, qu'à mesure qu'on grandissait on apprenait que le mal n'existe pas, que personne jamais ne voulait le mal, que les parents n'avaient jamais en vue que le bien de leurs enfants. (p. 89)

[That you must love your parents above all else, that ignorant little girls must be careful not to make judgments based on appearances, that as you grew older you learned that wickedness does not exist, that no one ever wished for wickedness, that parents never had anything in view but the good of their children.]

Lotte had written that children should only love their parents if the parents were good, and this statement of her own experience receives no acknowledgement whatsoever, but Lotte does not change her mind. The child sees her father as a wicked man, and when her mother invites him back into the family home, Lotte leaves forever.

She finds a job making flowers, gets her own room, makes friends, and survives more or less in the poverty of a working girl. She knows that she has no future unless she can find a man who will keep her, and so, steeling herself for the ordeal, Charlotte goes out with her friend Marthe to the Moulin Rouge. She uses her suffering caused by the rape as a bitter justification of her action:

Charlotte s'habilla très soigneusement, se croyant très résolue. Son père l'avait souillée, déshonorée, après tout il ne lui avait pas porté un si grand préjudice et sa mère avait eu raison de ne pas vouloir y attacher d'importance. Au contraire, il lui avait rendu service, ainsi elle n'avait aucune raison d'hésiter. (p. 175)

[Charlotte dressed very carefully, believing herself to be very resolute. Her father had soiled and dishonored her, but he had not inflicted such a great injury on her after all and her mother was right not to want to attach much importance to it. On the contrary, he had done her a favor, for now she had no reason to hesitate.]

Marthe finds a young man and leaves his friend with Charlotte.

Henri Lethoré turns out to be a young man with a social conscience, who is horrified that Lotte is afraid of him. He talks to her, feeds her, gradually wins her confidence, takes her home, gives her books, and finally falls in love with her. She returns his love. Charlotte's life is transformed. But despite his tenderness, she is still locked into the silence of her insecurity, born of the rape, and this undermines her all the time. Even a proposal of marriage cannot give her a sense of self-worth. Instead, she panics, remembering all the stories she has heard about unchaste brides sent home the day after the wedding.

We see that Charlotte's life displays the typical pattern of an incest victim. She is trapped in a web of private silence and public myth that invalidates her experience and gives her no means of healing herself. In this novel Henri is a sensitive and loving man who senses that Charlotte is troubled, but he is not capable of helping her break the silence of a lifetime, and Charlotte is not able to do it herself. She tries repeatedly but cannot tell him the unspeakable: that her father raped his own daughter without provocation; that she was a victim, deflowered, dishonored, and innocent. She has enough moral sense and character to care about what happened to her, but still has not enough strength and sense of self to be able to deal with the new situation, which threatens to bring to the surface the old trauma she has contained for so long. The strain is such that she falls ill, and decides that when Henri goes to fetch his sister (a doctor) for the wedding, she will commit suicide. In fact, ironically and symbolically, it is Henri who kills her. He is carrying her across the room when he trips, and she falls over the balcony. She dies several hours later.

Simone Bodève, author of this novel, was a self-taught woman whose writings depict and analyze the conditions of the working class with perspicacity and poignancy. It is not clear whether *La Petite Lotte* might be an autobiographical work, but what is both striking and strange is that thirteen years after the publication of this novel, she too fell through a window to her death, and there was a debate as to whether or not she had committed suicide.[6]

By chance Charlotte found a good man who recognized her needs and her intelligence; Henri would have understood her suffering and her position. Such is the taboo concerning incest, however, such was the sense of insecurity produced in the child by the rape that Charlotte's life was destroyed before it began. She was sacrificed to her father's weakness, as Gaude was sacrificed to her father's glory, but Charlotte had no means of overcoming what happened to her, whereas Gaude suffered less damage and had greater resources. Malvos and Bugeot are the antithesis of Aubier, yet all three think they love their daughters, all three determine their daughters' futures, and all three place restraints on their daughters' lives. The power of a father comes in various forms: intellectual, physical, emotional, and, as we are about to see, economic. In all cases the daughter is unable to escape the results of her father's behavior.

The immense difference that the presence of a good father makes in a girl's life is spelled out very clearly in *La Vie tragique de Geneviève* (1912), by Louise-Marie Compain.[7] This is a *roman à thèse* in which Compain shows methodically the differences between legitimacy and illegitimacy, wealth and poverty for a young woman at the turn of the century.

At the beginning of the novel Geneviève Duval leaves the orphanage for her first position in domestic service. She possesses a minimum of clothing, a photograph of her mother, and a little turquoise ring that the father she never knew had given to her mother. She is employed by Henri Varenne, a well-to-do civil servant in Caen. Varenne's daughter, Marguerite, becomes fond of Geneviève and tells the maid's story to her father. He sees a likeness between the two girls immediately, and recognizes the photograph and the ring. Much troubled, he confesses his past to his wife and tells her of his belief that Geneviève is his daughter. Called away on family business, he decides to settle the matter when he returns. Meanwhile, his wife turns Geneviève out on the excuse that she has a young man—a local workman who is attracted to Geneviève but whom she hardly knows. Abandoned, she turns to him, and by the time Marguerite has persuaded her father to look for Geneviève, Geneviève, pregnant and abandoned, cannot be found. The rest of the novel recounts Geneviève's struggles, her marriage, her husband's death, and the attempt at suicide in which she kills her children. Once she wrote to Marguerite, and the letter went astray; once Marguerite passed her in the street without recognizing her. Neither forgets the other. Meanwhile, Varenne dies; Marguerite moves to Paris with her brother and her mother, and studies medicine. She is part of the team that revives Geneviève, and she takes her in immediately. Geneviève is tried for murder and acquitted. One day, having been sent shopping for Marguerite, she is roused from her depression by a chance remark on the price of clothes. She decides to campaign for the rights of those who make them and who starve on the pay they receive.

We see again in this moral tale the recurrent patterns of the economically important disappearing men and the supportive woman, the social and sexual abuse of women that we have found throughout the novels of this period. Here, Geneviève's trial is Compain's trial of an unjust society. The novel is structured to underline the differences between Geneviève's hard, tragic life and Marguerite's comfortable one. They are daughters of the same father; they look alike, behave similarly, have similar tastes and talents. But fate decreed that Geneviève should be illegitimate, abandoned, uneducated, and poor; Marguerite was not. Compain's message to all her readers was, "There but for the grace of God go all of us." Her novel is a direct appeal for social reform. It also is a fascinating social document on poverty and a sensitive study of the main character, her problems, and her reactions.

In the novels mentioned in this chapter, we see a range of young women in different social and financial circumstances. The context is certainly that of the turn of the century, but the various relationships between fathers and daughters are relationships that still exist and have much the same effect on the lives of many girls today. It is true that modern feminist writers put much emphasis on the mother-daughter relationship as the basis of female autonomy, but the father still holds considerable sway over the lives of many women. Certainly all the abuses described in these works are still current. The mother-daughter relationship was less important in 1900 for the simple reason that virtually no mother existed who could support her daughter against her husband and win what the women wanted. Most wives were submissive to the point of invisibility (Yver shows it well in *Les Princesses de science*, cf. chapter 7); any autonomy a daughter could achieve came from her father. He could give material, physical, and emotional support which was respected in his social and family circle, or he could abuse his powers and be protected by the same circles. Without her father's support, a girl was prey to constant pressure and criticism from outside and to violent opposition within the home, or she was thrown out to fend for herself. A father, even a poor one, held the key to his daughter's future in both the public and the private spheres, and this power to give or withhold freedom or life itself recurs throughout this book. First and foremost, a woman of this period was a daughter of her father. Through the quality of this relationship she found her sense of self; by this relationship she was defined. Each father created or destroyed his daughter's future.

Profession

STRUGGLES AND SOLITUDE

In this period a woman who goes into a profession for love frequently does so because she is following in her father's footsteps and he has no son to do so instead. Thus she gets financial and emotional support. She is usually both strong and intelligent, or she would not have chosen to model herself on her father. In most cases this is a reaction to the totally submissive role of her mother, a role which she does not always escape totally but which she does understand and modify very considerably. The women who have been given a sense of self by their fathers succeed in their chosen professions. Those who study because they are poor and see no other salvation live their professional lives with difficulty, yearn for love and the emotional support of a husband, and usually abandon their work as soon as they can. The distinction between the two kinds of professional women comes from the kind of choices they made.

As we shall see in this chapter, which focuses on the novels of Gabrielle Reval and Colette Yver, Reval's women were for the most part forced into their situations by circumstance. They believe that as women, they should marry. Yver's women, however, are totally absorbed by their work. If men had not deliberately drawn their attention toward them, the women would not have thought about love and marriage. They are all self-sufficient beings—new women, like Laure Deborda (Compain: *L'Un vers l'autre*, chapter 7) and Sibylle Heursay (d'Ulmès: *Sibylle femme, Sibylle mère*, chapter 4). But as Germaine Lechaud said of Laure, society is not ready for them yet—and men certainly are not, either. Hence the women accept some measure of incompleteness, in full understanding of the positions they are in. What is curious is that, with the possible exception of Jean Cécile, the men seem totally unaware of those positions; they choose and love exciting women who are their equals, then set about destroying them with the methodical insouciance of little boys pulling wings off butterflies. In Yver's work more clearly than in that of her peers, we see man's refusal to allow woman to live according to her potential.[1] Yver reveals her male characters' attraction to and fear of strong, active, happy women, and she analyzes ruthlessly the strategies of dominance that masquerade under the name of love and that come into play as soon as a woman tries to be an adult in her own right. When women do not succeed professionally, it is because men have prevented them from doing so. Yver lays out the obstacles one by one. Her critical analysis of the destructive effects of patriarchal society on professional women has never been bettered. These are novels of pragmatic and subversive feminism.

Reval and Yver are the two novelists of the period who address the problems of the emerging class of professional women most directly and most fully. Reval deals exclusively with women's education and the teaching profession, whereas Yver concentrates mainly on women in the medical and legal professions. Her description of the feelings of intelligent, dedicated women and the attitudes of men toward them in *Les Cervelines* is a model of analytic perspicacity which has few peers to this day.

Reval's first novels recount the stages in the life of a potential schoolteacher. *Lycéennes* (High-School Girls) is situated in the final year of a Paris high school; *Les Sévriennes* (The Students at Sèvres) is the story of a class of students throughout the three years they spend at the Ecole de Sèvres; and *Un Lycée de jeunes filles* (A Girls' High School),[2] that of the first two years of a woman's teaching career. The effort described is enormous, the choices are hard, and the life is austere. *Lycéennes* (the least interesting of the novels) depicts the heavy demands made on the schoolgirls preparing the entrance examinations for the normal school, not only in terms of study, but also in terms of the requirement that they become rational, thus denying all emotion in their lives. Also, as models to the community they must be prepared to accept lives of total physical restraint. In this novel the new profession of teaching is clearly opposed to the traditional occupations of women as wife, "dancer" (i.e., a career in the theatre and aspirations to the demimonde of courtesans), and nun. The girl who is advancing happily and successfully toward a career in teaching is described as deficient in her femininity, a judgment presented as that of the girls themselves and put into the mouth of one of them. Her choice of autonomy and economic independence is seen as a choice against nature, a refusal of the possibility of love.

A similar message is expressed in *Les Sévriennes*, although it is presented more subtly. This novel recounts the lives of some half a dozen students as they move through the three years of normal school, from the announcement of the results of the entrance examination to that of the *Agrégation* (the competitive examination that leads to teaching the final years of high school and university in France). It is a lively and often humorous description of day-to-day discussions, worries, classes, interrelations, and increasing maturity told sometimes in the third person, sometimes through the diary of Marguerite Triel, and sometimes through the letters Berthe Passy writes to her father. The plot is very slight: Marguerite's close friend, Charlotte, fails the entrance exam the year Marguerite passes, but she arrives at the school a year later. Charlotte is engaged to a sculptor, and they cannot afford to marry unless Charlotte also has an income. Marguerite has no family; she thinks of Charlotte as a sister and gradually becomes fond of Henri also. Charlotte is found to have a weak heart and dies. After Charlotte's death Marguerite realizes that she is in love with Henri and he with her, but Charlotte, on her deathbed, had made him swear never to marry anyone else. Marguerite comes first in the *Agrégation* but refuses to take a teaching position; instead she goes to live with Henri. He will not break his promise, but she feels that she can and should give him happiness by agreeing to live as his mistress.

This plot is a mere thread of anecdotal interest added to the real theme of the novel, which is a reflection on the compatibility of love and teaching. Right from the beginning Marguerite Triel is shown to be superior to the other students because she is a more complete human being. She is intelligent and thoughtful. In her thoughtfulness she endeavors to combine both reason and emotion in a way that her companions do not, recognizing the important role feelings must play in any understanding of literature. Later, as a result of Charlotte's death and her own sorrow, she comes to the conclusion that "la vraie morale c'est la pleine expansion de la vie" (p. 261, "true morality is the development of life to the full").

Marguerite matures in real understanding in such a way that she rejects appearances and lives for true human values: justice, personal integrity, and love. In many ways she resembles Laure Deborda (*L'Un vers l'autre*). They are the ideal new women, intelligent, educated, independent, wise, and loving.

It is interesting to note that neither of them is allowed to be a teacher. Laure is told directly by Germaine Lachaud that such perfection as hers should be devoted to raising a family. Marguerite has disqualified herself from the teaching profession by her very autonomy, integrity, and strength of love. Reval may be right when she says in her preface to *Un Lycée de jeunes filles* that the *lycées* "aboutissent à l'idée socialiste en aidant à la libération des femmes par l'émancipation de leur cerveau" (p. ix, "arrive at the socialist idea by helping to liberate women through the emancipation of their minds"), but we note that the liberation of women's minds is not supposed to carry over into their behavior. Marguerite Triel cannot remain a teacher and live outside marriage with the man she loves, however honest and respectable they may be. The model of free love she is providing is too far ahead of her time. As we shall see in *L'Un vers l'autre* (cf. chapter 7), the unmarried woman usually is an outcast. Renée d'Ulmès' heroine Sibylle Heursay (*Sibylle mère*) is the only exception I have found to this social rule (cf. chapter 4), and she had nothing to do with teaching. The irony is that these early teachers are caught in a double bind. They are supposed to be both mentally emancipated and physically repressed—lay nuns, we might say. As Germaine Lachaud declared in *L'Un vers l'autre*, they are transitional beings deprived of the comforts of traditional roles yet caught by the old restrictions, aware of the new freedoms yet not allowed to practice them.

This bind explains, of course, why all the characters other than Marguerite fall into two distinct categories: those who need to earn a living, but are prepared to abandon their studies as soon as they can find husbands (Renée Diolat, who leaves Sèvres to marry; Adrienne, who tries to seduce a professor), and those who live for their studies (Victoire Nollet and Jeanne Viollet). The latter are described as deviants: Victoire is ugly, disagreeable, and dry; Jeanne unfriendly and (probably) lesbian. The message is clear: any woman with a normal desire to love and be loved has no place in the teaching profession.

The only character besides Marguerite who defies this categorization is Berthe Passy. Berthe, whose father is an impoverished poet, comes from Montmartre. Because of her unusual upbringing among his friends, she is a natural nonconformist, astute, cynical, witty, and irrepressible. She has no respect for the system within which she finds herself and as a result does not suffer from its pressures. Berthe is the one who survives best, and we find her again in *Un Lycée de jeunes filles*. She survives for much the same reasons that Charlotte was surviving (mentally, if not physically) and for which Marguerite leaves: affection and emotional support. Berthe loves her father and wants a job that will pay enough for her to give him a comfortable old age. Charlotte loves Henri and will teach so that they can afford to marry. Each thinks she can survive the rigors of the system because she will have someone to go home to. Neither sees teaching as an end in itself. During a discussion of their futures Charlotte describes the support a husband will give, and Berthe declares:

> Caissières et receveuses de postes. Comme elles, nous sommes des fonctionnaires, nous ferons notre devoir: c'est perdre son temps, que d'exiger de nous la vertu et le sacrifice des missionnaires. (p. 203)

> [Cashiers and postmistresses. Like them, we are public servants and we shall do our duty. It's time wasted to demand a missionary's virtue and sense of sacrifice from us.]

Later, in *Un Lycée de jeunes filles*, we see her living according to her own statement. She is a good teacher, hard-working, clear-sighted, fond of the children, and a fine colleague, but her sense of self depends on neither the judgment of her peers nor the affection of her pupils. She has the support of her father and interests in her life other than the school. Thus she does not suffer from the loneliness or the excessive fervor that destroy her single colleagues, or from the overwork that wears out those who try to combine their profession and a marriage which inevitably includes frequent pregnancies. Berthe does not have a high opinion of men and so is happy to remain unmarried, but she is unusual, as the author makes clear. In Reval's eyes marriage and teaching are incompatible; love outside marriage is impossible also. The choice must be made between the mind and the body, intellectual satisfaction and human affection.

In these circumstances, it is not surprising that many of the devoted teachers see themselves as missionaries. Victoire Nollet says, "Notre fonction de professeur n'est pas un métier mais un apostolat" (p. 205, "Our work as teachers is not a profession but a ministry"), and Marie Fleuret (*Un Lycée de jeunes filles*) demonstrates the same attitude toward her profession, though she lives it in a different way. Marie wants to draw out the soul of her pupils, to make them intelligent, sensitive women, whereas Victoire's aim is to turn them into impeccably logical, rational beings. Marie declares at one point:

> Tout esprit droit et bon doit être féministe. C'est le devoir de l'homme de préparer à son image la femme qui sera l'esprit de son esprit comme elle est la chair de sa chair. (p. 155)
> Je voudrais, moi, continua Marie avec franchise, que par respect de sa propre dignité la jeune fille prît pour principe de ne jamais rien faire qui puisse humilier sa conscience. (p. 156)
>
> ["Every straightforward, good mind must be feminist. It is man's duty to prepare in his own image the woman who will be mind of his mind as she is flesh of his flesh."
> Marie continued frankly: "I myself wish that out of respect for their own dignity young women would follow the principle of never doing anything that might humiliate their consciences."]

Un Lycée de jeunes filles is the chronicle of Marie Fleuret's brief career as a teacher. She lasts two years, at the end of which, worn out spiritually and emotionally, she is going blind. Without the help of Berthe Passy she would be destitute. Berthe and Victoire, characters in *Les Sévriennes*, are seen here as experienced teachers in the school to which Marie Fleuret comes directly from the Ecole de Sèvres. In this novel the fears expressed in the other novels are shown to be justified. The job is hard, the headmistress is ambitious for herself and demanding of others, colleagues are not friendly, and the people in the town ostracize the young women because they see them as revolutionaries who will lead their daughters astray. The townspeople think that lycées for girls are a political ploy to upset the status quo (as indeed they were[3])—"créer une femme nouvelle, tuer en elle l'esprit conservateur, l'esprit d'inertie ou de résistance" (p. 82, "to create a new woman and kill the spirit of conservatism, inertia or resistance in her")—and as a result refuse even to lodge the high-school teachers. Marie's only ally is Berthe. Through Berthe she meets an elderly, pious, kind, and thoughtful woman, Madame Ruissène, who takes her in, and becomes an affectionate supporter and a good friend. Madame Ruissène is a widow of independent means, able therefore to live according to her own decisions (a figure similar to Madame Duverger in Compain's *L'Un vers l'autre*).

Again we find a network of affectionate support of women by women within and opposed to the dominant male system. The prefect has withdrawn his daughter from the lycée, the inspector is a threat to the teachers, the town council wants to close the school, the rich men continue to send their daughters to be taught by nuns. There is no approval of women's education and no social support of the women involved in it, because all the influential men in town assume that freedom of mind is automatically joined to physical freedoms of a kind unsuitable to potential wives within a patriarchal structure. Women must be submissive and subdued.

Reval charts the vicissitudes of solitude and lovelessness, and the inhuman nature of the choices forced upon these women who have to earn their own livings. (Marie herself is courted by a lascivious poet, falls in love, and is on the verge of losing her virginity when she gathers her wits sufficiently to distinguish between lust and love. She survives the occasion physically intact but emotionally raped, more lonely and bereft than before.) If we look at the three novels in the order in which they were written, we see that the women Reval creates are less happy, less enterprising, less ambitious, and less idealistic from novel to novel. *Lycéennes* is the third novel, in order of writing, and it is there that the three main characters revert to the classic occupations of women: wife, "dancer," and nun, roles in which they expect to bask in the love of man or the love of God.

The picture Reval paints is grim indeed, especially as she seems to care about education for women and to see it as the way to social change. She pays tribute to the courage of the teachers in the preface to *Un Lycée de jeunes filles*:

> Depuis vingt ans qu'il existe, plusieurs générations de femmes sont passées là apprenant à se connaître, à juger leurs conditions. . . . Le Féminisme n'est plus aujourd'hui la tentative de quelques révoltées, c'est l'organisation raisonnable, disciplinée, de ces femmes instruites et courageuses. (p. viii)

> [During the twenty years it has existed, several generations of women have passed through it, learning to know themselves, to consider their situations. . . . Today, Feminism no longer represents the endeavours of a few rebellious women but is the reasonable, disciplined organization of these educated, courageous women.]

She recognizes that through education they are striving for equality of opportunity and social justice. However, she sees also the extreme vulnerability of these women who are obliged to fight constantly for their very survival, surrounded as they are by a hostile environment. From her descriptions of life as a teacher, the choice would seem to be not simply a personal choice between the satisfactions of the intellect and the satisfactions of the body, but also a social choice between being man's enemy or his servant. These professional women are caught constantly in political power struggles around the very existence of lay education for girls and in private power struggles to preserve the economic independence they have worked so hard to achieve.

It would seem (as we have seen already) that a woman also can survive if she has gained a sense of identity from a relationship with a liberating father. This is true, in very different ways, of both Berthe Passy and Victoire Nollet. Each girl gets a good education and has a goal in life which gives her strength, purpose, and a sense of being loved. Thus she is less vulnerable than most of the women around her. We must note, however, that Berthe remains outside any possible problem of love or servitude by remaining unmarried and lavishing affection on her father, whereas her colleague is following closely in her dead father's footsteps. (Victoire's life resembles in many ways that of Gaude Malvos.) Neither is living a "normal" life, though each is unabused and happy in her fashion. Autonomy still precludes love, and economic sufficiency brings exile from the ranks of social acceptability.

Reval prefers women who have a practical interest in what they are doing to women who have a quasimystical sense of vocation. Yver offers her readers women who combine the two in a practical sense of vocation, an overwhelming passion for the work at which they are very good. These women, too, are faced with having to decide between married life with men they love and the furtherance of their careers. Here, however, the subtleties of the painful choice lie in an analysis of each relationship in its social context, rather than in the general conditions of the profession itself.

Yver's novels *Les Cervelines* (The Brainy Ones, 1903), *Princesses de science* (Princesses of Science, 1907), and *Les Dames du Palais* (The Ladies of the Law Courts, 1909)[4] deal directly with the problem of whether professional women can expect to live a normal life with home, husband, and children.

In *Les Cervelines* the structure of the novel creates a comparison among the three major female characters: Jeanne Boerk, Marceline

Rhonans, and Henriette Tisserel. Jeanne Boerk is a very good doctor serving her internship in a hospital. She has no interest in love, no dreams
of marriage or of children except the sick ones in her care, no feeling but
comradeship for the men around her. Medicine is her passion. She is presented as an attractive, robust, direct woman of peasant stock. A gifted
doctor, she is depicted as being occasionally naïve and graceless outside
her chosen field. Above all she is uncomplicated; she has chosen the direction of her life and does not deviate from it. Henriette Tisserel, Paul's
sister, forms a complete contrast to Jeanne. She is delicately beautiful,
graceful, charming, and sickly. She lives for her brother, Paul, arranges
her life according to his comforts, even to the extent of denying her future
and possible marriage for him. She never expresses a desire or need, not
even mentioning her love for Paul's friend, Jean Cécile, until she is on
her deathbed. Henriette is the traditional self-sacrificing female; Jeanne,
the totally autonomous new woman. (Note that for once in literature the
roles are reversed; the traditional woman dies and the new woman
thrives.) Neither of them questions her role: both live alongside men
without having any emotional contact with them. Henriette lives for
men and is invisible to them; Jeanne lives without men, and for her they
are invisible except when they get in her way and annoy her, as Paul does
when he insists on declaring his love and as the medical students do by
their harassment at an official dinner.

Between these two poles of womanhood is situated Marceline Rhonans.
She is a brilliant historian who teaches at the local lycée, gives evening
lectures that half the town attends, and plans to go to the Middle East
to do original research for a new history of the ancient world. Already
symbolic divisions are created among a scientist who needs no emotional
satisfaction; a traditional woman who has neither knowledge nor emotional satisfaction; and a humanist who claims her right to both, thereby
becoming a complete human being. Marceline lives alone in an autonomy as great as that of her friend Jeanne, and is contented in her solitude,
though tempted from time to time by the idea of a husband and children.
She is happy until Paul Tisserel's friend, the doctor Jean Cécile, begins
to court her. Marceline then falls in love for the first time, and succumbs
briefly to the delight of unreason and sensuality. She would like to marry
and to complement the satisfactions of her intellectual life with equally
rich emotional experience. But in order to be Cécile's wife, she must give
up her career, and she is unable to make such a sacrifice. After much pain-

ful thought, she refuses to marry him and leaves on her research trip.

At first glance, the main theme of *Les Cervelines* seems to be the intellectual woman's refusal of marriage, but a more careful look reveals that the subject of the novel is men's refusal to accept any sign of autonomy in women.

The theme is stated overtly through Jeanne Boerk. She is not allowed to get on with her work in the hospital because on the one hand, her superior courts her assiduously, and on the other, she is constantly the butt of the remarks, pranks, and downright hostility of her fellow students. Each in his way is determined to reduce her to his idea of a woman—woman as sex object—and if they cannot use her as a woman in private they will try to humiliate her as a woman in public. The students are childish and annoying; Tisserel is protective. (As she has refused his love, he has no personal right to concern himself with her affairs, so he decides to use his right as a superior in whose tutelage he considers her to be.) The important issue throughout is that whether the men like the woman or not, they cannot bear to see her directing her own life. She must be seen as the possession of some man. For example, at the official dinner for the new director of the hospital, one of the students takes her necklace by force, intending to use it to create the impression that he obtained it together with other favors. Ultimately he returns the necklace not to Jeanne but to Tisserel, because he recognizes Tisserel's superior claim to Jeanne as his possession. Jeanne, "unclaimed," could be his. She is not allowed to be autonomous.

A more subtle version of the theme, played in emotional rather than physical terms, is shown in the relationship between Marceline Rhonans and Jean Cécile. First, Yver sets Cécile in context. His first declaration is one of antipathy for intelligent women. He says to Paul Tisserel that "ces femmes-là sont des êtres auxquels il ne faut pas s'attacher" (p. 8, "these women are human beings one should not become attached to"). He calls them "cervelines" (brainy ones) and defines them as women who have kept all the elements of womanliness, "tout, sauf le coeur, et le coeur souvent sauf l'amour" (p. 9, "everything except the heart and the heart often without love"). He declares his hostility to such "phantom" women quite openly, threatening to "[arracher] le charme, et [mettre] à nu la matière cérébrale qu'elles ont sous leur corsage" (p. 16, "to tear away the charm and lay bare the brain matter they have under their bodices").

It turns out that while in Paris, he fell in love with a successful woman writer who had refused to give up her independence to marry him. This is not surprising when we see that his idea of marriage was a totally traditional one:

> C'était sa vie dévouée toute entière, c'était l'union éternelle que la mort peut seule rompre, c'était le mariage tel que les parents de Cécile et toute son ascendance bourgeoise l'avaient connu et pratiqué depuis des siècles. (p. 37)

> [It was her whole life devoted to it, it was the eternal bond that death alone can break, it was marriage such as Cécile's parents and all his middle-class forebears had known and practiced for centuries.]

Cécile came to hate this writer because "son calme bonheur l'exaspérait trop" (p. 39, "her tranquil happiness exasperated him too much"), and it is by this experience that his attitude was formed. Later, when he decides to marry, he asks one of his Paris professors to find him a wife. He describes his requirements thus:

> Je la voudrais seulement silencieuse, souriante et très jeune. Ignorante surtout! ne sachant rien au monde que s'habiller bien; une toute petite cervelle d'oiseau, incapable de penser plus d'une minute (que peut-on bien faire d'une femme qui pense!) et dont je sois le mari, mais pas le lecteur. (p. 113)

> [I would like her to be just quiet, smiling and very young. Above all, ignorant! Knowing about nothing else in the world except how to dress well; an utter little bird-brain, unable to think for more than a minute (what on earth can you do with a woman who thinks!) and for whom I shall be a husband, not a reader.]

An appropriate girl—pretty and shortsighted—is found, but again the marriage does not take place, this time because the father does not consider Cécile to be a worthy son-in-law.

Cécile's subsequent behavior would seem to suggest that, having been hurt twice, he sets out both to hurt others and to fail again. He ignores Henriette Tisserel, who wants nothing more than to care for him, even though (or perhaps because) she fits his requirement of submission perfectly. Marceline Rhonans is the woman who attracts him, and she is, of course, very like Eugénie Lebrun, his first love.

Marceline is brilliant, hard-working, and self-sufficient. She thinks precisely and is not taken in by Jean Cécile's romantic language about eternal love. Reasoning from experiences around her, she makes a clear distinction between happiness and pleasure, and categorizes love as a short-lived pleasure. Yver creates an ironic reversal of expected ideas. Here, the woman sees the man as attaching too much importance to love:

> Ces pauvres hommes attachent à l'amour une importance étrange; ils voudraient tout y subordonner. Ce n'est pourtant dans la vie qu'un accident, un accident physique, tout au plus un plaisir, c'est-à-dire quelque chose de court, de transitoire. Tout le monde confond le plaisir avec le bonheur, c'est stupide. Le bonheur est permanent, le bonheur est un état; il naît de nous. Le plaisir est extérieur, il est en même temps agréable et inutile comme tout ce qui passe. (p. 179)

> [These poor men give a strange kind of importance to love; they would like everything to be subordinate to it. Yet it is nothing but an accident in life, a physical accident, at the very most a pleasure, that is to say, something short and transitory. It's stupid, everyone confuses pleasure with happiness. Happiness is permanent, happiness is a state, it is born of us. Pleasure comes from the outside, it is agreeable and at the same time useless, like everything that passes.]

This is the reasoning she falls back on when she finally chooses between marriage to Jean Cécile and her own life, for that is the ultimate choice she must make.

Jean is attracted by her brilliance, her fame, and her independence, but once he begins to take a proprietory interest in her he begins to enclose her. First, Marceline realizes that if she marries she must renounce all thought of her research project. Next, Madame Cécile, Jean's mother, insists that her son require a greater sacrifice. She says, "Mais cette femme-là te préférera toujours ses livres" (p. 268, "But that woman will always prefer her books over you"), and to prevent this from being so demands that Marceline must not lecture in public, for that is improper behavior (like being on the stage) nor must she teach. Jean does not dare ask such a sacrifice of her directly, but she understands what he intends to deprive her of when, after she says, "Vous serez toujours *le seul* pour moi, mon ami, dans le futur comme dans le passé" (p. 271, "You will always be *the only one* for me, my friend, in the future as in the past"), he replies, "C'est de vous seule désormais que j'ai à vous obtenir" (p. 271, "Now it only remains for me to win you from yourself"). Not content with separating her from other people, he must separate her from anything in herself that might distract her from him. Only the decorative and attentive shell of the vibrant woman to whom Jean was attracted, fascinated by her knowledge and art, is to be allowed to remain, a hollow woman of whom, as he wrote in his letter to his Paris professor, he is the husband, not the reader. Marriage with Jean is a prison in which Marceline's sense of self will languish and die.[5]

Yver makes it quite evident by the way she portrays Jean that what he is doing is diminishing Marceline, crushing her genius, and extinguishing her career, all in the name of love. It is also clear that he is an ordinary man for the period. Jean is not any more hypocritical, needy, and egoistical than many others, and his story is similar to many others in French literature. The difference lies in the perspective of the narrator of the novel. Seen from a woman's point of view, "traditional" relations between the sexes become negative. Male "love" is frequently possessive and oppresses women; marriage diminishes their potential activity and restricts their activity in the world. In sum, the traditional role women are expected to accept is superficial and unsatisfying mentally, emotionally, and frequently physically, too. As Jeanne Boerk says to her quite early in the novel, "Le mariage, ma chère, c'est bon pour les hommes" (p. 74, "Marriage is good for men, my dear"). It is certainly not good for Marceline.

Yver's depiction of Marceline is just as clear and psychologically accurate as her presentation of Jean. Marceline is an intelligent, clear-sighted, thoughtful woman who watches herself fall in love. It is a new experience, and she enjoys it. Also, she wants a more satisfying emotional life; desires love, a husband, and a family; and so is open to Jean's attentions without being taken in by his romantic notions. Nonetheless, she is a woman of her time and culture, and so as Jean becomes more possessive she at first exults in the idea of Cécile's domination: "S'il veut ma vie, je la lui donnerai et je sens qu'il la veut" (p. 234, "If he wants my life, I shall give it to him, and I feel that he does want it"). As Yver remarks, she is in love, "ce qui lui ôtait toute faculté de jugement qui s'exerce par comparaison" (p. 234, "which deprived her of any critical powers that operate by making comparisons"). It is when she receives Jean's letter that she realizes the full extent to which she is threatened: no research, no teaching. This marriage requires that to ensure Jean's happiness, she commit intellectual suicide. Yver makes no bones about the directness of her statement "Mourir n'est que cela" (p. 280, "Death is nothing other than that").

Yver shows the psychological development step by step. This analysis of the workings of an intellectual woman's mind is quite new in French literature and particularly interesting because it is not biased. We recognize that because she loves Jean and because love is new to her, Marceline forgets temporarily that what she wants is a whole life, incorporating both intellectual and emotional satisfactions. So at first she is prepared to go through with the sacrifices demanded. She tells herself (as many women have before her) that Jean will fill the terrible void that the loss of her intellectual activity will create. Together, they achieve a totally unrealistic level of ecstasy in love, and Marceline wills her own sacrifice. Yver underlines her condition: "Elle *désira*, plus encore qu'elle ne le résolut, l'immolation de tout à celui qu'elle aimait" (p. 282, "She desired, more than she chose, to sacrifice everything to the man she loved"). But Marceline has a sense of survival. She takes a week to make her final decision and, alone, without the excitement of a lecture and her adoring audience, without the cover of night, without Jean, she begins inevitably to apply reason to her situation. We see her work through a number of stages. First, she returns to her own thought that love does not last. Then, the opposition in the novel between Henriette Tisserel and Jeanne Boerk reasserts itself. Sounding like Henriette, Marceline thinks she can make Jean happy despite her own diminishment, but then she has a discussion with Jeanne Boerk in which they define the difference between "une cérébrale" and "une cerveline." A "cerveline" is a woman with no heart—like herself, says Jeanne cheerfully—whereas a "cérébrale" is a reasoning and intelligent woman who also has feeling for others and emotional needs—like Marceline. The difference is underlined further by their choice of scientific and humanistic studies. As the discussion develops Marceline sees her own state clearly:

> Elle était en train de sombrer dans un engourdissement. Elle n'avait pas *voulu* cet amour, elle y avait *cédé* comme n'importe quelle femme, et ainsi que dans la fable du lion amoureux, on exploitait cet état d'âme diminué et sans vigueur, on exigeait d'elle des renoncements insensés, la destruction de sa personnalité, l'abandon de son existence mentale, l'étouffement de cette progression lumineuse qui avait fait d'elle, jeune femme, un maître. (p. 295)

> [She was sinking into a state of numbness. She had not *wished for* this love, she had *given in* to it like any other woman and, as in the fable of the amorous lion, this diminished and weakened state of mind had been exploited,

senseless sacrifices had been demanded of her, the destruction of her personality, the surrender of her intellectual life, the stifling of that glowing
achievement that had turned her, a young woman, into an authority.]

She will not marry Jean. She has seen again what she understood before
she fell in love: she is happy as she is. She has autonomy, and "love"
would destroy her.

A number of other similarly destructive acts serve as a backdrop for
this attempted annihilation of Marceline. Jean Cécile tried to take
Eugénie Lebrun out of her calm and happy life, and Paul Tisserel tried
to impose himself on Jeanne Boerk. Thus the strong women were to be
forced into marriages which would diminish them and make them unhappy. Meanwhile, the weak women who want to be protected are refused marriage: Jean ignores Henriette's love for him, and Blanche's father overrides her love for Jean. After her father's death, Blanche is left
unmarried and unprotected in the world. Henriette's brother is so concerned with his own attempts to force his attentions on Jeanne that he
does not see how ill his sister is until it is too late. Paul's attitude toward
women kills Henriette's body as surely as Jean's attitude would have
killed Marceline's mind if she had married him.

Marceline and Jeanne are educated women with passionate interests.
We note that they stand alone, unencumbered by family pressure or direct
social pressure. In the way they support each other and respect each other's decisions, they provide yet another example of female friendship and
support in a hostile, male-dominated world. Yver makes the message in
her novel very clear indeed: women are happy when they are active, autonomous, and intellectually satisfied. They would, perhaps, be happier
still if they had families, but such a situation is not possible until men
stop thinking of love in terms of total possession of the woman and of
marriage as a wife's utter and invisible devotion to her husband's needs.
As things stand, marriage kills women so that men may live.

In *Les Cervelines* Yver shows the attitudes of two strong women faced
with certain specific men. The main analysis is of Marceline, who would
like to be both teacher and wife, to think and to love. That she should
choose between them is inescapable, but in this case her predicament
seems in part to be the result of particular experiences in Jean's life. In
subsequent novels, *Princesses de science* and *Les Dames du palais*, it becomes clear that such a choice is inevitable at some point for any woman

who has a profession. The choice may not always be made as clearly as Marceline Rhonans's decision was, however. Not many women think as comprehensively and lucidly about their lives as she does, and very few are free to make decisions for themselves in tranquillity, without social pressure or family interference. There is one strong unmarried woman in each of these subsequent novels, but she is not the central character. In *Princesses* and *Les Dames*, the subject is the dilemma of being married and having a professional life. The former tells the story of Thérèse Herlinge, a medical student; the latter, that of Henriette Marcadieu, a law student. The two novels are different in context but similar in structure and plot. Each presents a panorama of the profession within which is situated an intelligent young woman who marries a man already established in the same profession. In each case the woman's career rapidly overtakes that of her husband. He then suffers from general neglect, hurt pride, and envy. To save her marriage each young woman sacrifices her career, and stays at home to raise a family and care for her husband, both as his wife and his expert assistant.

Yver's sympathy lies with her heroines. They are competent, independent, and loving women whose success and happiness gall the men who "love" them. This love is revealed to be simple possessiveness and need for dominance, which come to the fore whenever the man's sense of pre-eminence is thwarted, be this when he feels that his intellectual endeavors are inferior to his wife's in the eyes of the world, when his creature comforts do not come before any other of his wife's material concerns, or simply when she thinks of her work while he is near. As soon as he is inconvenienced, he ceases to be able to accept his wife as an individual whose independence of mind he enjoys or himself as a modern, enlightened spouse; instead he sees himself as a husband who is imperfectly loved because his wife has not sacrificed her life for him. He suffers. Rapidly thereafter, he comes to think like an unreasonable, traditional, nineteenth-century man. He ceases to respect his wife's autonomy and claims, in word or behavior, that her professional activity is a threat to their marriage. Hence, once again the woman is forced to choose between the man she loves and her work—only this time, having been married for some time, she has much more emotional investment in the man, and so she gives in.

Once again the woman has had to sacrifice a completeness which gave her satisfaction and live in either an intellectual or an emotional void, because her man has been brought up to believe that he cannot be a real husband unless he controls every aspect of his wife's life. And above all, he cannot stand the thought that he is in competition with her because then his very sense of his own identity would be threatened. So she must withdraw from the game in order to protect his ego. She sees the injustice of the situation and agrees to play the inferior role of her husband's dependent because it is the only way in which she can retain both the man she loves and the work she loves. Henriette Mercadieu and Thérèse Herlinge both make such decisions. Yver shows these strong women making the best of a bad job and recognizing it as such. The author is perhaps telling her readers that the time is not yet ripe for a woman to have a husband, children, and a profession, but in the meantime she has revealed the injustice of the situation and presented women who have gained an awareness of their abilities and a sense of self.

In *Les Cervelines* we watched Marceline Rhonans analyzing her situation. She is a thoughtful and subtle woman, and Yver gives us a novel of careful observation and psychological analysis. The author has chosen a different mode of writing in *Princesses de science* and *Les Dames du palais*. Here, the main characters are surrounded by huge supporting casts, the problems are revealed by actions and reactions, the analysis by comparisons between characters in similar situations. These novels are full of movement, visual images, and graphic detail. One of the great strengths of these books lies in the variety of doctors and lawyers that the author creates. In no way is it possible to generalize, trivialize, and set aside women doctors or women lawyers as a result of these texts. The women are as individual as the men: rich and famous, poor and struggling, brilliant, hard-working, mediocre; researchers, teachers, students, and daily practitioners of their craft; celibate, amorous, married; of all ages and the full range from beautiful to ugly. Yver shows us women for whom work is a passion, an interesting job, or a means to survival, and she shows us those who leave the profession in order to marry. Alongside these women are the men who control the profession and who can make or break careers as they so choose. The support they give is always paternalistic and always qualified.

Yver substantiates in *Princesses* and *Les Dames* the declaration that she puts in the mouth of Jeanne Boerk in *Les Cervelines*: marriage is good for men. She goes on to illustrate that when for some reason this is not so, the men use all possible emotional blackmail on their wives until things have been rearranged to their liking. Yver sees the traditional husband as a pampered tyrant. Thérèse Herlinge's father is an excellent example. He is famous throughout the medical profession for his dinner parties. His wife, who has of course done all the preparation, is such a model hostess that she is able to signal her desires to the servants by her eye movements, and thus she maintains a perfect organization in total silence, never disturbing the great man and his guests. She has rendered herself invisible or, rather, has become the embodiment of the saying "[women] should be seen and not heard"—perfect illustration of the role of a wife in a patriarchal system.

The husband may be a dictator and the wife a slave, but that same man can give freedom to his daughter through education and his support. This is true of Herlinge and Marcadieu; we also know it to be true of the fathers of Victoire Nollet and Berthe Passy, of Hellé (chapter 5), and of a number of women in lesser novels. Conversely, a wife who refuses her husband's dictatorial ways, claims her right to education, and earns economic independence can, by her actions, change her husband's views and behavior.

As we shall see in the next chapter Louise-Marie Compain's heroine in *L'Un vers l'autre* entered the teaching profession in order to retain her sense of self and of the equality of women and men. The major theme of Compain's novel being the status of women within marriage, all question of the situation of professional women is secondary to the analysis of the relationship between Laure and Henri Deborda. Nonetheless, all the issues we have seen to be important in an examination of the lives of professional women are also stated unambiguously in *L'Un vers l'autre*. Laure's action in exchanging an unsatisfactory husband for a life of work and autonomy is in itself a strong statement that having a profession is a viable option to being married. That she should do so on a matter of principle illustrates her belief that a woman must have economic independence before she can live according to her own will and conscience. Subsequently, Compain shows by Laure's experience that the lives of working women are hard and lonely. She recognizes that only those who have an overwhelming sense of vocation survive more or less intact, because survivors must have the strength to withstand constant disapproval and social pressure.

The disapproval stems from two major causes: first, that working women are autonomous human beings in the public sphere, not wives;

second, because their behavior inevitably runs counter to that dictated by the implacably rigid nineteenth-century view of the role of a wife in a patriarchal society. As we know, such a woman should be pliant, comforting, and pure. She should remain in the private sphere, transforming her home into a literal and metaphorical nest of repose for her husband, wherein all her wishes are subordinated to his and all her spare time is spent making his life comfortable.[6] Her life and reputation are in the hands of her husband, for he is her tutor and guardian. In such an atmosphere of male domination the very existence of female professionals—teachers, doctors, lawyers—is an anomaly, so that it is not surprising that these women have to fight constantly for survival. Yver and Reval approach the issue from the point of view that any woman who chooses a career necessarily decides against marriage, and they make very clear the injustice of such a necessity. They want to reform attitudes toward women in the professions. Compain will use the same material in a struggle to change relationships within marriage. These authors are calling for more options and real equality for women.

Marriage

TRADITIONAL AND IDEAL

Marriage is still the expected fate of all young girls in 1900—and fate it is, because feminists and nonfeminists alike see marriage as something a woman must endure, rather than as the basic structure supporting a useful and happy life. A husband is an economic, social, and moral necessity, but only in very rare instances will he also be a supportive friend or an understanding lover. Usually he is a tyrant (successful or unsuccessful) under whose rule the wife lives quietly and unobtrusively, taking what pleasure she can in the details of her daily life. Indeed, the major virtue a woman can be blessed with, at this time, is that of finding happiness in a ray of sunshine or a bunch of violets. We have seen that characteristic already in Josanne Valentin in Tinayre's *La Rebelle* (chapter 3). Camille Pert, in her lugubrious manual of advice *Le Bonheur conjugal*,[1] recognizes the same source of strength in the wives she describes.

By the end of the nineteenth century, individual men treat women as the French have generally treated the peoples they have colonized—as inescapably inferior, amusing, or troublesome creatures that have to be governed for their own good. One novel on marriage, Myriam Harry's *Petites épouses* (1902),[2] even uses this dynamic of colonizer and colonized as its basic symbolism. Alain treats his Vietnamese wife/concubine as a pet: attractive but subhuman. He plays with her, decorates her, makes no attempt to understand her at all, and is surprised and vexed when he finds that she has a complete life of her own; that she gets what she can from him by lies, deceit, and trickery; and that she certainly does not dote gratefully and lovingly upon him as he would wish. Though accepted at the time as a male-centered and exotic love story—Alain's love for Frisson de Bambou—any gynocentric reading of the structures of the novel reveals that it is really the story of the total incomprehension of women by men, of a fundamental lack of interest, lack of caring, and total exploitation. For Alain, Frisson has no soul, and the most generous of his compliments comes when he finally thinks of her "presque comme une petite compagne avec laquelle on peut converser" (p. 281, "almost like a little companion one can talk to"). The example I have chosen is extreme, perhaps, but its essential points are exactly those of standard French marriage; in the latter, the situation of the wife is merely less easily recognized because of the veils provided by the conventions of description and the habits of mind of the reader.

A trenchant analysis of the situation is given by the heroine in Renée d'Ulmès' novel *Sibylle femme*. I quote it in full:

> Mais personne ne considère les actes en eux-mêmes; on s'attache aux seules formules.
>
> Sibylle était surprise du prodigieux respect qui s'attache au mariage, sans qu'il le mérite en rien. Le mariage, tel que l'ont édifié les religions, tel que le considèrent encore quelques rares personnes est, en effet, très grand et très noble: union indissoluble de l'homme et de la femme pour procréer d'autres êtres et les élever selon la justice et la beauté morale. Mais combien rare ce type idéal! Et que de mesquinerie, que de laideur dans la plupart des unions!
>
> Mariage sans amour, sans sympathie, sans estime, association d'intérêt ou de plaisir, rompue au premier heurt, comme une simple liaison.
>
> En observant les ménages autour de soi, on pouvait les diviser en trois types:
>
> Le ménage bien parisien. Grande fortune et haute situation, basé le plus souvent sur la prostitution légale d'une jeune fille à un homme riche, couvrant de son argent une tare quelconque. Prostitution d'un homme qui vend son nom ou sa jeunesse à une héritière vieille ou socialement inférieure à lui. Madame a des amants, monsieur, des maîtresses. On les voit, on les considère, on les recherche.
>
> Le ménage moderne. Deux égoïsmes associés. Chacun tire de son bord. Personne ne veut faire de concessions. On évite l'enfant; s'il arrive, c'est un accident qui ne lie en rien les époux et ne les empêche pas de divorcer.
>
> Enfin, le bon ménage. Les apparences sont correctes, on paraît s'entendre. En réalité ce sont les deux vies séparées de deux êtres qui n'ont ni goût,

ni idée commune, s'ennuient ensemble et ne se supportent que par convenance.

Tous ces ménages vivent entourés de l'estime générale parce qu'ils ont apposé leur signature devant un monsieur ceint d'une écharpe. (pp. 249–51)[3]

[But no one considers the acts in themselves; people cling to the formulas alone.

Sibylle was surprised at the enormous respect associated with marriage, which was in no way worthy of it. Marriage, such as religions have built it up, such as it is still viewed by a few unusual people, is indeed a very great and noble institution: an indissoluble union of man and woman to procreate other human beings and to bring them up in justice and moral beauty. But how rare this ideal kind is! And how much pettiness and ugliness there is in most unions!

Marriage—without love, fellow feeling or regard, an association based on self-interest or pleasure, broken at the first rude knock like a mere liaison.

By observing couples around you, you could divide them into three categories.

The typically Parisian couple: wealthy and in a high social position, most often based on the legal prostitution of a young girl to a rich man who is covering up some kind of defect with his money. Or a man who is selling his name or youth, prostituting himself to an heiress who is old or socially below him. Madame has lovers, her husband mistresses. They are visible, well thought of and sought after.

The modern couple: two linked egoisms. Each pulls his way. No one is willing to make any concessions. Children are avoided; if they come, they are accidents which in no way bind the husband and wife and do not stop them from getting divorced.

Finally, the good couple. All appears proper and they seem to get along well. Actually, these are two separate lives of two human beings who have no tastes or ideas in common, who bore each other and put up with each other only for propriety's sake.

All these couples continue to be well regarded by everyone because they have signed a document in front of a gentleman wearing a sash of office.]

D'Ulmès suggests that most marriages are financial alliances between people who have no interests in common at all. Tinayre gives a more comfortable picture of bourgeois marriage in *Madeleine au miroir* (chapter 3), where she describes the friendship that can be possible between husband and wife. In *La Rebelle* she also offers through La Tourette, Valentin's maid, a definition of a good working-class marriage: one in which the husband does not beat his wife and brings home most of his pay.

Camille Pert sets out the situation in *Le Bonheur conjugal* (1905), and a depressing situation it is, especially when we consider that Pert was in favor of marriage; this book is a guide intended to help young brides find happiness. She runs through a list of what young women should know when they marry. As what she has to say is useful as a context for the attitudes toward marriage that are depicted in the novels, it is useful to look at her comments at some length.

First, she discusses the choice of a husband and concludes that a young girl cannot possibly choose well, as she has no basis of values or experience, nor has she a real choice, since she is offered a maximum of ten men from whom to make her selection, so that all she can do is take the first one who comes close to her ideal and for whom she does not feel physical distaste. She then provides commentary and examples on the different kinds of marriage and of wives: love match, marriage of convenience, marriages in which the wife is a friend, an associate, a mistress, an equal, a good mother, and housekeeper. All her examples show how one can survive impossible circumstances. Her major conclusions are that men see women as inferior, and women must learn to work around that idea and not challenge it, because even a husband who is a declared feminist will not allow his own wife the rights he demands for women in general because he is absolutely sure that he is his wife's natural and legitimate master. Pert states that a woman must bear this in mind at all times and act accordingly in order to get what she wants within one of three contexts: she may act to please her husband, to seduce him, or to win. The relationship between them is always one of power and struggle. Any woman who wants to be her husband's equal, who has her own work outside the house and an independent income, is unacceptable as a wife because she is too virile for love "tel que le conçoivent la plupart des hommes" (p. 172, "as most men think of it").

Pert recognizes that birth control is necessary and legitimate. Indeed, she says bluntly that a woman who has too many children is committing suicide, and a man who imposes too many children on his wife is committing murder. On the other hand, she states that birth control can be bad for a woman's health and can even be criminal, depending on the methods used. (This whole argument is distorted because Pert entitles her chapter "La Fraude" (The Cheat), and despite her initial declaration of support, all her examples are negative.) She goes on to write about what she calls the dangers of marriage by which she clearly means venereal disease. She is mysterious in her presentation of the question itself, but provides a dreadful example of a doctor who gives a woman no treatment because, as the pharmacist would recognize the remedy, he could deduce the malady and thereby cause a scandal for the husband. Pert suggests divorce as the only alternative to lack of treatment and death.

The book ends with a brief chapter on unfaithful husbands and the various practical reasons their wives have for forgiving their misdemeanors. There is no conclusion. No conclusion is possible, indeed, because Pert would be obliged to state that social expectations and economic conditions force women to marry, and that marriage is a state of servitude that is hazardous for their physical, economic, and emotional health.

D'Ulmès states the problem in *Sibylle femme* and avoids it in a way by making Sibylle choose to remain unmarried. She does give Sibylle very clear opinions on marriage, however, as we have seen. Also, the distinction she makes between the acceptance, and even approval, given to the most scandalous behavior as long as the people involved are married to somebody—hence inviolably part of acceptable society—and the rigorous rejection of people, however sincere, honest, and honorable in their personal lives, who live outside the conventions of marriage is one that recurs time and again in novels of this period and that disturbs profoundly those authors who are concerned about the real condition of the women around them.

Within the institution of marriage, most women in novels seem to be unsatisfied, if not actually unhappy. The examples are many and various. First and most frequent are the bad marriages that result from the inability of an innocent, inexperienced young girl to choose a suitable husband. Jeanne Marni gives a clear example of such a situation in her novels *Pierre Tisserand* (1907) and *Souffrir* (1909).[4] Pierre Tisserand, the hero of both books, is a man of little money and great inconstancy. *Pierre Tisserand* is the story of his thoughtlessness and cruelty toward Claire La Plaine; his love for her stepdaughter, Henriette; and Claire's inability to warn Henriette of all Pierre's faults and weaknesses without appearing to be her jealous rival. The second novel tells how Henriette discovers little by little that her husband is mean, egoistical, a liar, an indifferent father, and an unfaithful husband, and that he was the unknown lover who made Claire suffer so much in the past.

The problem of choice is obviously one that preoccupies Marni, because between the two novels just mentioned, she published *L'Une et l'autre*,[5] in which Elise Surdier makes a good second marriage and her daughter Marie-Thérèse a good first one. This is a positive story, for a change, one in which the drama turns on the choices made. Elise and Lucien Terriel are gentle, indecisive people who would not have married if Marie-Thérèse had not taken it upon herself to tell a "fairy-story" to Lucien in which Elise's attitude toward him is made clear enough for him to have the courage to propose to her. Frédéric Stalder is an unworldly young man. He is attracted first to Marie-Thérèse, a modern, unsentimental, intelligent young woman with an abundance of opinions and absolutely no wiles. But upon the arrival of her gentle, gracious, beautiful, and naturally conquettish mother he gradually draws away from her, becoming fascinated by the older woman. He reaches the verge of suicide for Elise, but Marie-Thérèse saves him, and he recognizes her qualities. The novel offers two wise choices and two good marriages, both of which were created in *extremis*. *L'Une et l'autre* is the counterbalance to *Pierre Tisserand* and *Souffrir*. In both cases we follow the sentimental adventures of a mother and daughter who find themselves involved with a man who first loves the mother and ultimately marries the daughter. In the one novel, all seems likely to work out for the best, as Frédéric has solid values and virtues; in the other, both women suffer because Pierre thinks of no one but himself.

When we analyze the novels, we realize that in both cases the young girl is offered no other young man with whom she might compare the hero and has no real experience on which to base her judgment. Pierre Tisserand, the worldly man, abandons the passionate and sensuous love Claire offers in order to profit from Henriette's innocence and potential riches; Frédéric is seduced by coquettish femininity and softness away from Marie-Thérèse's good sense and directness, to which he returns. The men have a choice between two women; the girls have no alternative. The quality of each young man is in direct relation to the moral strength of the woman who brought him up: Pierre is as egotistical and inconsequential as Madame Tisserand; Frédéric has the solid humanitarian virtues of his sister Rosa. Each young woman has a supportive mother and is herself of strong character; nonetheless, the woman's position is the weaker, as she must wait to be chosen before accepting or refusing the offer. Marie-Thérèse is an exception because she takes action to influence the events around her. She it is who persuades Terriel to marry her mother; she it is also who understands Frédéric, prevents his suicide, and declares her love for him. Nevertheless, she would have returned home with her mother and stepfather without carrying the matter further if her stepfather had not taken her life in hand in his turn, so that eventually her life was determined because of male intervention. For Marni, the range of choices that a girl, even a strong-willed girl, can make concerning her life clearly is extremely limited.

Strength of character and endurance in women would seem to be essential, particularly in bad marriages. Claude Lemaître provides a striking example in *Ma Soeur Zabette* (1902).[6] The story of a community of sailors' women, the novel depicts a number of strong women of various sorts, in the center of which is Zabette, the victim of a striking and deliberate mismatch. Zabette is married to a simpleton because her mother owes money to his mother. Fortunately, her husband dies young, and Zabette is left to care for her son and her business interests.

At least Zabette is not poor as well as unhappy, and she does have an outlet for her energies, a useful occupation, and money of her own. In this she is much more fortunate than many of the women who are obliged to make similar marriages. This novel is remarkable for the number of competent women it depicts, yet it is the only one devoid of any female support system. All these women except Zabette work against one another's interests and toward one another's misfortune. Zabette is sacrificed by her mother and her grandmother, who find it normal that she should be selfless, obedient, and unhappy in their interests. All the women in the novel are discontented, ambitious, and frustrated by their conditions, even though they are in fact more independent than most women, all being autonomous widows. This is a novel of lovelessness caused this time not by the hostile male environment, but by a hostile, homophobic situation. These women do not like themselves and do not help one another. Zabette is the scapegoat for them, and her mismarriage is the symbol of their condition. In similar circumstances Hélène Barreaux in Camille Marbo's *Celle qui défiait l'amour* (1911)[7] chooses her own misalliance. When she was young her mother was being kept by a lover; they had no money, and Hélène, proud, innocent, and judgmental, could not bear her mother's moral position. To escape her situation she accepted an offer of marriage from a dull schoolteacher even though she loved a young artist. Later Hélène reaffirms that choice by refusing to go away with a man she loves. She sacrifices herself to wifely duty, respectability, and the hope of serenity.

Jacqueline Vallier in Marcelle Tinayre's novel *La Rançon* (1898)[8] does likewise, but the decision is not made without a long and very ironic struggle, during which Jacqueline learns morality and real values from the man she loves, only to leave him to return to her husband because of the very qualities he has taught her to respect. Jacqueline was given in a "mariage d'inclination," not a love match, and her husband is a good man. When she falls in love she thinks that she can live two parallel lives, but her conscience will not permit her to continue her double allegiance long. The novel treats the overwhelming power of love, the difficulties that are present when a choice must be made, and all the moral aspects of an arranged marriage.

These are some of the more striking novels that deal with the question of marriage. They are all vigorously and competently written, and interesting to read for the information they provide. The best of them, in terms of a well-made novel, is Tinayre's *La Rançon*, in which the author gives, as usual, a careful, subtle psychological analysis of the situation she has created and an interesting presentation of the moral complexities involved when a girl who has accepted a good husband for whom she feels a true "amitié conjugale" falls deeply in love with someone else.

All the marriages described here—and, indeed, all the others I have encountered elsewhere—are unsatisfactory for one reason or another. In each of them the wife has no emotional support from her husband. She spends her life giving herself for little return. Usually she has to find what contentment she can through her children, by good works, or in a sense of her own virtue. The only hope for better things comes when a woman finds a socialist humanitarian to love, as these men have a sense of social justice. Unfortunately, such stories, like all good fairy tales, tend to stop at the wedding. Most authors of this period seem incapable even of imagining a happy and successful marriage in which the woman is autonomous, unmutilated, and visible. Certainly, in the novels I have read, the union itself is not a source of joy and satisfaction; the woman has no sense of herself as a presence in the world, and the husband, even if not vicious, overbearing, drunk, unfaithful, or a financial disaster, is either unloved or unloving. Yet women continue to marry.

The only author who really addresses the question of marriage in terms of a young newly married girl who expects to live a full and happy life as her husband's equal and companion is Louise-Marie Compain, in *L'Un vers l'autre* (1903).[9]

L'Un vers l'autre (One Toward the Other) starts the evening before Laure Prevel's marriage to Henri Deborda and ends on the eve of a second beginning of their married life. Between the two points lies the extraordinary story of Laure's fight for her right to run her own life and Henri's gradual understanding of her position. (Henri Deborda and Noël Delysle [*La Rebelle*] are the only two heroes I have been able to find in French literature until early in this century who change their own beliefs and behavior as a result of their appreciation of the status and rights of the women they love.) Compain's novel has three sections. The first, "L'Un contre l'autre" (The One Against the Other) shows the progression of Laure's revolt against her diminishing liberty and self-governance, and Henri's increasing tyranny in the face of opposition. The second and third sections, "Seule" (She Alone) and "Le Retour" (The Return), are chronologically simultaneous, and present the modification of the initial positions of Laure and Henri as each understands more about the other's world. Laure is as loving and happy to see Henri in the last chapter of the novel as she was in the first; Henri is as ardent and well-intentioned as he was at the beginning of the book, but this time his intentions are founded in real thought and understanding, not merely in tradition and basic honesty.

Compain prepares the terrain carefully. One of the first things her readers learn about Henri is that he is stubborn but strictly honest; he has taken the risk of losing Laure because he would not promise to bring up his children as Catholics. Everyone pointed out that the promise was not binding, but Henri did not want to start his new life on those terms. Laure comments that her father had asked her whether she was sure she wanted to marry such an obstinate man, but she had been impressed by his integrity. It is, of course, Henri's respect for truth that will allow them to start again on a new footing. Meanwhile, other signs indicate the difficulties to come. Laure likes Henri's mother and sister, but senses the tyrant in her father-in-law. She is particularly irritated by his way of talking; he speaks in the first person singular at all times, apparently considering his wife and daughter to be mere extensions of himself:

Je partirai le surlendemain du mariage. . . . Cette phrase si courte et banale agaçait Laure. "Sa femme et sa fille sont comprises dans le 'je' sans doute. Elles font partie des bagages." (p. 9)

[I shall leave two days after the marriage. . . . This sentence, short and com-

monplace though it was, irritated Laure. "His wife and daughter are doubt-
less included in the 'I.' They are part of the baggage."]

But for the moment, she does not analyze her reaction further.

The next step in the preparation of Laure's reaction is taken when her
cousin, Madeleine Avilard, tells Laure how Robert Avilard, her husband,
has decided to send their son to boarding school against her wish. Laure's
response is, "Mais enfin, si les raisons de ton mari n'étaient pas bonnes,
il ne fallait pas y consentir" (p. 12, "Well, then, if your husband's reasons
were not good, you should not have agreed with him"), to which she receives the surprising (to her) reply, "Pas consentir! Est-ce qu'il m'a
demandé mon consentement?" (p. 12, "Not agree! Did he ask me to
agree?"). Thus she learns that a married woman has no rights. Her immediate reaction is "mais jamais je ne tolérerais . . . d'être ainsi traitée (p.
13, "but never would I tolerate . . . being treated that way"). That night—
the eve of her wedding—she begins to reflect on the question of a wife's
obedience and a husband's power. She had never seen an example of male
tyranny in her life and had always assumed that the vow of obedience
was a vestige of the customs of an early period which as such deserved
no attention. Suddenly she has the feeling that some essential element
has been omitted from her education, "qu'on avait peut-être négligé de
l'instruire des choses les plus importantes de la vie" (p. 19, "that perhaps
they had neglected to teach her about some of the most important things
in life").

The contrast between the positions of the man and the woman has
been established and the way prepared for the major themes of the novel:
the inferiority of women and the importance of the kind of education
given to children.

If we look first at the main characters, we see that Laure's education
has prepared her to see herself as a reasonable adult, whereas Henri was
convinced of the inferiority of women by his boarding-school education
and his experience at home. School deprived him early of the influence
of women and of the possibility to develop "ce sentiment fait de respect
et de tendre protection que le fils souvent éprouve pour sa mère et qui
le conduit doucement à aimer et à respecter la femme" (p. 25, "that feeling composed of respect and tender protectiveness a son often feels for
his mother and that gently leads him to love and respect women"). At
home his mother was always in the background, invisible, silent, and eco-

nomically dependent, even though the family income came from land she had brought as dowry. It is at this point that the discussion of Madeleine Avilard's concern for her son's education comes into true focus. Compain is criticizing the male-dominated education system for neglecting to educate young men to understand either women or their own developing emotions. The only feeling Henri has had for women is physical desire, and he is aware of no other form of love. Women signify temptation for him in all the traditional ways, so he is distrustful of the influence a wife might have on his career. For him an intelligent, loving wife is an impossible dream. Laure seems to be that dream, but for that very reason Henri's love for her does not change his fundamental attitudes. Unconsciously, he expects to marry a wife as submissive as his mother. Laure, on the other hand, has never learned that she should be a victim. The battle lines are drawn already by their upbringings and the struggle does not take long to get under way.

Compain sets up two areas of conflict: one public and one private, one general and one personal. These are the questions of the status of women in society and the reactions of Henri and Laure which rapidly become transformed into a microcosmic reflection of the larger issue.

Laure is observant and begins to analyze what she sees around her. She begins with male-female relations and reflects that there are some "où le désir régnait en tyran, avilissant les hommes et oppressant les femmes" (p. 32, "in whom desire held tyrannical sway, degrading the men and oppressing the women"). Her next step is to reflect on the situations of her friends who were married against their wills and of the status of a prostitute who gets on the train. Her thoughts are reflected in her attitudes, and she refuses to make a distinction between Henri's legally married colleagues, all of whom she finds to be in unsatisfactory relationships, and the unmarried couple in which the woman is an honest "wife" and mother. As far as she can see, the only difference between Marie Collard and herself is an arbitrary difference of birth and, therefore, of treatment. A man marries a young woman whose father has status and does not bother with the formalities otherwise:

> On épouse la fille du Conseiller Prevel mais celle d'un garçon de café, on la prend sans plus de formalités. Ça n'est pas une différence vraie, ça: une différence de père. (p. 40)

> [Counsellor Prevel's daughter is taken in marriage, but a café waiter's

daughter is just taken, without any other formalities. There is no real difference there: just different fathers.]

Hence the awareness of the social situation has a bearing on Laure's
behavior, and this behavior outrages Henri's conservative outlook, with
the result that the public issue becomes a private one. From a general
concern about appearances, respectability, and the reputation of women
Henri moves naturally to the question of Laure's reputation, which he
assumes is in his care. Here the clash of upbringing becomes very clear,
for such an assumption is totally outside Laure's experience: "Voilà une
raison que je n'eusse pas trouvé. Personne autre que moi-même ne peut
exposer ma réputation" (p. 47, "There's a reason I wouldn't have thought
of. No other than myself can imperil my reputation"). This is followed
by the discovery that not only does Henri think he has rights over her,
but he also thinks he is right and that she should accept that he knows
best.

We see that Henri is set in tyrannical ways which gradually filter into
the smallest details of their married life. He expects to be consulted before Laure accepts volunteer work. He forbids her to be seen with Marie
Collard. He reads her letters but does not show her his. He cancels her
choral work without consulting her. In a parallel development Laure becomes less conciliatory. At first she is hurt by Henri's tone, then outraged
that he should feel in a position to give her orders and finally furious that
he should control her actions.

Meanwhile, a very interesting psychological pattern develops in the
way they react physically to each other. Early quarrels end with a kiss
and reconciliation in love. Next, Henri argues to win, and when he suc-
ceeds in making her cry wants to take her in his arms to comfort her.
This is no longer equality in reconciliation but affirmation of victory.
Laure gradually becomes aware of the shift in their relationship:

> Ce n'est pas la première fois que je comprends que tu ne me considères
> pas comme ton égale, Henri. Ce n'est pas avec des baisers que tu peux ef-
> facer la blessure que tu m'as faite avec des pensées. (p. 68)

> [It is not the first time I have realized that you do not consider me your
> equal, Henri. It is not with kisses that you can erase the hurt you have
> done me with your thoughts.]

We see the dichotomy in Henri's behavior, and we see that his manifestations of love are becoming but another expression of his power over

Laure. He feels tenderness when she shows weakness, aggressivity when she shows strength.

> Il l'avait reprise entre ses bras et tout bas il continuait de lui dire des mots charmeurs et tout puissants pour l'alanguir, car il était sincère. A l'instinct dominateur se substituait une tendresse profonde.... A ce moment, il n'eût pu répéter les paroles orgueilleuses et dures.... Pourtant il ne les regretta pas, ne les jugea pas injustes, berça seulement la peine de Laure. Elle se laissa endormir, crut sentir sous les paroles de l'amant un repentir qui n'était point au coeur de l'époux, oublia la blessure faite à sa dignité de femme. (p. 69)

> [He had taken her back into his arms and continued to murmur beguiling, irresistible words to make her soften, for he was sincere. His instinct to dominate was replaced by deep tenderness.... At that moment, he would not have been capable of repeating the proud, hard words.... Nevertheless, he did not regret saying them and did not feel they were unfair; he simply soothed Laure's hurt feelings. She allowed herself to fall asleep believing that she sensed behind the lover's words a remorse that did not exist in the husband's heart, she forgot the wound to her woman's dignity.]

Compain offers a fascinating portrait of a man with confused values. As a result of his upbringing Henri expects his wife to be silent and submissive, whereas intellectually he appreciates her intelligence and personality. That the two sets of characteristics are not compatible does not seem to have occurred to him, nor does the fact that he might lose a battle with an intelligent wife "tant était naïve et profonde l'intime conviction de sa supériorité" (p. 74, "so naive and so deep was his belief in his superiority").

When Laure leaves the house in anger to go and settle her affairs for herself, Henri takes the last mental step into tyranny, violence:

> Ah! elle ne voulait point de la contrainte morale. Eh bien elle céderait à la contrainte physique, voilà tout. Il la ramènerait de force au besoin! Il fallait en finir une bonne fois avec cette manie d'insubordination. (p. 91)

> [Ah! she did not want any moral constraints. Well, she would yield to physical restraint, that is all there was to it. He would bring her back by brute force if necessary! Once and for all, there had to be an end to this mania for insubordination.]

He does not actually lay a hand on her because, as she sees him following her, she falls. The direct opposition is diffused for a time because she then miscarries—which is, of course, a symbol of their discord and the fact that nothing vital can develop from such a relationship. The issue of a mother's involvement in her child's education now becomes the focus of their discord, but the real issue is the fact that the only way a married woman can obtain what she wants is by making her husband's life a misery, because she is not considered a reasoning adult. Laure finds the situation humiliating, and the reply she gets is even more so:

> —C'est cela qui est humiliant qu'elle n'ait que le droit d'ennuyer son mari, non pas celui d'intervenir comme un être doué de raison.
> —"Bah! la raison n'a jamais passé pour être le privilège de ton sexe. Vous avez d'autres charmes.
> —Oh . . . Quelle étrange alliance de l'amour et du mépris vous faites, vous autres hommes. (p. 103)

> ["What is humiliating is that she only has the right to annoy her husband, not to intervene like a human being gifted with reason."
> "Bah! Rationality has never been known to be the prerogative of your sex. You have other charms."
> "Oh . . . what a strange combination of love and scorn you men are."]

Having come to regret her marriage, Laure reflects upon her situation and that of all women. She reaches several very important conclusions. First, she reflects that public esteem is given to wives, and not to honest women such as Marie Collard, because it is only by such obvious social pressure than men can render desirable "ce servage déguisé du mariage" (p. 110, "the disguised serfdom of marriage"). Then, realizing that the only autonomous woman she knows is Madame Duverger, the director of the normal school, she wonders whether one has to be economically independent in order to live by one's own conscience. Her next thought is one of revolt against her husband, in whom she sees "l'esprit qui avait opprimé son sexe" (p. 110, "the way of thinking that had oppressed her sex").

However, Laure still loves Henri, and she tries to come to terms with the opposition she feels within herself between the person who needs a sense of self and dignity, and the loving woman who is happy to serve her master on his terms. She reflects at length in many of the same terms as Josanne Valentin (chapter 3).

For a time she considers the possibility of leaving Henri, and leave him she does the day she sees in his face that he is using his caresses to make her obey him. The letter she leaves for Henri reads:

Je t'ai compris Henri, et puisque mon amour est devenu pour toi le signe de mon asservissement, je te quitte et je rentre chez mon père. (p. 116)

[I have seen through you, Henri, and since for you my love has become the sign of my bondage, I am leaving you and going home to my father.]

She returns home and explains very clearly to her father her reasons for leaving Henri:

Mon mari ne me considère point comme son égale et de ce fait me dénie le droit de me gouverner moi-même, celui de diriger mes enfants. Mon infériorité radicale est pour lui un dogme. Je souffre trop de ce jugement que je sens planer sur toutes mes actions; c'est pourquoi j'ai rompu le lien qui m'attachait à lui. (p. 121)

[My husband does not consider me his equal and therefore denies me the right to govern myself or guide my children. My fundamental inferiority is a dogma for him. I suffer too much from this judgment that I feel hovering over all my actions; that is why I broke the tie that bound me to him.]

Nobody understands. Henri does not beat her; he is not unfaithful. Why leave him? Her father thinks she is unreasonable; her stepmother thinks she is crazy; the pastor who married her (Henri's uncle) declares she is proud (and incidentally decides not to send his daughters to the lycée, as educated girls come to a bad end). Finally, demoralized and miserable, she goes to see her cousin Madeleine, who not only understands but also approves and supports her:

En t'écoutant parler il me semblait que je me comprenais mieux moi-même. . . . Tu m'as fait du bien et tu en feras à d'autres . . . [sic] à celles qui, comme moi, souffrent d'être de petites créatures sans conséquence et se disaient qu'elles étaient faites pour un autre rôle. . . . Crois-moi, tu as bien fait; je te l'affirme. (p. 147)

[Listening to you talk, I felt I understood myself better. . . . You have been good for me as you will be for others . . . those women who, like me, suffer from being little unimportant creatures and who told themselves they were made for another role. . . . Believe me, you have done the right thing, I assure you.]

We have again reached the heart of the most important problem for women of this period: what are the relations between love and autonomy? Yver made Marceline Rhonans decide they were incompatible. Tinayre arrives at a compromise: if a woman is autonomous in her public behavior and her husband's equal in his mind and in his heart, she can allow him to be her master in the intimacy of their lovemaking. The crucial point is, of course, the sincerity of the equality in mind and heart. This is the obstacle that Laure and Henri run afoul of. Henri does not think of Laure as his equal, with the result that any gesture of loving sacrifice on her part is transformed into confirmation of superiority and dominance on his. Hence their loving relationship is transformed into a power relationship between master and slave, where all her sacrifices are taken for granted as his due.

Compain provides a detailed description and careful analysis of the changing dynamics of this relationship, and makes Laure grow in awareness of her social condition and of her sense of self. However, she does not call into question the traditional idea that a woman in love wants her partner to be dominant. The only writer to challenge that perception will be Rachilde in *Monsieur Vénus* (chapter 9).

In this first section Compain makes clear the rooted attitudes men have toward their own power and privilege, and their unwillingness to question the status quo. She shows the ferocious and unreasonable defense of their position, and the sense of domination that is part of the expression of what men call their love for women. Henri Deborda's attitude toward Laure is not fundamentally very different from Alain's feeling for Frisson de Bambou. On such a basis it is not possible to create a marriage partnership of the kind Laure expects.

Having set aside the question of love for the time being, Compain then explores autonomy. Laure proceeds to act reasonably upon the conclusions she has drawn from her own experience: she refuses to live in servitude, and so sets out to obtain economic independence so that she may live with dignity according to her conscience. She obtains her teaching diploma and goes to work in a normal school. There she finds a friend in Germaine Lachaud, the principal. Germaine is young, efficient, and idealistic about her work; she approves Laure's decision, admires her, and supports her in her teaching. During this period Laure realizes how hard life can be in the work world. The situation is much as we have seen in Reval's novels (chapter 6). The school inspectors are unjust and tyrannical; certain of Laure's colleagues are difficult and unpleasant; the work is time-consuming and sometimes boring. The experience gives her an insight into Henri's life and makes her realize that it really is more comfortable to be a bourgeois wife than a working woman. She also comes to admire her colleagues, who work so hard in the face of great opposition to try to give an education to girls. Again, in reaffirmation of what we have seen elsewhere, Compain depicts Germaine as proud of what they are doing: "Nous préparons des races nouvelles de femmes plus raisonnables, plus capables de mériter ce respect de l'homme qu'elles réclament" (p. 249, "We are preparing new generations of more reasonable women, women more capable of deserving that respect of men that they demand"). But as a woman who sees herself and women like her as odd transitional creatures: "Nous sommes des archéoptérix, des êtres de transition, point aimables par eux-mêmes peut-être mais beaux par ce qu'ils annoncent" (p. 250, "We are archaeopteryx, transitional creatures who are not perhaps likable in themselves but beautiful for what they foretell"). According to Germaine, Laure is the kind of woman these teachers are trying to produce: developed in mind and heart, the perfect modern wife.

Compain's interest lies in improving the conditions within marriage, so here she quite ruthlessly makes the professional woman appear to undervalue herself. Germaine urges Laure to return to her husband, as she is too fine a specimen of womanhood to remain in the teaching profession. It is not until the very end of the novel that we realize that in Compain's view, devoted women such as Germaine will be the wives in the new society, in which men will treat their spouses with respect, honor them as equals. These are the women who have rejected the servitude of marriage and in so doing have accepted a life without love, for they are the best of women. As Laure states:

> Un jour, prochain sans doute, les hommes s'apercevront bien que ce sont les meilleures d'entre nous, les virtuelles épouses à jamais stériles, qui se sont éloignées. Alors ils retourneront vers elles comme tu est revenu vers moi. L'humanité sera enfin unie et bienheureuse. Peut-être nos enfants connaîtront ces jours? (p. 310)

> [One day, probably soon, men will notice that it is the best of us all, the forever sterile wives-to-be, who have moved away. Then they will turn back toward them as you came back to me. Humanity will finally be united and blessed. Perhaps our children will see that day?]

So Compain seems to agree with Colette Yver. The time for equality in marriage has not yet arrived for most women. As she says, Laure was born before her time.

Laure gains in wisdom and experience throughout the separation. Henri does so also, but his growth starts more slowly. At first he settles into his rights and his righteousness, and waits for Laure to return to him, but when summer comes, he goes to visit his family and suddenly sees them with new eyes. He finds the way his father treats his mother and sister unacceptable, but does not see yet the parallel with his own life. Gradually, however, he begins to remember arbitrary actions imposed by his father and his grandfather. At about this time also, he goes to the wedding of a friend and hears the pastor proclaim that a husband should love his wife and a wife fear her husband. He tells himself that he never wanted to make Laure fear him; he wanted to protect her. But at this his conscience pricks him, and in self-defense he thinks of all the historical justifications for his right to superiority. The integrity we were told about at the beginning of the novel, however, is beginning to surface, and he wonders why, if this reasoning is true, he suffers when he sees his mother victimized. The search for truth has begun. Henri recognizes that his father treats him as he treated Laure.

Just as Laure learned to appreciate her feelings for Henri in contrasting her life with him with those of her colleagues, so Henri explores his attitudes in a parallel development. First he realizes that he is used to the love and comfort Laure provided, and he no longer likes living as a bachelor. Then he listens to his colleagues discussing a feminist conference, where the conclusion had been that there is more human dignity in working than in sitting waiting for a husband. One of the men argues that for financial reasons, married women should be allowed to work. Another quotes Dumas in response: "Qu'elles restent femmes, pour rester nos maîtresses" (p. 295, "Let them remain women so that they remain our mistresses"). Henri thinks that both men are wrong, the first because he sees liberation as economic liberation only, the second because he sees women as objects for men's use. Finally he pays a visit to a prostitute. Suddenly the difference between love as a joyous gift from one to another and love as power over an inferior becomes clear to him. He realizes all he lost when Laure returned to Paris, recognizes how he had treated her, and understands why she left him. Now they can start again.

Compain writes that they become a new couple, freed from old tyrannies and united in the plenitude of a rediscovered love. The ideal marriage is about to be accomplished. Laure, Henri, and Germaine, the perfect couple with the ideal teacher and as yet unrecognized wife, walk out of the book together. (Henri and Laure can be found as a happily married couple with children, doing good socialist works, teaching in the popular university, and giving support to pregnant and unmarried women in another of Compain's novels, *L'Opprobre* (1905),[10] so all their good intentions bear fruit.) Never does Compain challenge the idea that the best life for a woman is life as a wife and mother. Though after a magnificently romantic apotheosis on a mountaintop in the sunset (in flagrant opposition to the careful realism of the rest of the novel), she does recognize that that life could and should be improved considerably in order for women to find fulfillment in it.

Compain's novel is careful and courageous. She shows clearly the traditional attitudes men have toward women and marriage, their automatic use of emotional, economic, and physical power to dominate their wives. She takes pains to reveal the little manifestations of tyranny that can make daily life so unpleasant and gives them their real importance. Not only that, but she also shows how very difficult it is for a woman to explain her position and her grievances to a man who has never shared any of the experiences which cause her humiliation and suffering. Meanwhile, her characters remain human: we can identify very easily with the quarrels and reconciliations and the resulting confusion of values.

That education is essential for women and that a different education is necessary for men are major concerns if society is to be changed. Compain's educated women are variously pleasant and unpleasant, but all are interesting and able to survive well. Madame Duverger and Mademoiselle Lachaud are admirable: models of idealism, careful thought, hard work, and humanitarian behavior. Together with Laure they oppose the rigid bigotry of Henri, his father, and his uncle. Valuable human qualities characterize these women, and the world as they see it would indeed be a better place. On the global scale such a vision is perhaps utopian, but on the scale that Compain gives us, her ideal is possible (if improbable); all it requires is that every man should have the integrity of Henri Deborda and every woman the courage of Laure Prevel so that equality may be achieved. Laure and Henri's children did not see their parents' dream come to pass. For many women Compain's novel is, alas, almost as apposite today as when she published it in 1903. All that has changed is the rhetoric of marriage—and that only in the Western world.

In all the novels in this chapter marriage is seen as a taking possession of women by men. The ways in which this happens are many; some are much less pleasant than others. Rare is the woman like Laure Prevel who has the education, the determination, and the family support necessary to fight successfully for her rights within marriage. Laure is the only wife I have found who demands and proves her equality. She takes her life into her own hands for the purpose of obtaining both her rights and the respect and love of her husband. She is an unusually successful woman and a powerful model in this period, in which the ultimate aim—as stated by all the novelists, however feminist they may or may not be—is that all women should live in a love relationship with a man.

These authors are pragmatists. Given that most women cannot earn a decent living in the Belle Epoque, the reformers choose to strive for better conditions within marriage rather than encourage women to go out and starve. French culture had little or no place for the single woman, and these authors, even the most courageous of them, are products of their time. Even so, by their trenchant criticisms of marriage as servitude for women, they all subvert to some degree traditional relations between husband and wife. By their examination of marriage from women's perspective they provide material for reflection, and by their suggestions for reform they encourage change in the public sphere and in the daily lives of their readers.

Love and the Choices II
COLETTE

As Colette is the only woman writer of the period to have received critical attention over the years, the only one whose name comes to mind readily, and one of the few well-known women writers in the whole of French literature, it is essential and inevitable that she should have a place here among her peers.[1] It is as a woman writer in relation to her peers only that I intend to consider her in this book. In this way the choice of novels to be discussed imposes itself: *La Retraite sentimentale* (1907), *L'Ingénue libertine* (1909), and *La Vagabonde* (1910).[2] We have the novel Colette writes by herself to close the series of Claudine tales, the first three of which had been written in collaboration with Willy; the story of Minne reclaimed, reworked, retitled *L'Ingénue libertine*, and republished by Colette as a work for which she assumes sole responsibility; and *La Vagabonde*, the first novel she is free to write as she sees fit.

The three texts provide us with a selection of heroines whose preoccupations and decisions fit interestingly into the issue of love as a lifestyle as it has been seen so far in these chapters. Colette touches on many aspects of female desire, on love, on marriage and emancipation for the individual woman. Her descriptions of adolescent girls add piquancy to those in Gabrielle Reval's novels; her characters have life and charm. The comparison between Colette's work and that of Marcelle Tinayre is an interesting one. It is possible to see a parallel between *L'Ingénue libertine* and *Avant l'amour*, between *La Retraite sentimentale* and *La Rançon*, between *La Vagabonde* and *La Rebelle*, but there is a great difference in attitude between the two authors. Tinayre wants to help women reconcile autonomy and love, and thus emancipate themselves. Hers is a critical and analytical view of male-female relationships on emotional, practical, and sexual levels. In contrast, Colette's presentation of love is restricted to the various modes of desire, sensuality, and love. The accuracy of her perception and expression of female sensuousness completes the view of women that we have seen already, but does not add anything fundamentally new to the picture because Colette has a traditional attitude to women which makes her see emancipation in terms of sexual freedom only; this emancipation is "naughty." The result is that although Colette's women may be faced by the same choices as some of the heroines of the other writers discussed here, their decisions are not the same and not necessarily made for the same reasons, for they are frequently women of a different breed.

Claude Pichois, author of the preface to the Pléiade edition of Colette's works, did not realize how right he was when, after listing Colette Yver, Lucie Delarue-Mardrus, Marcelle Tinayre, Gérard d'Houville, and Anna de Noailles, he wrote:

> Colette s'apparentera à elles, mais d'épiderme seulement, n'ayant jamais levé la bannière du féminisme, ni confondu le rocher de Sapho avec celui de Prométhée. (p. XXII)[3]

> [Colette's connection with them goes only skin deep as she never raised the banner of feminism nor confused Sappho's rock with the rock of Prometheus.]

His conclusion is correct, but the reasons for it seem to me to be inaccurate. His analysis of the works of the women he lists and compares with Colette is traditionally androcentric: he thus misinterprets their aims and strengths. He is right to say that Colette is neither feminist nor lesbian, despite her behavior, because her interests and her sensuality are directed toward men within an unchallenged patriarchal system. For her, two women can be together only because the men around them are temporarily hostile; they are not united by real love or even real voluptuous pleasure:

> Deux femmes enlacées ... l'image mélancolique et touchante de deux faiblesses, peut-être réfugiées aux bras l'une de l'autre pour y dormir, y pleurer, fuir l'homme souvent méchant, et goûter, mieux que tout plaisir,

l'amer bonheur de se sentir pareilles, infirmes, oubliées. (*La Vagabonde*, Pléiade, p. 1207)

[Two women enlaced . . . the melancholy and touching image of two weak creatures who have perhaps sought shelter in each other's arms, there to sleep and weep, safe from man who is so often cruel, and there to taste, better than any pleasure, the bitter happiness of feeling themselves akin, frail and forgotten. (p. 188)][4]

In *La Retraite sentimentale* Colette establishes an opposition between the monogamous loving wife, Claudine, and Annie, the divorced woman seeking constant sexual fulfillment. Claudine is fascinated by Annie's adventures and persuades her to recount her experiences in full. Annie does so, in a prurient mixture of shame and pride. Claudine lives Annie's adventures vicariously from the moment she teases the first response out of her friend:

> —Annie . . .
> —Oui . . . quoi?
> —Péronnelle . . . cette danse de l'Amour, ces torsions de bayadère . . . ça ne vous rappelle rien?
> —Allons, Annie! Je vous vois assez, moi, en travers d'un lit d'hôtel étranger, roucoulante et les reins creusés . . .
> Les trucs les plus éculés réussissent toujours! Annie saisit la perche que je lui tends.
> —Oh! voyons, je ne faisais pas tant de bruit que ça, Claudine!
> Cette pudeur! ces mains qui éloignent l'image du péché! Si je ne connaissais pas Annie, depuis l'autre soir je me tromperais. Qu'elle parle! qu'elle parle! C'est le seul plaisir un peu coupable qu'elle puisse m'offrir.
> —L'extase silencieuse, alors?
> Elle tourne les épaules, mal à l'aise:
> —Ecoutez, Claudine, je ne sais pas comment vous pouvez, au grand jour, sous ce soleil, parler si tranquillement de . . . de ça!
> —Vous trouvez plus naturel de le faire? [. . .]
> —Oui avoue-t-elle enfin. Plus naturel, et plus facile aussi. . . . Je sens que je ne vais pas m'ennuyer. (pp. 861–62)

> ["Annie . . ."
> "Yes, what is it?"
> "Peronnelle . . . this love dance, these dancing-girl contortions—doesn't that remind you of anything?"
> "Come on Annie, I can see you fairly easily, lying across the bed in some foreign hotel, cooing, arching your back . . ."
> The most daring tricks are always successful! Annie rose to the bait I offered her.

"Oh, come now, I didn't make as much noise as that Claudine!"

Such modesty! Those hands pushing away the image of sin! If I hadn't learned to know Annie since the other evening, I'd be taken in. If only she'd talk! If only she'd talk! It's the one slightly guilty pleasure she can offer me.

"So it was silent ecstasy, then?"

She turned her shoulders away uneasily: "Listen Claudine, when it's broad daylight and the sun's shining, I don't know how you can talk so easily about . . . that!"

"Do you find it more natural to *do* it?"

"Yes," she admitted at last. "More natural, and easier too."

I felt I was not going to be bored.][5]

The tone is set. Annie is properly naughty—she is sexually emancipated and socially ashamed ("Je ne veux pas trop diminuer à vos yeux" (p. 67, "I don't want to sink too far in your estimation"), and the recounting of her adventures will not differ very much from traditional writing of the same kind (such as Diderot, *Les Bijoux indiscrets*) except that the female experience is being described not only by a woman to a woman within the text, but also by a woman author. The novel remains a "roman libertin" of the usual sort, in which the telling of past exploits alternates with an affair in the present. In this case, Claudine, continuing her vicarious interest in Annie's life, sets up her friend with Marcel, Claudine's stepson, who is homosexual. The result is frustration for Annie, humiliation for Marcel, and some outlet for Claudine's ambiguous feelings for her stepson—feelings of her need to dominate him violently, be it by a beating or by a caress.

We realize that the distinction that Claudine makes between herself and Annie—that Annie feels desire, whereas Claudine feels love and thus is faithful to Renaud even after his death—is a very fine one. Claudine declares:

Moi, moi, l'amour m'a rendue si fortunée, si comblée de plaisirs dans ma chair, de tourment dans mon âme, de toute son irrémédiable et précieuse mélancolie, que je ne sais vraiment pas comment vous pouvez vivre auprès de moi sans mourir de jalousie. (p. 864)

["As for me, love has made me so happy, so deeply satisfied physically, so emotionally excited; love, with all its irremedial and precious melancholy, that I really don't know how you can live close to me without dying of jealousy." (p. 63)]

Yet it is clear that she does feel some desire for Marcel's "chair fraîche" and also for Annie.

She can maintain her original statement only insofar as infidelity with other men is the only infidelity that counts. In Colette's world, lovemaking between women is foreplay for heterosexual lovemaking; lesbian relationships have no autonomous existence and therefore cannot harm "real" relationships. Like Annie, then, Marcel does not count because he is homosexual and, hence, not a man. Claudine can diversify her desire and remain faithful to Renaud as long as her contact with other men comes only through Annie's stories. Claudine's desire finds an outlet in her imagination—thus she becomes the virtuous woman with whom the female readers of *La Retraite sentimentale* may identify and justify themselves, while at the same time suggesting to male readers, by her very attitude, that the women around them may well be more interested in amorous exploits than their social behavior might imply.

Colette creates a neat division between emotion and practice, maintaining the traditional mind-body dichotomy used by the upholders of patriarchy to prove the wickedness of women, while commenting upon it. The "mind" is, in fact, concerned with sexual pleasure rather more than is the "body." Claudine is obsessed by Annie's actions and judges them:

> Elle a appris la volupté sans amour, elle est tombée sans noblesse, et, quoi qu'elle m'aît dit l'autre soir, sans en ressentir l'humiliation. (p. 864)

> [She had learned sexual pleasure without love, she had fallen without nobility, and in spite of what she told me the other evening, without feeling any humiliation. (p. 63)]

Annie's attitude is much simpler: for her the body dominates utterly—it "thinks" for her. It is also the traditional attitude attributed to women: women cannot think; they live through their feelings and emotions; and are the eternal temptresses, always ready to give in to their inexhaustible sensuality. Annie is the essential female. Claudine is a "better" woman because she restrains her desire, not because she does not feel it. She also feels herself to be superior (and Colette sustains this judgment) because she has learned to see the world as men see it. What she calls love for Renaud is, rather, total male-identification, as we see in the comment on Annie which follows Annie's affirmation of her body:

O jolie petite peau qui savez si bien quitter votre âme! Je suis seule, et je
nous compare l'une à l'autre. Je n'ai jamais étudié une femme autant que
vous, parce que je méprise instinctivement mes soeurs vos pareilles, et que
je ne me connais point d'amies. (p. 897)

[O charming little body that knows so well how to leave your soul! I'm
alone, and I make comparisons between the two of us. I've never studied
a woman as much as you, for I instinctively despise my sisters who resemble you, and I have no women friends at all. (pp. 121–22)]

She denies her a soul, in time-honored fashion, expressing her scorn for
all women like Annie. In this context the attraction that draws Claudine
toward Annie and Marcel becomes even more ambiguous, because the
implication is that she is looking at them as a man would. She describes
her encounters with Renaud as a "savoureux antagonisme"—a virile
struggle in which the attitude is "Je t'aurai avant que tu m'aies" (p. 897,
"I'll get you before you get me," p. 122). Claudine is set up as pseudo-man
(she and Renaud even share a number of gestures and characteristics [p.
135]) poised between Annie, the real woman in traditional terms, and
Renaud, the real man. Not for nothing is Marcel the same age as
Claudine, and Claudine looked upon as Renaud's child as well as his wife.
Marcel and Claudine are improper examples of their sexes, ironic echoes
one of the other as the creations of the patriarch.

The reign of Renaud, the all-powerful and all-loving father-husband in
the earlier Claudine novels, seems to come to an end in this one. He returns home to die, this man who has the right to say to Claudine during
their lovemaking:

Je te tuerai, si un autre homme que moi voit tes yeux, tes yeux qui sont
chargés de rancune au moment où ils me doivent le plus de reconnais-
sance!" (p. 897)

["I'll kill you if any other man but me sees your eyes, your eyes which fill
with resentment at the moment when they owe me the most gratitude!"
(pp. 121–22)]

Resent him as she may Claudine continues to live in his shadow, to remain faithful to a dead love, to the man she feels will watch over the rest
of her life "et pour qui je garde, sans dormir, mes paupières fermées, afin
de mieux le voir" (p. 955, "and for whom I keep my eyelids closed, without sleeping, in order to see him more clearly," p. 223). End of novel. Her

life of male domination is not over because she chooses to remain within the context established by Renaud.

The whole of *La Retraite sentimentale* is a comment on male domination; Annie, Claudine, and Marcel are all oppressed in one way or another. Annie and Marcel, held in thrall by their desire, may well find pleasure in their sexual life but are nonetheless victims of their numerous menfolk. That such is their position is made clear by their behavior toward Claudine, who, in the absence of Renaud, takes the male role in the household. They have what Colette describes elsewhere as "a slave mentality."

Claudine and Marcel are governed by Renaud, whether they are happy within the relationship or not. Marcel's attitude is ambiguous; Claudine expresses wholehearted love and devotion, though her statements are somewhat compromised by her attitude toward Annie and Marcel, as we have seen already. Whatever her imaginary and vicarious unfaithfulness, however, she does not rebel against the life Renaud laid out for her, and even after his death remains the person her "father" created. Claudine has moved toward an identification with Renaud, and Marcel has shifted away from such an identification, with the result that neither of them has Renaud's power and authority. Each has been changed in nature by the overpowering presence of the father figure; each has been deprived of the characteristics that could constitute a threat. Marcel seeks constant love and approval from men (as Annie does), whereas Claudine, who responds only to Renaud, has become a metaphorical eunuch, symbolically sterile, and without a future. Pseudo-man already, she is also endowed metaphorically with pseudo-motherhood, for it is she who looks after those who are obviously slaves—Marcel and Annie. As we have seen, a union of slaves is not feasible. After the disaster of their night together, Annie and Marcel leave Casamène in search of new masters; Claudine remains as custodian of the old order.

Antoine, in *L'Ingénue libertine*, is much less a patriarch than Renaud is. To begin with, he is much closer in age to Minne, the cousin he loves and ultimately marries. Although he carries the authority of a husband, he does not add to it that of a father. He tries to impose his will at one point by having Minne followed by a private detective, but abandons the idea and offers her freedom and total support instead. Antoine offers sexual freedom and is given love in exchange, but the situation in *La Retraite sentimentale* has only been modified. Minne is as dependent on Antoine as Claudine was on Renaud, although she is not male-identified in the same way. The mind-body division in this novel comes between the adolescent Minne of the first part, who lives in her imagination, and the physical Minne of the second part. Here, despite appearances, is still the separation between chastity and voluptuousness, because the young Minne is totally ignorant of all things sexual. The male-identification comes from Minne's acceptance of her romantic role, as defined within a male-dominated world of crime and violence.

Minne's real world is less obviously male-dominated than that of Claudine because Minne has no father. The father figure in the novel, Uncle Paul, is Antoine's father, whose main functions seem to be embarrassing Antoine, reassuring Minne's mother, and annoying Minne. Curiously, the basic structure of the novel is the same as that of *La Retraite sentimentale*. There are the same four main characters: a man who is father to his own son and to a young woman of similar age, a mother figure, a gauche young man, and a young woman who is trying to find herself through sexual freedom. But this time attention is turned fully on Minne (the Annie figure), who is loved exclusively by her mother and by Antoine.

In the first part of the novel Minne is depicted as a romanesque adolescent, totally ignorant of her ignorance concerning sexuality—she thinks two copulating snails are a double snail and defines rape in terms of tomb robbery.

> Alors, je demande à maman: "Qu'est-ce que c'est, violer une sépulture?" Maman dit: "C'est l'ouvrir sans permission." Eh bien, violer un cadavre, c'est l'ouvrir sans permission. Tu bisques? (pp. 694–95)[6]

> [So I asked Mamma: "What is violating a tomb?" Mamma said: "It's opening it without permission." Well, violating a corpse is opening it without permission. Are you cross?]

Her innocence is purely physical and factual, however, for her concept of passion is developed in the extreme and drawn entirely from the emotional attitudes purveyed by popular magazines. Minne is utterly obsessed by an idea of love derived from pulp fiction. She imagines herself as a gangster's moll, queen of the underworld, and regales her startled cousin with tales of her lover, the murderer. Antoine has more knowledge, more prudence, and less imagination than Minne.

He is in love with her and unsure of himself—seventeen years old, with pimples and an awakening desire for women which he transposes alternately onto Minne and the buxom servant—so he has difficulty in dealing with Minne's fantastic pronouncements. His awareness of love and sex is part of his physical experience, whereas Minne's concept of love is verbal and idealistic, in her head only; she is both innocent and ignorant.

She is totally unaware of the danger that her apparent attitude might bring upon her. She imagines herself to be in love with a vagrant whom she saw several times sitting at the corner of her street, and one night, thinking he has come for her, she dresses up in her "criminal" clothes and sets out after an unknown man. She wanders around in the dark, expecting to find the romance and excitement of the fictional underworld; instead she gets lost and meets only miserable creatures, prostitutes, and drunken men from whom she has to flee, arriving home covered with mud from a fall and totally disillusioned:

> Je comprends! je comprends à présent! je fais un rêve! mais comme il dure longtemps, et comme j'ai mal partout! Pourvu que je m'éveille avant que le vieux m'attrape! (p. 731)
>
> [I understand, I understand now! I'm dreaming. But how long the dream is lasting and how I ache all over! If only I can wake up before the old man catches me.]

The real mud on her clothes and in her hair is symbolic of the social mud that will stick to her person as a result of her escapade, and a sign that the mind and body cannot be brought together lightly. (If chastity goes looking for voluptuousness, the result is a besmirched reputation.) In her fright and fever Minne cries her innocence to Antoine, but it is too late. The reality of her fear and appearance make him believe her tales: "Il pleure sur Minne, il pleure aussi sur lui-même puisqu'elle est perdue, avilie, marquée à jamais d'un sceau immonde" (p. 734, "He wept for Minne and he also wept for himself because she was lost, debased, branded for ever with a hallmark of filth," p. 93). Minne has the reputation of a fallen woman.

This first part of *L'Ingénue libertine* is clearly fantastic in the way in which Minne lives out her dream, but it does throw light on the attitude and development of adolescents of the period. Antoine is realistic; his knowledge of love comes from his emotions and his body. He tells the truth. Minne is a mystery to him because none of what she tells him about love is true, yet any of it could be real because he has no experience of women against which to measure her unpredictable behavior. Minne is a mystery to Antoine, and love is a mystery to Minne. She is trapped by her own imagination. Adolescent girls are ignorant; they are given stories about love that feed their imagination and then are open to moral disaster and social disgrace. A girl must not only be pure, she also must be seen to be pure, and coming home in the middle of the night covered in mud is not reassuring behavior.

The second part of the novel, starting as it does with the statement "Je vais coucher avec Minne" (p. 735, "I am going to sleep with Minne," p. 98) follows on from the image Minne projected in the first part. Minne is still searching for the ideal love, only now she is married to Antoine and is taking lovers systematically to try to find satisfaction. The first part of the novel was talk and wild imagining; this part is sexual action unsupported by emotion. Each is as unrealistic as the other. Each becomes an apprenticeship: the first in disillusion and reality, the second in sensitivity and love.

Here Minne is no more awakened physically than she was as an adolescent, and her behavior is still outrageous, only now, instead of announcing that she has a lover, she walks into the current lover's room and takes off her clothes, thus announcing her intention. She assumes that men are interested only in her body and her beauty, and so is astounded when an elderly friend who desires her refuses to take her to bed. He gives her two reasons: first, that she is upset by the idea of making love with him; second, when he learns that she has never yet felt pleasure, that he is old and ugly and would add to her disillusionment. This gesture of care and friendship is the first step in Minne's emotional development. The second comes when Antoine, after having her followed because he suspects that she is deceiving him, decides to give her the freedom she seems to need:

> Je voudrais que tu m'aimes assez pour me demander tout ce qui te ferait plaisir, mais *tout*, tu entends, même les choses qu'on ne demande pas d'ordinaire à un mari (p. 820)
>
> [I wish you'd love me enough to ask me for anything that would give you pleasure, *anything*, you understand, even things one doesn't normally ask from a husband (p. 208)]

She realizes that he does it for love. Suddenly she feels tenderness for Antoine and in recompense offers the only thing any man has ever wanted from her when he said he loved her: her body. But this time, instead of thinking of herself, she makes an effort to give pleasure to Antoine and for the first time in her life reaches orgasm.

> Enfin elle tourna vers lui des yeux inconnus et chantonne: "Ta Minne . . . ta Minne . . . à toi" tandis qu'il la sentait enfin défaillir, froissée contre lui, moirée de frissons. (p. 823)

> [At last she gazed up at him with a look he had never seen before and murmured "Your Minne . . . your Minne . . . all yours" While at last he felt her happy body surge against him in waves. (p. 211)]

Clearly the lesson is that a man who does not try to dominate a woman will be loved better, that a woman gives herself freely to a man who does not try to impose his will upon her in life or in love. The problem for the reader is that the woman is still the man's responsibility and possession. She may give her body to whomsoever she chooses, but she has no real freedom other than that which her husband may give. Minne, the fairy-tale queen, has found her prince and apparent love and happiness. As in the other fairy tales, she is seen only in terms of her beauty and men's desire for her. She exists only as a body whose sensuality must be aroused, for in that physical satisfaction lies her emotional identity. There is no change in the concept of women here, only an apparent emancipation, because for a woman "l'Aventure c'est l'Amour, et [qu']il n'y en a pas d'autre" (p. 743, "the great Adventure was Love and [that] there was no other," p. 106).

The one new thing that *L'Ingénue libertine* adds to the knowledge of women provided by women writers before the First World War is an appreciation of the care a lover takes to give pleasure in his lovemaking and a full, sensuous description of an orgasm, the achievement of which provides the structure of the second part of the novel.

Claudine found emotional satisfaction in her role as daughter, complete with an Electra complex lived out to the full. Minne finds full physical satisfaction as a wife. Neither of them is her own person. Renée Néré in *La Vagabonde* rejects all sexual satisfaction because it is not compatible with emancipation, and thus claims her full autonomy as a self-sufficient, though incomplete, individual, but she does it for the wrong reasons.

The structure of *La Vagabonde* is similar to that of the previous novels, but with an important modification. Again we find the four central figures of father, mother, and young couple. But this time the young female character is split into mind and body, both within Renée herself and between Renée and Fossette, her dog, which is presented as the total sex-object, receiving jewels, gifts, and caresses in exchange for devotion to a master.[7] Both male characters are divided also. There are two opposed husband-father figures—Taillandy and Hamond—and two young men vying for a place in Renée's life—Max and Brague. Or, according to interpretation, two possessive husband figures—Taillandy and Max—and two emancipating friends—Hamond and Brague. Margot, the mother figure, plays an unusual role: she is against marriage. Taillandy is Renée's ex-husband, whom she left because he was interested only in other women and in money. She spends long evenings with Hamond discussing their past misfortunes—his wife left him—and their distrust of love relationships. Margot, Renée's ex-sister-in-law, shares their negative attitude. Brague is Renée's professional partner; it is in his interest that she remain free of all emotional entanglements. And so it seems, for once, that a female character is surrounded by people who are not trying to push her into marriage.

Despite appearances, however (Brague aside), none of them is against love. Hamond actively encourages Renée to meet Maxime Dufferein-Chautel, who has been coming regularly to the theater to see her, in part because Max is an old friend of Hamond but really because Hamond is distressed by the thought that Renée might live without love.

Renée refuses her Prince Charming who comes to save her from hard work and modest circumstances, not because she has any idea of autonomy or ideal of feminism, but because she is afraid of being caught in the trap she was in during her previous marriage. Her first reaction is to refuse to see Max:

> C'est que . . . ce garçon est *un homme*. Malgré moi, je me souviens qu'il est un *homme*. Hamond, ce n'est pas un homme, c'est un ami. Et Brague, c'est un camarade.
>
> Le malheur est que je ne sais pas flirter. Manque d'aptitude, manque d'expérience, manque de légèreté, et surtout, oh! surtout! le souvenir de mon mari.
>
> Si j'évoque un instant Adolphe Taillandy dans l'exercice de ses fonctions, je veux dire travaillant, avec l'âpreté, l'entêtement chasseur qu'on lui

connaît, à séduire une femme ou une jeune fille, me voilà refroidie, contractée, toute hostile aux "choses de l'amour." (p. 1125)

[It is because . . . this fellow is a *man*. In spite of myself I cannot forget that he is a *man*. Hamond is not a man, he is a friend. And Brague is a comrade.

The trouble is that I do not know how to flirt. I have neither the disposition, nor the experience, nor the light touch necessary, and above all—oh above all—I have the memory of my husband.

If for a single instant I call to mind Adolphe Taillandy when he was on the job, by which I mean working, with the ruthless unswerving pursuit characteristic of him, to seduce a woman or a young girl, I immediately grow frigid, shrinking and utterly hostile to "the business of love." (pp. 81–82)]

Max Dufferein-Chautel seems very different from the portrait she draws of Taillandy, however. He seems simple, straightforward, and patient in love, letting Renée ensnare herself by her own weariness and the pleasure of taking physical comfort from someone affectionate. But the moment of comfort is followed swiftly by a warning for Renée, as Max calls her "mon enfant chérie" (my darling child) just as Taillandy used to do. She recoils at once this time, but as Max profits from every occasion to caress her, though carefully following her lead and rhythm, and as she is susceptible to the pleasures of voluptuousness, her barriers fall:

·Je remue imperceptiblement la tête, à cause des moustaches qui frôlent mes narines, avec un parfum de vanille et de tabac miellé. . . . Oh! . . . tout à coup . . . malgré moi . . . ma bouche s'est laissée ouvrir, s'est ouverte, aussi irrésistiblement qu'une prune mûre se fend au soleil. . . . De mes lèvres jusqu'à mes flancs, jusqu'à mes genoux, voici que renaît et se propage cette douleur exigeante, ce gonflement de blessure qui veut se rouvrir et s'épancher, la volupté oubliée. (pp. 1159)

[I move my head imperceptibly, because of his moustache which brushes against my nostrils with a scent of vanilla and honeyed tobacco. Oh! . . . suddenly my mouth, in spite of itself, lets itself be opened, opens of itself as irresistibly as a ripe plum splits in the sun. And once again there is born that exacting pain that spreads from my lips, all down my flanks as far as my knees, that swelling as of a wound that wants to open once more and overflow—the voluptuous pleasure that I had forgotten. (p. 126)]

She also slides into her old ways and behavior—those of Fossette, who was delighted to welcome *a man* into the house once again. We remember Marie Avenal betrayed by her sensuousness into becoming the passive

victim of a demanding master. The issue is the same: a woman's pleasure
overrules her will, according to both Colette and Delarue-Mardrus. A
woman is controlled by her physical responses. Here we see that Renée's
independence has gone, and she seems to fall in love. But love is not simple at thirty-three after a broken marriage, and some instinct or residual
memory prevents her from becoming Max's mistress in the full sense of
the word, even though their lovemaking is more and more important to
her:

> Pour mon plaisir et pour mon inquiétude, le hasard a mis, en ce grand
> garçon d'une beauté simple et symétrique, un amant subtil, créé pour la
> femme et si divinateur que sa caresse semble penser en même temps que
> mon désir. Il me fait songer,—j'en rougis—au mot d'une luxurieuse petite
> camarade de musichall, qui me vantait l'habileté d'un nouvel amant: "Ma
> chère, on ne ferait pas mieux soi-même! (p. 1163)

> [For my pleasure and to my disturbance chance has willed that in this tall
> young man, with his straightforward, symmetrical good looks, there is a
> subtle lover, born for women, and so skilled at divining that his caresses
> seem to know the thoughts behind my desire. He makes me think—and
> I blush for it—of the saying of the lascivious little music-hall comrade who
> boasted of the cleverness of a new lover: "My dear, one couldn't do better
> oneself!" (p. 131)]

The pleasure Max gives her may well lull her fears, but does not make
her forget her experience and her newly acquired independence. When
Hamond suggests that she should marry Max rather than be his mistress,
her refusal is categorical, and her description of marriage as constant servitude is devastating. Colette builds the novel on the complexity of
Renée's responses to Max and the increasingly visible attempts of Max
to control her life and her choices. Independent Renée becomes a subservient animal, fawning for Max's caresses, and then, recognizing her position, reacts and reclaims her body, her mind, and her future.

The novel moves back and forth between incompatible attitudes as
Renée understands her position. The security Max offers is tempting, but
given that he views marriage and motherhood as ways of trapping Renée,
how much independence can she expect in the future? She is increasingly
tormented by her awareness of her position: she loves Max; she is afraid
of being left alone; she enjoys her sensuality and recognizes the subordi-
nate role she has taken on once again: "Femelle j'étais, et femelle je me

retrouve, pour en souffir et pour en jouir" (p. 1184, "Female I was and, in pain and in pleasure, a female I find myself to be again," p. 158). She never seriously considers losing her economic independence, however, and is vexed when Max suggests that he might buy her out of her obligations to go on tour with Brague because he is not taking her work seriously.

When Renée exerts her independence, Max uses attempted rape to prevent her from leaving. It is adroitly done, but rape nevertheless, and a clear manifestation of the social code that a man may commit any violence or perfidy to obtain possession and control of the woman he desires, whatever her view of the matter may be. (Colette understands the situation well enough, but only in *La Vagabonde* does she choose to criticize social attitudes toward women in any way.)

Renée recognizes the power play for what it is, but while Max is with her, she can maintain a belief in the possibility of a happy life with him which nullifies her experience. It is when she is away from him and when she has survived the withdrawal symptoms of physical passion that she sees him ever more clearly. Max writes about their future, which he is arranging without consulting Renée at all, and she is more and more haunted by echoes of Taillandy's behavior. Each time a coincidence occurs she says she feels as though she has swallowed a shard of glass. Each time it seems more likely that the second marriage will be much like the first.

Taillandy was unfaithful; now Renée is older. How much more likely is it that Max—who is younger than she is to begin with—will turn to more beautiful women. She is afraid to risk her peace of mind a second time: afraid of growing old, being betrayed, afraid of suffering once more. That is the reaction of her mind. Meanwhile, her body is loath to give up its newly rediscovered pleasures. She must win the struggle and escape.

Colette depicts a Renée who is wary of Max, who, once she is away from his physical presence, can survive the withdrawal symptoms of passion and make a choice to avoid a second marriage which is coming to resemble the first. But it is clear that for Colette, Renée's major struggle is with her own sensuality. A woman's body reduces her to subservience, and it is not conceivable in Colette's world for a woman to be both autonomous and loving. Renée describes her struggle like this:

Comment y parvenir? tout est contre moi. Ce premier obstacle où je bute, c'est ce corps de femme allongée qui me barre la route—un voluptueux corps aux yeux fermés, volontairement aveugle, étiré, prêt à périr plutôt que de quitter le lieu de sa joie. . . . C'est moi cette femme-là, cette brute entêtée au plaisir. "Tu n'as pas de pire ennemie que toi-même!" Eh! je le sais, mon Dieu, je le sais! (pp. 1217–18)

[But how to achieve it? Everything is against me. The first obstacle I run into is the female body lying there, which bars my way, a voluptuous body with closed eyes, deliberately blind, stretched out and ready to perish rather than leave the place where its joy lies. That woman there, that creature bent on pleasure, is I myself. "You are your own worst enemy." Don't I know it, my word, don't I know it. (p. 203)]

Renée does indeed win. She breaks her engagement with Max and goes away alone, but she does not leave with any real satisfaction. She has no sense of emancipation or delight in her own independence. Rather, she sees herself as diminished. Hurt by her first experience of marriage, she is unwilling to undertake another adventure into the future with a man, for she sees any man as necessarily a tyrant. Her only experience of a relationship with a husband has been that of master and slave. Unwilling to be a slave to a man again, and afraid of being a slave to an increasing fear of aging as well, she decides, rather, to live as an old maid for whom no love is perfect enough and who therefore refuses to share her life with anyone. She has chosen freedom, tranquillity, and solitude.

For Colette, the choice seems to be between voluptuous slavery and chaste independence. She does not question the inequality between women and men, although she seems to be aware of it at times. For her, women are their bodies. Women take delight in sensuality, and enslavement to men is the price they pay for their pleasure. This is a different solution to the problem of male-female relations from that attempted by Marcelle Tinayre in *La Rebelle*, where Josanne Valentin wrestles with the question of public status, her independence, and her capacity to give herself in love. Tinayre does not solve the problem satisfactorily for the modern reader, who feels that Josanne relinquishes too much of her autonomy in the bedroom, but at least Josanne is allowed to be whole—to work, to marry, to have a child, to love passionately, and retain her capacity for reasoning and decision-making. In Colette's world a woman without a man does not suffer, nor does she experience joy or satisfaction. The socially imposed obligation that a woman must choose between pain plus pleasure and sexless serenity remains unchallenged.

Colette's gift to literature lies in the perspicacity and sensuousness of her descriptions of women in love with men. She does not question the circumstances which surround the lovemaking. To her, emancipation is the freedom to find sexual satisfaction. Women exist as specifically female beings through their senses only; their relation to the male of their species is the same as that of pet cat or dog to beloved owner. Colette seems to have no problem at all with the ratios she establishes. At one level Fossette is to Renée as Renée is to Max. When the relationship of devotion to protection is properly measured, security and satisfaction are had by both partners. At another level Fossette is to Max the sensuous animal Renée refuses to be. The opposition is the same as the one that exists between Annie and Claudine in *La Retraite sentimentale*, and the symbolism makes the situation even clearer. For Colette, a woman is an uneasy mixture of the nature of man and animal. She must choose the one with which she will identify in order to gain a presence and a sense of herself, if not exactly an identity. There is no concept of a harmony of mind and body in these novels; one must always dominate to such an extent that the other is excluded. In this Colette remains firmly in the Western androcentric tradition of woman as whore or virgin. Those who accept their sexuality are caught in the politics of power and domination. They allow themselves to be used in exchange for pleasure or security. The others are condemned to perpetual chastity, and in this they remain as much victims of society as do the others. Used or unused, they remain objects in a men's world. There is no concept of autonomous womanhood here.

Perversion and Social Criticism

Perversion tends to be born of the dark side of love and frequently finds its expression in morbid sensuality. By far the most interesting writer in this vein is Rachilde, though Anna de Noailles also uses morbid and negative emotion as a major theme. A brief look at Noailles' novels *La Nouvelle espérance* (1903), *Le Visage émerveillé* (1904), and *La Domination* (1905)[1] will serve as an introduction to the rather extraordinary works by Rachilde.[2]

La Nouvelle espérance and *La Domination* have similar subjects. In the first Sabine is depressed: her child has recently died and her husband, Henri, is frequently away on business. After two unsuccessful attempts at love she meets Philippe Fourbier, a philosopher, psychiatrist, and sculptor, to whom she is attracted and whom she subsequently seduces. Between Sabine and Philippe there is no warmth. Their love is passionate, wild, and black. When they separate, Philippe returns to his wife; Sabine goes to visit her cousin Jérôme and his wife, Marie, but Marie asks her to leave because her presence separates Marie from Jérôme and Jérôme keeps Marie from Sabine. Sabine returns to Paris alone; she becomes more and more depressed, and is to commit suicide (with morphine) at midnight. The book ends as she writes a letter to her closest (male) friend and a clock begins to strike midnight.

During the course of the novel Sabine is gradually transformed into the archetypal wicked temptress. As the book goes on, all the other characters move away from her, and there are fewer and fewer descriptions of her surroundings, even at the end, when she is wandering compulsively around her house. This novel closes in on Sabine as she closes in on herself. A woman with nothing else to do but think of herself and her passion, she turns into a siren figure and becomes progressively more destructive, first of others and then of herself. She is incapable of living simply and being happy.

Antoine Arnault, the hero of *La Domination*, is a parallel figure, an arrogant young man who destroys all love offered to him and who tries to make his mistresses kill themselves for love. Sabine's men get older and more famous (also more attached to their family and career). Antoine's women get younger and more aristocratic. In both cases the chain of lovers is somewhat a cliché. Sabine moves from her cousin to her husband's best friend and then to a famous psychologist. Antoine starts with a Parisian writer's "modest" daughter, then a Creole with "animal beauty," followed by a pale, fragile countess and her "vulgar" maid. His final love is the countess's half-sister, who is descended on one side of her family from Spanish royalty. She is the opposite of her sister in all things: dark-haired, of a somber and tormented disposition. She dies of love just a few days before Antoine dies also. Antoine Arnault collects his women from all over Europe; they swoon and fall. Unfortunately Antoine is a shallow and obnoxious young man rather than the brilliant, tormented, and somber person he is supposed to be in order to match his royal mistress, so the novel is less successful than *La Nouvelle espérance*. Sabine is rather shallow too, but Noailles's brand of sensuousness works better in describing a woman. The siren myth is effective, but Antoine is a feeble Don Juan, even though the decadent atmosphere of the novel as a whole is quite successful.

Le Visage émerveillé is the retelling of another standard perversion: that of the voluptuous nun. Sister Sainte-Sophie keeps a diary for one year, during which she makes the acquaintance of a young man who first comes to her window and then spends the night in her room quite regularly. Finally, he has to leave the district and begs her to go with him, but she refuses because an ex-nun is not well received in the world. She makes a distinction between love for an ordinary woman and love for a nun: a nun is desirable because each time she makes love she is aware of the evil of her action. A nun has a greater sense of sin, and so the voluptuousness of the conquest is greater. The ultimate proof of a man's pride and power is his ability to seduce the bride of Christ. What could illustrate more obviously the traditional fate attributed to a fallen woman than a nun's rejection of heaven in exchange for paradise on earth and hell hereafter?

In her writing, Sister Sainte-Sophie is shown to be self-indulgent, hypocritical, pampered, weak, and sensuous. (Noailles perhaps intended her to be of a loving and sensuous nature, but that is not how she appears today.) The main interest of the novel lies in the way she is able to change the direction of her sensuousness without any great problem. At first, she loves God through the comforts and pleasures of convent life, then she transfers her love to Julien, justifying and exalting her emotions in exactly the same terms as before. She remains in the convent because her life will be easier and more secure there than outside.

At one level the novel is a study of the various kinds of voluptuousness available to nuns—chaste voluptuousness. A nun who had been married is considered to be different from the others. Sister Colette and the Mother Superior both have a memory of being loved and cherish the images of the men in their past. Others draw acute pleasure from the flowers and creatures around the convent. Sister Catherine is a mystic who has stigmata and who writes prayers that are declarations of her passion. It is a curious piece that portrays love as a self-indulgence slightly tainted with perversion. Like Anna de Noailles's other novels, it lacks the energy to convince its readers of its plausibility.

Energy is certainly not lacking in Rachilde's novels, and plausibility is not a concern. She is usually situated among the Décadent writers and shares many of their characteristics. Her books are consciously perverse. Gabrielle Reval defines Rachilde's characters in this way:

> Cette humanité baroque et farouche se délecte dans la cruauté, s'enivre dans la perversion, goûte un plaisir démoniaque dans le triomphe des vices ou dans la défaite qui accroît sa volupté. (*La Chaîne des dames*, p. 157)[3]

> [These strange, wild human beings revel in cruelty, become intoxicated with perversion, take demonic pleasure in seeing the triumph of vices or defeat that increases their voluptuous delight.]

Reval sees Rachilde's writing as an act of protest against the state of humanity, as a scouring of souls, as deeply hidden fantasies take public, written form. This assessment may indeed be accurate at one level. At another level, these are novels that can be read as astringent criticisms of the socially accepted forms of love between men and women, of the roles allowed to women in their relationships with men. They are deliberately nightmarish parodies of male and female attitudes toward sexuality and marriage.

If we look first at the last novel Rachilde published before the 1914–18 war we find a quiet little book, almost pastoral in its structure and style. *Son Printemps*[4] is the story of a group of girls who are all "Children of Mary." The central figure is Miane; she is richer, more protected, and better educated than the village girls, and more isolated also, as she has been brought up by her grandmother. Miane is trying to understand love. She struggles to reconcile the idealistic notions she has been taught with the experiences of her friends. Her own concept of love is symbolized by a picture of Cupid; her emotion is expressed in the fantasy that she is in love with Paul, the sacristan's son, who looks like Cupid. First, she must come to terms with the physical reality of her grandmother's maid's pregnancy and miscarriage. Next, she faces the social reality that for economic reasons, her friend Joanille is married at fifteen to an alcoholic man of thirty. Finally, she struggles to understand how one might die for love. Her friend Marie is a "little saint," exalted in the hope that her death will save the life of her sick brother. All these girls suffer in the name of love; all but Miane accept their fate. Miane questions the priest, has a spiritual crisis, and worries more and more. Finally, when Paul leaves the village and her grandmother tears up the picture of Cupid, Miane drowns herself. She had said that if she could not understand love she would want to go and ask God for his explanation. We must assume that this is what she does.

Love certainly takes strange forms for the fifteen-year-olds of Miane's village. For one, it is the physical fact of pregnancy, and the accompanying shame and castigation. For another, it is marriage to a brute. For another, mystic devotion and unhealthy exaltation leading to death. Miane has more literary fantasies of love than do her companions, but she has no real understanding of reality and no one from whom she can obtain the knowledge she needs. She goes to her death in spiritual and intellectual frustration.

This innocent little novel is in fact a parable of the abuses society heaps on adolescent girls. All the proffered relations with men are unhealthy and unacceptable. The title, *Son Printemps*, is ironic, and criticism of society is implicit in the stories told. Most of Rachilde's novels are more violent and more bitter in tone than this one, but they all deal with some aspect of the theme of *Son Printemps*. All the main characters are searching for love.

The most outrageous comment on male-female relations is made in *Monsieur Vénus* (1889).[5] Raoule de Vénérande, a rich heiress, is struck by the beauty and grace of Jacques Silvert, her florist's brother. She sets him up in a luxurious studio, visits him frequently, marries him, provokes a duel in which he is killed, and creates a mortuary chamber in which there is a wax model of Jacques. The wax doll has body hair, teeth, and nails taken from the corpse, and an inner spring which moves the mouth when it is kissed. Raoule visits the chamber every night, sometimes dressed as a woman, sometimes as a man. She is living out the comment that she made to the Baron de Raittolbe early in her relationship with Jacques: "J'aimerai Jacques comme un finacé aime sans espoir une fiancée morte" (p. 90, "I shall love Jacques without any hope as a fiancé loves a dead fiancée").

At one level this is the story of a somewhat masculine woman who loves a weak man, who uses her wealth and power to feminize him and force him to play the role of her mistress. Jacques has an androgynous beauty: he is compared to paintings of both Venus and Cupid at various times in the novel. Raoule provides him with clothes of an ambiguous nature: flowing velvet robes and shirts with barely a suggestion of a collar. At first Jacques is upset by this, but gradually he becomes accustomed to the garments which harmonize with the silk and lace of his surroundings. Raoule forbids him to go out, then to smoke, to see other people, or let anyone but her touch him. When she discovers that the Baron de Raittolbe forced his way into the studio one night and saw Jacques sleeping naked, she beats Jacques. He becomes her possession, allowing her to use him as she wishes. In every possible way he becomes a kept woman, "un homme faible comme une jeune fille" (p. 56, "a man as weak as a girl").

At first Jacques is vexed and ashamed of his role, but by the end, when Raoule suggests to him that he should rehabilitate himself in order to marry her, he refuses:

—Parce que je vous aime, comme vous m'avez appris à vous aimez . . . que je veux être lâche, que je veux être vil et que la torture dont vous parlez c'est ma vie maintenant. Je retournerai dans une mansarde; si vous l'exigez, je redeviendrai pauvre, je travaillerai, mais comme vous voudrez de moi je serez encore votre esclave, celui que vous appelez: ma femme! (p. 125)

["Because I love you, as you have taught me to love you . . . because I want to be cowardly, I want to be vile and because the torture you speak of is now my life. I shall go back to an attic room; if you so demand, I shall become poor again, I shall work, but as you want me, I shall still be your slave, he whom you call "my wife"!]

When she reminds him of the delight of their first embrace, he cries and murmurs, "Ce n'est pas ma faute, à moi, si je ne m'en sens plus la force" (p. 125, "It is not my fault if I no longer have the strength"). His energy has been sapped, his identity destroyed; in effect he is as dead as the life-sized wax doll at the end of the novel.

That a woman should so destroy a man is an unthinkable perversion. That a man should do likewise to a woman is a frequent occurrence in literature. In reversing the roles, Rachilde makes clear how outrageous the relationship is. Raoule de Vénérande humiliates Jacques constantly; she keeps him prisoner; she chooses his clothes, his home; she refuses to allow him pleasures of his own; she shows him off to other men; she beats him; and finally, in the midst of great scandal, she marries him. And she can do all this because she is high in society, very rich, and very determined. He is poor and simple, and by the time he realizes that the marvelous comforts she offers have to be paid for in service, it is too late for him to escape. On a second level *Monsieur Vénus* is a criticism of the abuse of women that takes place in the name of love as a result of male passion for beauty and voluptuousness.

On yet another level, the novel presents a search for an alternative way of loving. Raoule tells Rattolbe that women find men unsatisfactory lovers because they give women no pleasure. She states, "Nous désirons l'impossible, tant vous nous aimez mal" (p. 86, "You love us so badly that we long for the impossible"). She goes on to explain that men are so occupied by their own pleasure that they forget to love their partners. She wants the emotion of love; because she is autonomous and independent, she expects love to be active, and so she describes herself as "amoureux d'un homme et non pas d'une femme" (p. 88, "in love with a man and not with a woman"). Again, she explains further:

On ne m'a pas aimée assez pour que j'aie pu désirer reproduire un être à l'image de l'époux ... et on ne m'a pas donné assez de jouissances pour que mon cerveau n'ait pas eu le loisir de chercher mieux. ... J'ai voulu l'*impossible*. ... Je le possède. ... C'est-à-dire non, je ne le posséderai jamais! (p. 89)

["I have not been loved enough for me to want to reproduce a being in a husband's image ... and I have not been given enough pleasure for my brain not to have had the time to find better ones. ... I wished for the impossible. ... I have it. ... That is to say, no, I shall never have it!"]

In the context of this search for the impossible, the reader's perspective on *Monsieur Vénus* changes yet again. Now Raoule's insistence that Jacques become a woman while she plays the role of a man takes on a different significance. Each is learning to understand the other by becoming that other in the love relationship. Jacques learns to be observed, admired, decorated, made love to. He learns to be gentle, submissive, and to await the pleasure of his master. Raoule meanwhile takes care of all the material concerns of the couple, goes out, is accosted by prostitutes, gives love, dominates her mistress. Then, when these reversed roles have been explored to the full, Raoule steps back into her place and invites Jacques to a ball, where he appears as a normal man. She announces her engagement to him, and he begins to learn all the skills of a gentleman.

When Raoule and Jacques first made love, Raoule fed Jacques hashish so that he would be haunted by the dreamlike splendors of the night without having any precise memory of having possessed her. From then on she makes love to him but receives no pleasure herself, she says. Clearly they do not have intercourse again. Subsequently, as we have seen, Jacques is too effeminate to be able to take on the man's role even when encouraged to do so. The impossible remains unattainable. It would seem that Jacques cannot take on female characteristics and remain a man, whereas Raoule can combine the nonphysical attributes of both sexes with impunity.

Rachilde poses two problems. Does a strong and active person always fall in love with someone weaker than him/her self? In which case, must we assume that any man loved by an autonomous woman will necessarily be emasculated by the active part she plays in their lovemaking? Is a man sensitive enough to understand a woman's position in the traditional relationships of men and women necessarily too weak to survive as a husband in society? If the situation is that which these questions suggest, Raoule and her like, "l'élite des femmes de notre époque" (p. 86, "the elite of the women of our time"), as she says, are going to remain unsatisfied. A standard marriage is not for them. Indeed, their choice is there in *Monsieur Vénus*: they can turn to virtue, like Raoule's aunt, or to vice, like Raoule herself. In terms of love, the future is bleak until the male need to dominate can be removed from sexual relations.

Men's preference for "dead" women is a theme that Rachilde reiterates in *La Tour d'amour* (1899).[6] In the novel she tells the story of two lighthouse keepers living off the coast of Brittany. The old keeper is silent and strange, almost an animal in the eyes of the newly appointed sailor. At first, the young man, Jean, takes his shore leaves. One evening, a young girl he expected to marry failed to meet him; the same night he killed a prostitute. Thereafter, he ceases to leave the lighthouse. Gradually, Jean realizes that the old man is a necrophiliac; he rescues corpses from the reef after shipwrecks. Thus he gets a new woman from time to time and attaches her hair to his cap so that it surrounds his wizened face. The young man is horrified by this and has hallucinations, but after the old man dies, Jean stays on as senior keeper and continues to tend the light.

The tower itself is a very phallic image, and the men tend it continuously. The sea itself is not an explicit symbol of woman, though clearly it is the living force that threatens the fragile structure, and Rachilde does describe mussels as women's eyes. By comparison, the men find that the corpses that float by and can be brought in from the reef are more desirable than the living women on shore with whom Jean had trouble. The old man keeps a woman's head in a bowl locked in a room halfway up the tower and has Jean destroy it just before he dies. The animal attitude of a man preying on a woman's body is chillingly portrayed. The tale is macabre; the comment upon woman as sex object is unmistakable.

Rachilde has shown the perversion inherent in certain kinds of sexual relationships. In *L'Heure sexuelle*,[7] she explores the distinction between pure and commercial love. Louis Rogès has two mistresses, with whom he behaves quite correctly. One night after he has been dreaming of Cléopâtre (of whom he has a little ivory statuette), he is accosted by a strange prostitute with compelling eyes and a curious bejeweled dress. He goes with her and develops a pure passion for her because she looks like his Cléopâtre. (Her name is Léonie, but he calls her Reine.) She thinks he is crazy because he is not interested in using her services, but she puts up with his visits. He sends her ivory-white roses when she is in the hospital with syphilis, takes her into the country for an outing, and finally persuades her to live in his house. Meanwhile, he gradually severs relations with Mathilde Saint-Clair and Julia Noisey (to whom he always sent pink and red roses, respectively), all for his ideal. Léonie does not care for Louis; he knows that she will leave him as soon as the man she loves has served his prison sentence for murder. The novel is carefully crafted: Mathilde and Julia are balanced against Léonie and Cléopâtre; three men friends against three women; Louis's mother, whom he detests, against the aunt he loved and ran away with as a youth.

The novel opens with Louis's dream about the Orient, and this is picked up later in a long story about Cléopâtre and a tiger. The tiger attacked Cléopâtre's elephant, killed some of her servants, and was itself hurt and taken captive. It became a favorite of Cléopâtre. One day Cléopâtre's brother repudiated his sister and sent her into exile instead of making her his queen. It was said that he had seen her lying naked with the tiger.

The tale is relevant to several relationships within the novel. When Cléopâtre is Léonie, the tiger is the dangerous man she loves, the murderer who killed one of her clients, the royal animal who is her equal. In this version Louis Rogès may be seen as Cléopâtre's brother, the man with position and power. If, however, we center the tale on the repudiation and exile, Cléopâtre could well be Louis's aunt, who was cut off by her sister (Louis's mother) because she had made love to Louis. Louis then becomes the tiger, but with the wrong Cléopâtre. This is a tale of passion and has full romantic decor.

The rest of the novel has somewhat the tone of an eighteenth-century novel—licentious rather than full of spleen and decadence in the Baudelairean mode. Louis Rogès writes scandalous love stories himself, and *L'Heure sexuelle* uses most of the standard clichés and thrills of literature of that kind: when Louis bursts in on what he expects to be a quarrel between Julia and Mathilde, for example, he finds them in bed together, and after a token amount of shouting and vituperation, he joins them; Léonie knifes Louis while they are out in the country; Louis reminisces over the way his aunt caressed him when he was a child.

These are not perversions. The perversion in this novel is the way in which all love is transacted finally as prostitution. Léonie is pure because she is a professional who sells her services openly. Julia and Mathilde prostitute themselves much more than Léonie does. Léonie keeps love and sex distinct. Her body can be bought, but her affection is not for sale. She will not let Louis kiss her—her lips are for the man she loves. All Julia's and Mathilde's moral values are set aside when sexual pleasure, which they call love, is available. They have no concept of real love, and so make no distinction between emotion and physical lust.

Among the older generation the confusion between love and prostitution is expressed in terms of money. Louis's mother comes to see him—a most unusual occurrence—to tell him that his aunt is dying. She wants Louis to visit the aunt (despite the fact that the family forbade him to do so after the scandal) in order to make sure that they get their share of her money. In essence, his mother wants to be paid for his services and her trouble; her attitude is that of a brothel owner. Louis is disgusted. He goes to visit his aunt, an action which gives them both pleasure, and unbeknownst to her burns the will. Their love remains pure, as does his relationship with his family. He had left the family and changed his name in order not to owe his services for their money.

Again, Rachilde writes a cynical criticism of society into an apparently scandalous and slightly exotic text. What society calls love is usually a commerce in bodies. Whether it be sexual love or family affection, the components of the "love" are the same. One person provides the money, and the other person provides the service. Only those people who deal openly can remain pure because they can distinguish between prostitution and real love. All such people (Léonie and Louis) are exiled from their rightful place in society, just as Cléopâtre was exiled for recognizing the power of the royal tiger. Here the distinction is not between men and women, but between the pure and the impure.

If love has become a prostitution of bodies, then inevitably marriage, which is the social expression of a certain sort of love, is going to be tainted by this same commerce. This is the rather surprising subject of hidden criticism in *La Jongleuse* (1900).[8]

The story of *La Jongleuse* is curious: Eliante Donalger, a Creole widow of thirty-five, ensnares a young medical student, Léon Reille. She keeps him in an unbalanced emotional state because sometimes she appears as an impeccably correct bourgeois widow, and sometimes as an extremely erotic, exotic snakelike creature, always dressed in stark black. (On one occasion, at a party for Missie's girlfriends and Léon, she appears in a leotard and juggles with knives.) Never does she allow Léon to touch her, and she continuously urges him to marry her niece, Missie, who is the absolute opposite of her: a large, gangling, modern young woman, dressed in white. Despite his refusal to consider the match, she announces the engagement publicly, and he is obliged to appear to go along with it, at least in public. One day Eliante sends Léon a note inviting him to spend the afternoon and evening at her house, then to return in secret at night. The day is spent with Eliante, Missie, and a friend. First, the young women dance for him; finally, Eliante performs a wild Spanish dance. Léon returns later and is led by Eliante into her bedroom in pitch darkness. The next morning he thinks he is dreaming because Eliante is approaching the bed with her knives, yet she is beside him. As she begins to juggle, the woman beside him wakes and gasps: it is Missie. As he realizes that it is not Eliante besides him, she lets a knife fall on her throat. The next year, Léon's wife, Missie, gives birth to a daughter.

The mother seduced the young man for her daughter. This is not the usual way of looking at the role of the mother of a daughter of marriageable age, but it is an accurate, if fantastic, description of the marriage market of the period.

The exoticism of the entire novel is build on clichés about women's behavior pushed to extremes. Eliante is the archetypal dark lady. This is the description of her which opens the novel:

> Cette femme laissait traîner sa robe derrière elle comme on peut laisser traîner sa vie quand on est reine. Elle quittait la salle flambante, emportant sa nuit, toute drapée d'une ombre épaisse, d'un mystère d'apparence impénétrable montant jusqu'au cou et lui serrant la gorge à l'étrangler. Elle faisait de menus pas, et la queue d'étoffe noire, ample, souple, s'étalant en éventail, roulait une vague autour d'elle, ondulait, formant les mêmes cercles moirés que l'on voit se former dans une eau profonde, le soir, après la chute d'un corps . . . ce qui sortait de son enveloppe funèbre semblait très artificiel: une face de poupée peinte, ornée d'un bonnet de cheveux lisses, brillants, à reflets d'acier, des cheveux se collant aux tempes, trop tordus, trop fins, si fins qu'ils imitaient la soierie, un lambeau de sa robe noire, cette gaine satinée presque métallique. (pp. 25–26)

> [This woman let her dress trail behind her the way life can be trailed behind one when one is a queen. She was leaving the blazing room, taking her darkness with her, wrapped as she was in a deep shadow, in an apparently impenetrable mystery that rose high on her neck, clasping her throat tightly enough to strangle her. She took small steps and the train of black material fanning out full and flowing, rolled in a wave around her, undu-

lated, forming the same shimmering circles that can be seen in deep water in the evening after a foreign body has fallen in . . . what emerged from this funereal envelope seemed very artificial: a painted doll's face, adorned with a cap of smooth gleaming hair, glinting like steel, the hair clinging to her temples, too twisted and too fine, so fine that it imitated silk, like shreds of her black dress, that satiny, almost metallic sheath.]

She pauses in the deserted antechamber watching for someone and is reflected in the mirror together with a marble nymph holding a torch:

Deux jumelles se tournant le dos, celle-là très nue, répandant du froid dans les transparences électriques, celle-ci merveilleusement habillée, moins réelle encore et ces muets fantômes éveillaient l'idée d'une prochaine catastrophe. (p. 26)

[Two twins back to back, the farther one very naked, spreading coldness into the bright electric light, the nearer one marvelously dressed but even less real, and these mute phantoms gave rise to the idea of impending catastrophe.]

A young man follows her down the stairs and steps on her gown:

Toute l'étoffe se roidissant en barre de fer et le costume correct, la gaine chaste, se détachait peu à peu de la femme, la livrant aux transparences électriques plus nue, malgré sa noirceur, que la statue de marbre. (p. 27)

[All the material stiffened like an iron bar and this correct costume, this chaste sheath, gradually detached itself from the woman, revealing her in the electric light, more naked than the marble statue, in spite of her blackness.]

A catastrophe has been predicted, and the colors of the novel have been set. There will be black women and white women, clothed and naked, yet it is the dark woman who, even clothed, will reveal most of all.

The primary juxtaposition is between Eliante and Missie. Eliante dresses in black; Missie, in white, childish clothes. Missie is young, modern, educated, and verbally shameless. She is direct, innocent, and unsophisticated in her dealings with men. Eliante is older, proclaims her old-fashioned attitudes, and is indirect, perverse, and subtle in her relations with Léon. The comparison of Missie to the other white figures in the novel seems preposterous at first. The others are naked and erotic; they are also menacing when joined with Eliante.

Eliante appears in various guises: in a black evening dress, over which she throws a brilliantly colored wrap when she goes outside; a black day

dress; deep mourning that makes her look at least forty; a black silk leotard that reveals her entire body; and finally, in a scandalous echo of her
first dress and shawl, a Spanish dancer's costume of red and yellow which
left her breasts bare. Under the skirt she again wore a black silk leotard:

> Mais le maillot laissait transparaître la chair, se moirait, eût-on dit, d'une
> espèce de sueur laiteuse, et on finissait par apercevoir, très distinctement,
> la chair blanche de tout le corps comme on apercevait les jambes nues sous
> ses bas. (p. 244)

> [But her flesh could be seen shining through the leotard, shimmering, one
> might say, with a kind of milky sweat, and finally there the white flesh
> of her whole body could be seen very clearly as her legs showed naked
> under her stockings.]

In this way, at the end of the novel the white woman and the black one
of the opening scene become one. And although Léon does not know it
yet, Eliante remains as cold as marble, so that he can only observe her
as an erotic figure and a love object as he has before.

The night of the opening scene, he returns home with Eliante, and she
shows him a human-sized alabaster vase that has an almost human
beauty:

> Le pied, très étroit, lisse comme une hampe de jacinthe, surgissait d'une
> base plate et ovale, se fuselait en montant, se renflait, atteignait, à mi-
> corps, les dimensions de deux belles jeunes cuisses hermétiquement
> jointes et s'effilait vers le col, avec là, dans le creux de la gorge, un bourrelet
> d'albâtre luisant comme un pli de chaire grasse, et plus haut, cela
> s'épanouissait, s'ouvrait en corolle de liseron blanc, pur, pâle, presque
> aromal, tant la matière blanche, unie, d'une transparence laiteuse, avait la
> sincérité de la vie. Ce col s'évasant en corolle faisait songer à une tête
> absente, une tête coupée ou portée sur d'autres épaules que celles de
> l'amphore. (p. 46)

> [Its very narrow foot, smooth as a hyacinth stalk, emerging from a flat, oval
> base, slender, swelling out as it rose to achieve, half-way, the dimensions
> of two beautiful young thighs joined fast together, and tapered towards the
> neck where, in the hollow of its throat, a roll of alabaster gleamed like a
> fleshy fold; higher still it blossomed forth, opening out like the corolla of
> a convolvulus, so white, pure, pale and almost perfumed that the uni-
> formly white, milkily transparent material seemed to possess the genuine-
> ness of life. That neck, widening into a corolla, suggested an absent head,

one that had been cut off or was borne on shoulders other than those of the amphora.]

Eliante explains her feelings toward all things beautiful, explains that for her voluptuousness, pleasure, is a state of being, that she does not need specifically sexual pleasure and is humiliated because men think only of taking her to bed. Then, her black body beside the white one in a reversal of the image in the mirror, she caresses the amphora until she reaches orgasm.

> Eliante, à présent dressée au-dessus du col de l'amphore blanche, se tendit comme un arc de la nuque aux talons. Elle ne s'offrait point à l'homme; elle se donnait au vase d'albâtre, le personnage insensible de la pièce. Sans un geste indécent, les bras chastement croisés sur cette forme svelte, ni fille ni garçon, elle crispa un peu ses doigts, demeurant silencieuse, puis l'homme vit ses paupières closes se disjoindre, ses lèvres s'entr'ouvrirent, et il lui sembla que les clartés d'étoiles tombaient du blanc de ses yeux, de l'émail de ses dents; un léger frisson courut le long de son corps—ce fut plutôt une risée plissant l'onde mystérieuse de sa robe de soie,—et elle eut un petit râle de joie imperceptible, le souffle même du spasme. (pp. 50–51)

> [Eliante, stretched now above the white amphora's neck, was arched like a bow from the nape of her neck to her heels. She was not offering herself to the man; she was giving herself to the alabaster vase, the one unfeeling figure in the room. Without any indecent gesture, with her arms inno-cently folded on that slender form, neither girl nor boy, she clenched her fingers a little, in silence, then the man saw her closed eyelids open, her lips part and it seemed to him that starlight fell from the whites of her eyes, the enamel of her teeth; a light shudder ran through her body—rather, it was a light breeze rippling the mysterious waves of her silk dress—and she gave, imperceptibly, a little gasp of joy, the very sigh of orgasm.]

Léon is shocked, furious, and frustrated. She tells him that he cannot add to her pleasure and forbids him to touch her. She has given him all she can *show* of love to a man.

Showing love is what she continues to do on those occasions when she receives him in her own rooms, instead of in the communal rooms of the house she lives in with her brother-in-law and niece. In public she always appears as the correct widow. The opposition of black and white recurs the next time he visits her. This time the black of Eliante's costume is juxtaposed with a number of figurines which were made in China for her

husband. As these are made of wax and ivory, they recall the juxtaposition of flesh and stone in the earlier scenes. The poses are similar, too:
one of them recalls the women back to back in the mirror, another that
of Eliante arched against the amphora. The erotic image is developed further:

> Le corps n'adhérait à ce que lui servait de lit de repos que par la nuque
> et les talons. Cette petite femme . . . ne cachait plus rien avec ses mains
> longues, franchement écartées, au contraire, et très indicatrices. Eliante fit
> tourner la statue et, de nouveau, Léon en retrouva une autre, n'adhérant
> à son lit de repos que par sa nuque et ses talons. . . .
> —Regardez maintenant entre les deux soeurs? dit Eliante. Le contour des
> deux formes vues dos à dos, ne se tenant que par la nuque et les talons,
> donnait un dessin d'une effroyable obscénité. (p. 118)

> [The body touched what served it as a resting place only at its nape and
> heels. That little woman . . . no longer hid anything with her long hands
> that were, on the contrary, openly spread apart and very revealing. Eliante
> turned the statue around and again Léon came upon another of them,
> touching her couch only with her neck and heels. . . .
> "Now look between the two sisters," Eliante said. The outline of the two
> shapes seen back to back, touching each other only at the neck and heels,
> created a terrifyingly obscene pattern.]

Eliante shows Léon a series of figures in ever more revealing positions,
and gradually he realizes that they all look like her. Again, Eliante is
showing herself making love. Again, Léon is the frustrated observer. He
is surfeited with exoticism and sees Eliante as a vampire, which indeed
she is, though she is sucking his blood for someone else. That night, as
Missie knocks on the door, Eliante kisses Léon:

> Trop d'exotisme!
> Eliante Donalger ne lui apparaissait plus qu'en beau fantôme, un vampire
> au ventre argenté glissant, ondulant. . . .
> Alors elle fut près de lui, l'entoura de ses bras souples, et penchant son
> visage sur le sien elle le baisa aux lèvres, et durant que Missie,
> impérieusement, frappait une seconde fois, il tint, serrée contre sa poitrine,
> cette femme toute pâmée d'amour. (p. 125)

> [Too much exoticism!
> Eliante Donalger no longer appeared to him as anything but a beautiful
> specter, a vampire with a silver belly, slithering undulating. . . .
> Then she was next to him, wrapping him in her supple arms, and lower-
> ing her face onto his, she kissed him on the lips; while Missie knocked

imperiously for a second time, he held close to his breast this woman all
swooning with love.]

The sequence of events is such that Léon never knows what will hap-
pen. He is fascinated by Eliante, in love, horrified, and gradually drawn
into her schemes. The next time the erotic Eliante appears she reveals
another aspect of her skill: juggling with knives (or, as Léon observes,
juggling with men). Again her black body is opposed to white ones, this
time those of the young women at Missie's party. The scene here, where
she lets a knife fall onto her chest in a mock death, and the mention of
the headless amphora both prepare the final scene, when all the symbols
come together.

At the beginning of the novel Eliante leaves a respectable ball; the man
who follows her becomes aware of her lithe, animal presence and exoticism as she drapes an Oriental shawl over her black garments and moves
off. He goes home with her, feeling that he is following his fate and excited because he expects to make love. The movement of the last scene
is identical. Missie and her friend dance stately dances for and with Léon;
then, at the end, Eliante appears in her Spanish costume and performs
her wild dance. All her savage, animal grace is revealed. Léon is waiting
impatiently for nightfall: Eliante has invited him to return. At the end
of the dance, however, Eliante says she will kill the dancer and destroys
her costume. Missie is dressed in a Turkish costume, which is a distant
reminder of the amphora, for Eliante bought it as if she were buying a
slave from "les intermédiaires habituels, j'allais dire: *les entremetteurs!*"
(p. 47, "the usual intermediaries, I was going to say: the procurers!"). That
night Léon gets into bed with a naked woman and makes love (the figurines) and when he wakes up Eliante is juggling at the foot of the bed. As
she dies, he realizes that his white woman is Missie and that Eliante was
the "entremetteuse" who sold him a headless woman in two senses.
While he was making love to the woman beside him in the dark, he was
not at all aware that her head was not the right one. He had kissed Missie
as Eliante had kissed the air above the amphora. Eliante herself no longer
has a head on her body. Eliante has sacrificed herself for Missie, and her
mission accomplished, she has withdrawn from the scene. Her niece is
married.

In tone and style this novel is reminiscent of *Monsieur Vénus* and is
even more successful in its fantastic romanticism and morbid sensuality.

Like *Monsieur Vénus* it is satisfactory on a number of levels. It can be read as a macabre tale or as a piece of elaborate social parody. It can also be interpreted as an experiment in alternative ways of loving. Eliante talks of a sort of pan-voluptuousness, elicited as a response to anything beautiful. For her, dancing and juggling are all part of love. But her love remains independent of sexual union because men then get jealous and possessive, as did her husband. She writes in a letter to Léon that she burns with the sacred fire that makes saints, martyrs, and great courtesans, and she has not met her equal. She looks on men as her children:

> J'ai cru un moment que *j'éléverais* un homme dans le sentiment de mon genre de beauté, qu'il me viendrait un enfant vraiment né de mon amour et *semblable à moi*. Que je pourrais perpétuer la folie du plaisir. (p. 168)
>
> [I believed for a while that I would *rear* a man with a feeling for my kind of beauty, that a child would come to me truly born of my love and *like me*. That I could perpetuate the madness of pleasure.]

Modern women are her worst enemy—they are born weary and reason too much—so that men cannot find all they desire in one woman, needing one for "a voluptuousness that has no conscience" and another for "passionless comradeship." Eliante herself is out of phase, she is overwhelming and frightening, she is all men's dreams, she is the "eternal feminine," both desirable and dangerous. She saw in Léon the right kind of desire, she says, but did not want to overpower him, so would not give herself to him. (A nice excuse.) In no way is it suggested that Eliante commits suicide because of any failure in her relationship with Léon. She sees herself as an all-mysterious goddess of a love beyond mere human comprehension, and is world-weary.

In some ways Eliante is the projection of Louis Rogès's dream of Cléopâtre in *L'Heure sexuelle*. She is the siren displaced by the modern woman. She is the great goddess reincarnate. Men dream of her, but marry the Missies of society. She is the ultimately desirable woman to men because she is unattainable. She is a source of both frustration and desire. By her very existence she is a criticism of Léon Reille's attitude toward women. He follows her into the street! From then on all the scenes that take place at night could well be creations of his desire and fear of her. He depicts her as cold, yet unnaturally and permanently aroused (the amphora), shamelessly seductive and immoral (the figurines). She is hard-hearted; how otherwise could she play with men as she does without their touching her heart (the juggling with knives)? In sum, she is an animal with strange, ungoverned passions (the dance). Yet she is a dream which ceases to exist when he wakes up beside his wife—a wife whom he does not love and whom he feels that he was tricked by her guardians into marrying. At this point *La Jongleuse* becomes a man's reaction to his mother-in-law, and we return yet again to social criticism of the question of marriage.

By way of the perversions of Rachilde's characters, we return to all the major issues raised by the lesbian writers at the beginning of this book. Once again, men are perceived as separate from love as women live it. Once again, the attitudes men have toward women are negative. Once again, women are perceived to be divided within themselves, either into lover and mother or lover and prostitute, and their desires are shown to be generally considered unnatural. Once again, the relations between men and women are revealed to be commercial transactions. Rachilde borrows the trappings of decadence, as Renée Vivien used those of art nouveau; and like Vivien, she appropriated the style for her own purposes, transforming its androcentric taste for perversion into a gynocentric criticism of society. And yet again, the measure against which her creations are judged is that of virtuous, nineteenth-century bourgeois morality.

Toward the Concept of
a New Woman

In contrast to the virgin, bourgeois wife, and harlot of the nineteenth century, the Belle Epoque has provided a new kind of woman. By 1900 the new woman, as she was called, was a phenomenon whose presence could not be denied. She makes an interesting literary heroine, although in life she was rarely appreciated because her modern attitudes were profoundly subversive of traditional society. For feminists and socialists, competent, independent, educated, and thoughtful women were seen as necessary to the better world to come, where there would be justice and equality for all; but even they recognized that such women, forced to live under the constraints of turn-of-the-century France, were transitional beings, constantly struggling for the right to fulfill their potential. "We are archaeopteryx," says one of Compain's characters, wryly and rightly.

The popular view propagated by the press was that new women were man-hating, man-imitating, cigarette-smoking shrews who were fighting for rights that no real woman either wanted or needed. Camille Pert claimed that these women were totally unnatural, refusing motherhood and prepared to go to dangerous extremes to exploit their belief in free love. To substantiate her claim, she even wrote a novel entitled *Les Florifères* (The Flowerbearers),[1] in which all the "modern" women undergo sterilizing operations to remove their ovaries[2] in order to take their pleasure where they wish without fear of a pregnancy which would spoil their social lives. The novel is totally superficial, and like all Pert's work, it both condemns and profits from the movement for the emancipation of women. Here, the idea that new women refuse their "natural" role is combined with the implication that women are victims of a repressive system such that they feel obligated to remain beautiful in order to satisfy male desire. To achieve that end they ruin their health with abortions and sterilization; if they fail they commit suicide.

Bad though this novel is, it does provide one of the first epitaphs for traditional marriage: as soon as there exists reliable contraception, certain sorts of abuse of women will come to an end. The novel also gives one of the first warnings of the dangers of male-dominated biotechnology.

Although Pert presents her characters as new women, she is actually describing the mores of social butterflies concerned only with fashion and transitory pleasures. The real new women are independent, critical, and provided with a social conscience: as they are presented within the novels of the period, so they were in reality, if we consider the lives of the authors themselves.

Whether one approves of them or not, it is obvious that at the turn of the century there was a growing number of active, thinking women who were demanding more room than before for themselves, their needs, and their values. Because they had the public ear and eye, the journalists and writers among them were the most visible members of the group. They were also some of the most openly criticized because, as one might expect, they were seen as a threat not only by traditional women[3] but also by their male colleagues, professional critics all, who were afraid that women writers in general were flooding the market and that feminist writers were upsetting their public. A lot of column inches were devoted to these authors and to the question of women's emancipation.

As the statements of social injustice made by the most important women writers could not be denied, these women were perceived to be dangerous. Whenever they could not be repressed, they were ridiculed.

> There is a New Woman, and what do you think?
> She lives upon nothing but Foolscap and Ink!
> But though Foolscap and Ink are the whole of her diet,
> This nagging New Woman can never be quiet![4]

This attack in *Punch* has the advantage of brevity; in Paris, Jules Bertaut spends nine pages of his book *Le Paris d'avant-guerre*[5] in a lampoon of women writers. He describes in great detail what he calls "la petite fonctionnaire des lettres" ("the little pen-pusher of literature") in order to affirm that whatever her aspirations, she always remains fundamentally and totally woman, adding snidely, "Personne, au reste, n'en avait douté et il avait suffi de lire dix lignes de sa prose pour s'en apercevoir" ("Besides, nobody had ever doubted it and ten lines of her prose were sufficient for it to be obvious"). Not only is it particularly galling to find this attack on his contemporaries coming from the pen of a historian and critic who made his career writing about famous women of previous centuries, but also, the terms of the attack itself make it quite clear that in 1900 women's interests are not considered to be the stuff of literature, and that women's style is ipso facto inferior.

Individual writers did get good press from certain critics, but it is interesting to note that when they did, the critic had usually managed to transform the work under review into a study of male concerns.[6] Given the paucity of material within any given novel that the critic could use to support such a misreading, it is small wonder that some authors were considered to be inferior and were set aside. Emile Faguet was one of the few who showed constant appreciation of good novels by women,[7] but even he rarely escaped androcentric readings and was frequently patronizing in his criticism.

At the time of publication, all the women in this volume were reviewed regularly, some in journals of general literary interest, other in magazines published for or by women, and many of them were widely read. Some of them were respected in the literary community, held office in literary societies, were decorated for their efforts, and had a considerable, if transitory, presence. Their fate has been that of most writers of best-sellers at any time.

The problem lies in the fact that a number of them deserved a measure of survival. It is true that their subject matter was topical, that their concerns were social and their writing realistic, but such attributes do not necessarily exclude an author from posterity, Balzac and Zola being good examples of the contrary. One of the major reasons why the women wrote the way they did is that women's experience was changing substantially in the Belle Epoque, and the authors were observing, recording, analyzing, and encouraging the shifts. They had little time for introspection and none for problems of writing for its own sake.

These are political novels, for the most part, and the writers were *engagées*; they were not providing novels of private life or romances of the kind disparaged as "women's books," despite the implications made by some of the reviewers. The style of the novels differs from what we are used to today, because these authors were addressing a wide audience with clear expectations of the way a novel should be set in context, and they chose not to violate certain of these expectations but, rather, to use them subtly for their own ends. We must remember that the novels had to appear bland and innocuous on cursory inspection, or most wives would not have been allowed to keep them in the house. This is literature of careful subversion. Some of the novels contain overt argument for reform; in most it remains covert—a literature of critical realism and apparent accommodation in which the surface message carried by the conclusion of the plot line runs counter to the tone throughout its development.

Gradually, from the variety of writings an image of the new woman emerges. She is, above all, a woman determined to escape from the constraints of home life, who looks askance at marriage because it represents another set of restrictions. Above all, she believes that education can provide the way for a woman to become psychologically and financially self-sufficient, freeing her to claim her place as man's equal in the home and in the workplace. She demands freedom of movement, freedom to dispose of her body and affections as she sees fit, and economic emancipation, too.

This new woman would be an entirely bourgeois concept[8] if it were not for the fact that middle-class socialist women tried hard to improve the lot of the working classes, both in education and working conditions. Among the novelists, Louise-Marie Compain was particularly known as an expert on women and work,[9] and Harlor for her efforts in the field of education.[10] Other notable women were fighting for the same ends. Although they are not novelists, I would like to draw attention to Nelly Roussel, Hélène Brion, and Madeleine Pelletier in particular, because some of their works are now available and are directly relevant to the context of this study, if not to its specific concerns. Nelly Roussel's lecture "L'Eternelle sacrifiée" ("She who is always sacrificed") is an uncompromising denunciation of inequality.[11] Hélène Brion's brochure "La Voie féministe" ("The Feminist Way") is a tract directed at male socialists and union workers in order to make them understand the needs and sufferings of women and work with the feminists for the betterment of society.[12]

Madeleine Pelletier wrote a treatise on education. "L'Education féministe des filles" ("A Feminist Education for Girls"), concerned with all aspects of an education which provides information, independence, and advancement in ways that are astute and sometimes seem remarkably modern; she also addressed the questions of sexual emancipation, the right to abortion, women's right to work, and other feminist issues.[13] These politicians and theorists pursued the same lines of thought as the concerned literary women of the period.

In the novels written around 1900 the characters presented as new women are educated already and tend therefore to belong to the bourgeoisie, while the younger characters are sometimes girls from poorer families who grow into independent women in the novels. This pattern occurs more frequently as teaching becomes recognized as a way for a girl with no dowry to earn a decent living. Still rare is the book that deals with working-class characters on their own terms, not observed or commented on by a new woman.

Whatever their age, station, and aims in life, the major problem to be faced by the women characters, be it at the theoretical or practical level, is always love. This is not, as is all too frequently assumed, because novels for women always talk about love and emotion, women knowing nothing else, but rather because in French culture, love is the central issue for women of all ages and stations in life.

Inevitably, "love" is defined in many different ways. All women refer to the feeling they have for their husbands as "love," whether it be desire, adoration, affection, respect, or fear.[14] In general, steady husbands are preferred by working women, generous ones by the bourgeoisie and adoring ones by the idle rich. In fact, marriage is the practice and love is the rhetoric for most women in most novels, though there is, of course, the occasional wild passion and the rare love match. We must remember that most girls of this period had few men to choose from, that an arranged "mariage d'inclination" was the norm, and that fortunate was the woman who found kindness and attentiveness in a husband who was to her taste. The dream of the perfect lover was universal, and many writers pandered to the taste for romance.[15] Camille Pert makes the situation all too clear: in her manual of advice to young women, entitled *Le Bonheur conjugal* (Marital Happiness),[16] she depicts marriage as an inevitable torment to be survived as best one can.

Normally it was assumed, for the comfort of most of society, that if a woman was with a man, she loved him, and that henceforth her love for him would become the dominant feature of her life, overruling all other concerns. Traditionally a woman's love was expected to be total devotion: a woman in love gave all she had to the man she loved, whom she delighted, cherished, nurtured, and obeyed.

How such an all-encompassing expectation of self-sacrifice could be reconciled with any sense of independent self-worth, however modest, was the primary problem that had to be faced by any author interested in emancipation. If no reconciliation was possible, the whole concept of love had to be redefined within the culture so that new relations among men, women, and children were made possible. In novel after novel we see the female characters struggling first to believe that they have the right to exist as people without denying their lives as daughters, lovers, wives, or mothers, and then to achieve that right without losing all sense of themselves as normal, loving, and lovable women.

As the feminists such as Brion, Harlor, Lacour, and Roussel pointed out in their political and theoretical writings, such a redefinition of the concept of woman, with the subsequent changes in the perception of women's position and roles in society, might not have been difficult if accomplished in conjunction with a concomitant shift in the definition of men. What was well-nigh impossible was a unilateral reform of the relations between men and women made by women only; that is, by a group that was undereducated, undervalued, underpaid, legally and practically powerless, and taught to think their slave mentality a virtue. Yet the attempt was valiantly made. Within the movement for reform it was the feminist novelists of the period who analyzed women's problems in the private sphere; charted the public advances; and encouraged, informed, and subverted their readers so that there was a gradual but visible adjustment of roles in French society before 1914.

The 1914–18 war changed the structure and priorities of French society, with the result that the egalitarian new societies postulated by socialists and feminists in the late nineteenth century have still not come into being.[17] Victor Hugo's proud and much-quoted statement that the eighteenth century had proclaimed the rights of man and the nineteenth century would proclaim the rights of women never did apply, and now, a hundred years after the death of Hugo, it is beginning to look as though the twentieth century will not manage much more than the rhetoric either. If we confine our comments to France, England, and North

America—the transatlantic community of 1900[18]—we find that women are still the poorest members of society; still earn low wages; still live the dichotomy of work and home; are still judged by social expectations based on the values and assumptions of the bourgeois nuclear family; and are still unprotected from violent, abusive, and alcoholic husbands. The conditions for unmarried mothers are better, fewer women stay in unhappy marriages, education for girls has improved, there are more professional women—though we have the same problem as Yver's doctors, teachers, and lawyers—and we do have a greater life expectancy. Nonetheless, such improvements are minimal when we consider the extent to which the industrial-technical world of 1990 differs from the industrial-commercial world of 1890 in everything except its androcentric values and behaviors.

In many ways the years between 1968 and 1990 are similar to those between 1895 and 1913. In both periods we see not only a mounting political pressure and an interest in women's affairs, with a concomitant proliferation of conferences on the status and rights of women, but also the publication of increasing numbers of women's journals of all kinds and the opening of more professions to women.[19] In both periods there develops a violent antifeminist backlash in which attention is focused on the traditional role of woman as wife and mother at home. As far as I can tell, there is very little difference between the demands of the Christian Feminists described by Léopold Lacour in *Humanisme intégral* [i.e., feminism] in 1897 and the movement of reactionary women (Phyllis Schlafly, et al.) in North America today. In their way, those women also are trying to change the circumstances of our lives, but they are working for more security in dependence—to take the risk of desertion out of marriage—while others want independence and autonomy. These poles of opposition have not shifted either in the past hundred years.

This book is about women concerned with women. Whether they be self-declared feminists or not, all the novelists discussed expose aspects of women's oppression. Most of them seem conscious of the implications of their material. Some lecture, some analyze, some prefer subversive description, and a few of them seem to have created critical structures unawares. Whatever their strategy, they have something important to say about human experience from a female perspective. They bear witness to the struggles and aspirations of their age, to the gradual emergence from the nineteenth-century bourgeois ideal of feminine submissiveness into a sense of female autonomy.

> Gynocriticism is a part of the praxis through which the voices of the silenced are becoming heard. Not only is gynocriticism naming and identifying what has never been named or even seen before, it is also providing a validating social witness that will enable women today and in the future to see, to express, to name their own truths. (p. 108)

So wrote Josephine Donovan in "Towards a Women's Poetics" (*Tulsa Studies in Women's Literature*, vol. 3, nos. 1–2, spring 1984), and what she says is very appropriate to this study of women novelists writing in France between the turn of the century and the First World War. Not only is this an attempt to name and bring back to public notice a number of women who were active and important in their day, but it also is a description of the various stages in the development of active, independent, modern woman: the new woman of the twentieth century. Unfortunately it is also a saddening witness that many of the fundamental issues have changed remarkably little for women in the Western world in the past century.

NOTES

I. Away from the Bourgeois Ideal

1. See for example Joan Kelly-Gadol, "The Social Relation of the Sexes: Methodological Implications of Women's History," *Signs*, vol. I, no. 4. summer 1976, pp. 809–24.

2. Article 213, "La Femme doit obéissance à son mari."

3. For example, the publication of *L'Athénée des dames* (Paris: F. Buisson, 1808). This was a women's newspaper which appeared in two editions only.

4. Deborah Pope, "The Development of Feminist Consciousness in Women's Writing in France in the First Half of the Nineteenth Century" (Ph.D. Thesis, University of Bristol, 1979).

5. For a detailed history of the social movements of the nineteenth century, I refer the reader to standard works such as Maïté Albistur and Daniel Armogathe, *Histoire du féminisme français* (Paris: Editions des femmes, 1977); Marie-Hélène Zylberger-Hocquart, *Femmes et féminisme dans le mouvement ouvrier français* (Paris: Ed. Sociales, 1981); Richard J. Evans, *The Feminists* (London and Sydney: Croom Helm, 1977); Claire Goldberg Moses, *French Feminism in the Nineteenth Century* (Albany: State University of New York Press, 1984); or perhaps Charles Turgeon, *Le Féminisme français* (Paris: Librairie de la Société du Recueil Général des Lois et des Arrêts, Ancienne maison L. Larose et Forcel, 1902).

6. Marguerite Thibert, *Le Féminisme dans le socialisme français de 1830 à 1950* (Paris: Marcel Giard, 1925).

7. Patrick Kay Bidelman, *Pariahs Stand Up! The Founding of the Liberal Feminist Movement in France 1858–1889* (Westport, Conn.: Greenwood Press, 1982).

8. Jean Rabaut, *Féministes à la Belle Epoque* (Paris: Editions France-Empire, Collection Si 1900 m'était conté . . . , 1985), and James McMillan, *Housewife or Harlot: The Place of Women in French Society 1870–1940* (Sussex: Harvester Press, 1981). Avril de Sainte-Croix, *Le Féminisme* (Paris: V. Giard et G. Brière, 1907).

9. Notably in 1900 the International Congress on the Condition and Rights of Women, involving Clémence Royer, Maria Desraimes, Maria Pognon, and Marguerite Durand.

10. Albistur and Armogathe list twenty-six titles published at some time between 1891 and 1914 (op. cit., vol. 2, pp. 547–48).

11. Béatrice Slama, "Femmes écrivains," in *Misérables et glorieuses: les femmes au 19e siècle*, ed. J. P. Aron (Paris: Fayard, 1978), pp. 213–43, states that there were 1,219 women members of the "Société des gens de lettres" and thirty-two members of the "Société des auteurs dramatiques" (p. 214).

12. Anne-Marie Thiesse, *Le Roman du quotidien: Lecteurs et lectures populaires à la Belle Epoque* (Paris: Le Chemin Vert, 1984).

13. Léopold Lacour, *L'Humanisme intégral* (Paris: Stock, 1897).

14. Nina Baym makes this point in relation to readers in the United States in "Novels, Readers and Reviewers: Responses to Fiction," in *Antebellum America* (Ithaca, N.Y., and London: Cornell University Press, 1985), p. 186.

15. Biographies are provided here only for those authors who are not discussed in the body of the book.

Gyp is the pseudonym of Gabrielle Marie Antoinette de Mirabeau, Comtesse de Martel de Janville (1849–1932). She married M. le Comte de Martel de Janville in 1869. In 1882 she began writing under the name A. Ouiche and illustrated books under the name Bob. An observer of frivolous Parisian society, she had a vast output and a vast following.

16. Gérard d'Houville is the pseudonym of Maria Hérédia, Mme Henri de Régnier (1876–1963). (Her maternal grandmother was Louise Gérard d'Houville.) She was a member of a literary clan; her father, José-Maria de Hérédia, was a famous Cuban-born poet. She wrote poetry and novels, and was drama critic of *Le Gaulois, Le Figaro, La République*, and *Le Temps*. She was awarded the Grand Prix de littérature in 1918, the Prix Osiris in 1935, the Prix de Poésie Fabien d'Artigues in 1937, and the Grand Prix de Poésie in 1958. In 1937 she was elected to the Académie Mallarmé (poets), the first woman ever to receive that honor.

Georges de Peyrebrune is the pseudonym of Mathilde-Georgina-Elisabeth de Peyrebrune, Mme Judicis de Mirandole, Mme Numa-Paul-Adrien Eimery (1848–1917). She first published poems when she was fifteen years old, then moved to Paris and published her first "best-seller," *Marco*, in serial form in the *Revue des deux mondes* in 1890 and 1891. (Calmann-Lévy republished it in book form in 1892). Her second novel was "crowned" by the French Academy. She was subsequently a member of a jury of the "Vie Heureuse" Prize (which became the Prix Fémina).

17. Jeanne Landre (1874–1936) worked as a schoolteacher and then as a journalist. She published in *La Fronde* and was a founder of the Ligue des Femmes de Professions Libérales. She served on the jury of the Prix Minerva. In 1925 she became a Chevalier of the Légion d'honneur and in 1935 vice president of the Société des Gens de Lettres, only the second woman to be elected to that post.

18. Daniel Lesueur was the pseudonym of Jeanne Loiseau, Mme Henri Lapauze (1860–1921), who wrote poetry, adventure stories, and serial stories for newspapers, and translated Byron. She was a member of the jury of the "Vie Heureuse" Prize (Prix Fémina). Her first book, *Fleur d'avril*, was "crowned" by the French Academy, and she was the first woman ever to be given the Légion d'honneur for literature (1910). She was also secretary of the Société des Gens de Lettres for a time.

19. Anne Martin-Fugier, *La Bourgeoise* (Paris: Grasset, 1983), and also *La Place des bonnes: La domesticité féminine à Paris en 1900* (Paris: Grasset, 1979).

20. Karen Offen, "Depopulation, Nationalism and Feminism in Fin-de-Siècle France," in *The American Historical Review*, vol. 89, no. 3 (June 1984), pp. 648–76.

21. Karen Offen, "The Second Sex and the Baccalauréat in Republican France, 1880–1924," in *French Historical Studies*, vol. xiii, no. 2 (Fall 1983), pp. 252–86.

22. Pierre de Coulevain, *Eve Victorieuse* (Paris: Calmann-Lévy, 1901). Pierre de Coulevain is the pseudonym of Mlle Augustine Favre de Coulevain

(1871–1913), who was born in Territet, Switzerland. She was better known abroad than in France, and her books were translated into English and Spanish. She was a member of the original (1904) Jury of the "Vie Heureuse" Prize (Prix Fémina).

23. Léopold Lacour, *L'Humanisme intégral* (Paris: Stock, 1897). Paul and Victor Margueritte, *Femmes nouvelles* (Paris: Plon, 1899).

24. Liane de Pougy, *Idylle saphique* (Paris: Stock, 1897). Jeanne Marni, *Pierre Tisserand* (Paris: Plon, 1899), *Souffrir* (Paris: Felix Juven, no date [1909]). Colette, *La Vagabonde* (Paris: Pierre Ollendorf, 1910).

25. Harlor, *Tu es femme* (Paris: Plon, no date [1913]). Harlor is the pseudonym of Jeanne Fernande Clothilde Désirée Perrot (1871–1970). She was the daughter of Amélie Sylvia Ragon (Mme Richard Hammer), a noted feminist propagandist and longtime president of l'Union fraternelle des femmes, and Eugène Dominique Perrot, and was educated at the Collège Sévigné. In her youth she was a noted pianist who played in concerts chez Pleyel. Her career was in journalism, and she first wrote as a critic in *La Fronde*, the feminist-socialist newspaper published by her friend Marguerite Durand. Ultimately she became the first librarian of Bibliothèque Marguerite Durand, the feminist library in Paris. She was a novelist, art historian, and political activist. In 1900 she acted as the recording secretary of the education section of the Conference on the Rights of Women, held in Paris, and she was the general secretary of the Republican League ("Droit et Liberté") and all her life lectured on feminism. In 1931 she received the Prix de l'Académie and the Prix George Sand.

26. Marcelle Tinayre, *La Rebelle* (Paris: Calmann-Lévy, 1905). Louise-Marie Compain, *L'Un vers l'autre* (Paris: Stock, 1903). Renée-Tony d'Ulmès, *Sibylle femme* (Paris: Ollendorf, 1904).

27. Camille Marbo, *Christine Rodis* (Paris: Stock, 1906). Danielle Lesueur, *La Nietzchéenne* (Paris: Lemerre, 1908). Valentine de Saint-Point, *Un Inceste* (Paris: Léon Vanier, 1907).

28. Rachilde, *La Jongleuse* (Paris: Mercure de France, 1900).

29. Colette Yver, *Les Cervelines* (Paris: Felix Juven, 1903), *Princesses de science* (Paris: Calmann-Lévy, 1907), *Les Dames du Palais* (Paris: Calmann-Lévy, 1909), *Dans le jardin du féminisme* (Paris: Calmann-Lévy, 1920).

II. Men and the Issues

1. Shari Benstock, *Women of the Left Bank* (London: Virago Press, 1987).

2. Liane de Pougy, *Idylle saphique* (Paris: Librairie Nilsson, 1901; republished Paris: Éditions Jean-Claude Lattès, 1979). All references are to the 1979 edition. Renée Vivien, *Une Femme m'apparut* (Paris: A. Lemerre, 1904). A new and different edition was published by Lemerre in 1905. All references are to the 1905 edition. Lucie Delarue-Mardrus, *L'Ange et les pervers* (Paris: J. Ferenczi et fils, 1930).

3. Liane de Pougy is the pseudonym of Anne-Marie Chassaigne (c. 1870–1950). In her youth she married a naval lieutenant named Pourpe. The marriage did not last long, and Liane de Pougy became one of the famous courtesans of the Belle Epoque. She was famous both for her beauty and for her necklace of 357 matched pearls. She occasionally appeared on stage at the Folies Bergères and once went to St. Petersburg as an "actress," but the tour was a fiasco. In 1910

she married Prince Georges-Grégoire Ghika and became respectable. After the death of her husband she became a lay sister in a convent in Lausanne, where she stayed until her death.

4. Lucie Delarue-Mardrus (1880–1945) was the sixth daughter of a Normandy laywer. In 1900 she married Dr. Mardrus, translator of *1001 Nights*, and left him in 1914. Primarily a poet, dramatist, and novelist, she also practiced painting, music, and Arabic. She was also one of the first jury members of the "Vie Heureuse" Prize (Prix Fémina). In 1936 she was the first recipient of the Renée Vivien Prize for poetry. She traveled quite extensively and lectured in Europe, Brazil, and the United States; however, she died poor and on her deathbed reconverted to Catholicism.

5. Renée Vivien is the pseudonym of Pauline Mary Tarn (1877–1909). A lesbian poet who was born on Long Island of a British father and an American mother, she lived in France most of her life. All her writing was done in French. As well as poetry, she wrote occasional pieces of prose. In 1935 Baronne Zuylen de Nyevelt née Rothschild founded a poetry prize named after her.

III. Love and the Choices I: Marcelle Tinayre

1. Marcelle Tinayre (1877–1948), born Marguerite-Suzanne-Marcelle Chasteau, married the painter and engraver Julien Tinayre two weeks after she passed the Baccalauréat. Her first two books, *Vive les vacances* (1885) and *L'Enfant gaulois* (1887), were written under the name of Ch. Marcel, after which she published under her own name. During her working life she was a journalist for *La Mode pratique, La Vie heureuse, Madame et Monsieur,* and *Le Temps.* She was on the list of recipients of the Légion d'honneur (Chevalier) 1908, but wrote a satirical piece on the award (too soon) and was removed from the list before it was signed by the minister. In 1938 she received the prix Barthou from the French Academy.

2. *La Rebelle* (Paris: Calmann-Lévy, 1905).

3. *Madeleine au miroir* (Paris: Calmann-Lévy, 1914).

4. *Avant l'amour* (Paris: Mercure de France, 1897; Calmann-Lévy, 1906).

5. *La Rançon* (Paris: Mercure de France, 1898; Calmann-Lévy, 1906).

6. *Hellé* (Paris: Mercure de France, 1899; Calmann-Lévy, 1909).

7. *La Maison du péché* (Paris: Calmann-Lévy, 1909).

8. *L'Ombre de l'amour* (Paris: Calmann-Lévy, 1910).

9. *Avant l'amour* was republished by Flammarion in a collection called Select-Collection (Paris, 1940). All page references are to this edition.

10. *Hellé* was republished in an undated joint edition between Calmann-Lévy and Nelson. Page references are to this edition.

11. All published in Paris by Calmann-Lévy.

12. André Gide, *L'Immoraliste* (Paris: Gallimard, 1902). The novel structure rests on two reciprocal journeys. The first one, from Paris to Algeria and back to Normandy, depicts Michel's illness, rebirth, and growth into love, responsibility, and a sense of the future. A period in Paris provides the pivot of the novel. The second journey duplicates the first except that Marceline, his wife, is ill, and she dies in Algeria. It is the depiction of Michel's refusal of responsibility and of his destructive attitude toward possessions and the future. The novel itself provides the final return to Paris.

13. My thanks to Angèle Segger for her clarification of this aspect of Josanne.

14. Marcel Proust, "Un amour de Swann," in *A la Recherche du temps perdu*, vol. I, *Du Côté de chez Swann* (Paris: Grasset, 1913).

IV. Maternity: The Pitfalls and the Pleasures

1. Lucie Delarue-Mardrus, *Le Roman de six petites filles* (Paris: E. Fasquelle, 1909), *Marie, fille-mère* (Paris: Fasquelle, 1906). Renée-Tony d'Ulmès, *Sibylle femme* (Paris: Ollendorf, 1904), *Sibylle mère* (Paris: Ollendorf, 1909). Valentine de Saint-Point, *Un Inceste* (Paris: Léon Vanier, 1907).

2. Renée-Tony d'Ulmès is the pseudonym of Renée and Berthe Rey. All I have been able to discover is that Renée was a friend of Jean Lorrain and that both sisters were at St. Jean-Cap-Ferrat one Sunday in 1901 at a reception given by M. Andre Pollonais, mayor of Villefranche. A passing reference suggests that both died shortly after the 1914–18 war. These novels were written by Renée alone.

3. Valentine de Saint-Point, *Trilogie de l'amour et de la mort:* (i) *Un Amour* (Paris: Leon Vanier, 1906); (ii) *Un Inceste* (Paris: Léon Vanier, 1907); (iii) *Une Mort* (Paris, *La Nouvelle Revue*, 15 December 1909–1 March 1910). It was published in one volume in 1911, but I can find no trace of a copy of this edition.

V. Daughterhood: Creation and Destruction

1. Marcelle Tinayre, *Hellé* (Paris: Mercure de France, 1899; Calmann-Lévy, 1909).

2. Marcelle Tinayre, *L'Ombre de l'amour* (Paris: Calmann-Lévy, 1910).

3. Gabrielle Reval, *La Bachelière* (Paris: Editions de "Mirasol," 1910). Reval (1870–1938) attended the Ecole de Sèvres (Agrégée, 1893), taught at the lycée for girls at Niort until 1899, when she married and became Mme Logerot. Her second husband was the poet Fernand Fleuret. She wrote for *L'Oeuvre* and *Le Journal*, and during the course of her career lectured all over Europe. She was made Chevalier de la Légion d'honneur, and was a member of the jury of "Vie Heureuse" Prize (Prix Fémina). In 1934, she was awarded the Prix du Président de la République and in 1935 the Portuguese order of Santiago de L'Epée.

4. Yvette Prost, *Catherine Aubier* (Paris: Armand Colin, 1912). As a writer Prost's name is linked to Harlor and to the feminist movement. (See chapter 1, note 25.) Most of her work was published in the 1930s and 1940s. *Catherine Aubier* was translated by Frank Alvah Dearborn as *The Saving Pride* and published in New York by Dodd Mead and Co. in 1912. Her dates are 1886–1949.

5. Simone Bodève, *La Petite Lotte* (Paris: Bonvalot-Jouve, 1908). Simone Bodève is the pseudonym of Mlle Jeanne Chrétien (1876–1921). Born into a working-class family, she received primary education only, but taught herself English and German, then science, which one of her brothers was learning. All her adult life she was a shorthand typist for an electrical company (Paz and Silva).

6. Bodève died in 1921 as the result of falling out of a fifth-floor window. It was reported as suicide. This was contested in an article in *La Voie des femmes*, 28 April 1921.

7. Louise-Marie Compain, *La Vie tragique de Geneviève* (Paris: Calmann-Lévy, 1912).

VI. Profession: Struggles and Solitude

1. Colette Yver is the pseudonym of Antoinette de Bergevin, Mme Auguste Huzard (1874–1953). Her parents were of Breton origin, but her father was from Martinique and her mother from Guadeloupe. Yver tells us she took her name from a shop in Yvetot. It is said that when she was six, she dictated her first novel to her thirteen-year-old brother. At seventeen, she published a successful book for children entitled *Mlle Devoir* and several more between 1891 and 1900. Her first adult novel, *Les Cervelines*, was read by Auguste Huzard at the publishing house of Juven; he claimed to have married her because of it. Widowed at thirty-seven, she worked for the church, then for the sick, especially to raise money for Praz-Coutant sanitorium (Savoie). She was awarded the "Vie Heureuse" Prize (Prix Fémina) in 1907 for *Princesses de sciences* and subsequently became a member of the Fémina Jury. In later life she wrote on religious subjects.

2. Gabrielle Reval, *Lycéennes* (Paris: Ollendorf, 1902), *Les Sévriennes* (Paris: Ollendorf, 1900), *Un Lycée de jeunes filles* (Paris: Ollendorf, 1901).

3. Karen Offen, "The Second Sex and the Baccalauréat in Republican France 1880–1924," in *French Historical Studies*, vol. XIII, no. 2 (fall 1983), pp. 252–86.

4. Colette Yver, *Les Cervelines* (Paris: Felix Juven, 1903), *Princesses de Science* (Paris: Calmann-Lévy, 1907), *Les Dames du Palais* (Paris: Calmann-Lévy, 1909).

5. It is convenient that Jean should be able to put the responsibility on his mother and on Marceline herself. Here is his letter:

> "Chère Marceline, vous avez formulé vous-même ce que je n'aurais jamais eu la force de vous dire. Ce que vous pensez, en effet, ma mère l'a souhaité; elle vous le demande. Je ne vous l'aurais jamais demandé. Je vous voyais, en vous donnant à moi, me donner votre liberté de travail, votre temps, vos conceptions d'avenir, mais non pas ce qui fait de votre oeuvre comme une mission, ce qu'on aime enfin pour l'avoir choisi, embelli, pour ce qu'on lui a donné et pour ce qu'il a rendu: le métier. Eteindre, Marceline, ce flambeau lumineux de votre enseignement, taire ces conférences où se complaisent tant d'intelligences fines sur qui vous entretenez une adorable autorité, renoncer à ces apothéoses délicates que vous offrent les esprits, à ces triomphes qu'on vous a faits parfois, où je vous ai connue un soir, mon amie, c'est, il me semble, commettre en même temps une grande injustice et un grand sacrilège; est-ce assez que votre bonté d'un côté, et de l'autre l'immense tendresse que je vous porte pour les motiver?" (pp. 276–77)

["Dear Marceline, you have put into words what I would never have had the strength to tell you. What you are thinking is indeed what my mother wished; she is requesting it of you. I would never have asked you for this. In giving yourself to me, I saw you giving me your freedom to work, your time, your concept of the future, but not what makes your work a vocation, that which, in the end, one loves because one has chosen and embellished it, because of what one has given to it and because of what it has given back: one's profession. To put out that glowing flame of your teaching, Marceline, to silence those lectures that are so pleasurable to so many fine intellects over which you hold worshipful sway, to give up those subtle apotheoses that you offer to people's minds, those triumphant moments you have sometimes been offered, as on the evening when I met you, it seems to me that this would be committing both a great injustice and a sacrilege against you; is your goodness, on the one hand, and the enormous tenderness I feel for you on the other, enough to motivate this?"]

6. Anne Martin-Fugier, *La Bourgeoise* (Paris: Grasset, 1983), *La Place des bonnes* (Paris: Grasset, 1979).

VII. Marriage: Traditional and Ideal

1. Camille Pert, *Le Bonheur conjugal* (Paris: Librarie Universelle, 1905). Camille Pert is the pseudonym of Louise Hortense Grille, Mme H. Rougeul (1865–1952). She wrote vast numbers of slightly improper novels that are definitely not feminist.

2. Myriam Harry, *Petites épouses* (Paris: Calmann-Lévy, 1901). Harry (1875–1958) was born in Jerusalem. Her father was a Russian-Jewish archaeologist who converted to Anglicanism; her mother, a German doctor. She married Emile Perrault-Harry. Multilingual and much traveled, especially in the Middle East, she became a journalist and novelist. She wrote novels with a distinctive and exotic flavor. She was awarded the "Vie Heureuse" Prize (Prix Fémina) in 1904 and Légion d'honneur (Chevalier), but was refused the Prix Goncourt for *La Conquête de Jérusalem* because "the author is a woman and we really cannot create such an annoying precedent" (J. K. Huysmans, quoted in *La Fronde*, 1 February 1905).

3. Renée-Tony d'Ulmès is a pseudonym for two sisters, Renée and Berthe Rey. Renée alone is responsible for *Sibylle femme* and *Sibylle mère*.

4. Jeanne Marni, *Pierre Tisserand* (Paris: Ollendorf, 1907), *Souffrir* (Paris: Félix Juven, 1909). Jeanne Marni is the pseudonym of Jeanne-Marie-Françoise Barousse, Mme Marnière (1854–1910). Daughter of a distinguished "femme de lettres," she published her first story in *Le Monde illustré* when she was eight years old. She trained for the stage and was an actress for a short time, and began publishing only after 1885, when she was widowed. She wrote stories in *Le National*, then novels and plays. Under the names "Lucienne" and "E. Voilà" she wrote in *La Vie parisienne*, using "J. Marni" only after 1896. Her essays and articles were collected and republished in volumes. She was a member of the original jury of the "Vie Heureuse" Prize (Prix Fémina).

5. Jeanne Marni, *L'Une et l'autre* (Paris: Pierre Lafitte, 1908).

6. Claude Lemaître, *Ma Soeur Zabette* (Paris: Ollendorf, 1902). Claude Lemaître is the pseudonym of Elise-Marie Chignot, who was born in 1873 in Saintes (Charente-Maritime). She is generally considered to be a good provincial writer.

7. Camille Marbo, *Celle qui défiait l'amour* (Paris: Fayard, 1911), republished under the title *Hélène Barraux* (Fayard, 1926). Camille Marbo is the pseudonym of Marguerite Appell, Mme Emile Borel (1883–1969). Her father was rector of the University of Paris; her husband, an ex-minister for the navy and member of the institute who founded the *Revue des mois* in which Marbo collaborated. They also organized La Maison des Etudiants and a hospital. She was awarded the Prix Fémina in 1913 for *La Statue voilée*, became a Chevalier de la Légion d'honneur

in 1926, and was the first woman President of the Société des Gens de Lettres in 1937, reelected in 1946.

8. Marcelle Tinayre, *La Rançon* (Paris: Mercure de France, 1898).

9. Louise-Marie Compain, *L'Un vers l'autre* (Paris: Stock, 1903). Compain (I have been unable to find dates) was an active socialist and a recognized expert on women's work and labor law. She lectured on economics and the conditions of working-class women. In 1911 she was a delegate to the Congress of International Alliance for Female Suffrage in Stockholm and in 1913 to the 10th International Congress of Women: Feminine Works and Institutions and Women's Rights, Paris 1913. She was also founder and secretary general of the "Foyers des campagnes" movement, which set up centers for meetings and activities in villages.

10. Louise-Marie Compain, *L'Opprobre* (Paris: Stock, 1905).

VIII. Love and the Choices II: Colette

1. Gabrielle Sidonie Colette (1873–1954). Married Henry Gauthier-Villars (Willy), 1894; Henri de Jouvenal, 1912; Maurice Goudeket, 1935. She wrote her early books in collaboration with Willy and after their divorce worked for a while in music halls, also as the literary director of *Le Matin*. She was awarded the Légion d'honneur (Chevalier) for literature. She is so well known that it is only in the interest of consistency that I give information here.

2. Colette, *La Retraite sentimentale* (Paris: Mercure de France, 1907), *L'Ingénue libertine* (Paris: Ollendorf, 1909), *La Vagabonde* (Paris: Ollendorf, 1910).

3. Colette, *Oeuvres*, principal ed. Claude Pichois (Paris: Pléiade, 1984). All references in French are to this edition.

4. *The Vagabond*, trans. Enid McLeod, in *7 by Colette* (New York: Farrar, Straus and Cudahy Inc., 1955). All translations are from this edition.

5. *Retreat from Love*, trans. Margaret Crosland (London: Peter Owen, 1974). All translations are from this edition.

6. *The Innocent Libertine*, trans. Antonia White (London: Secker and Warburg, 1968). All quotations are from this translation.

7. I am indebted to Mair Verthuy (Concordia University) for this observation.

IX. Perversion and Social Criticism

1. Anna de Noailles, *La Nouvelle espérance* (Paris: Calmann-Lévy, 1903), *Le Visage émerveillé* (Paris: Calmann-Lévy, 1904), *La Domination* (Paris: Calmann-Lévy, 1905). Anna, la Comtesse Mathieu de Noailles (1876–1933), was born Princess Anna-Elizabeth de Brancovan, of a Rumanian father and a mother sometimes said to be Cretan, sometimes Turkish. She received the Légion d'honneur for literature and was the first woman awarded the rank of Commandeur. Best known for her poetry, she received the Grand Prix de Littérature from the French Academy in 1921 and in 1922 was invited to become a member of the Belgian Royal Academy of Language and Literature.

2. Rachilde is the pseudonym of Marguerite Eymery, Mme Alfred Vallette (1862–1953). She started writing at age fifteen and wrote for the theater under the pseudonym of Jean de Chilta. For most of her life she was the literary critic

of the *Mercure de France*, which she founded with Alfred Vallette. She is usually included in the Décadent group of writers (1880–90).

3. Gabrielle Reval, *La Chaîne des dames* (Paris: Crès, 1925).

4. Rachilde, *Son Printemps* (Paris: Mercure de France, 1912).

5. Rachilde, *Monsieur Vénus* (Paris: Brossier, 1889; republished, Flammarion, 1977). All references are to the 1977 edition.

6. Rachilde, *La Tour d'amour* (Paris: Mercure de France, 1899; Crès, 1914; facsimile Crès published Paris, Le Tout sur le Tout, 1980).

7. Rachilde, *L'Heure sexuelle* (Paris: Mercure de France, 1898).

8. Rachilde, *La Jongleuse* (Paris: Mercure de France, 1900; republished Paris, aux éditions des femmes, 1982). All references are to the 1982 edition.

X. Toward the Concept of a New Woman

1. Camille Pert, *Les Florifères* (Paris: Simon Empis, 1898).

2. Léopold Lacour, *L'Humanisme intégral* (Paris: Stock, 1897).

3. Anne-Marie Thiesse, *Le Roman du quotidien* (Paris: Le Chemin Vert, 1984). Among the interviews with readers reading before 1914 is one with an agricultural laborer's daughter, born in 1899, who worked in a factory from the age of thirteen: "I also read a novel by Marcelle Tinayre, *La Rebelle*, in which she recounted her own life. This book has created a scandal and I was criticised a lot by my workmates for reading it. The novel was about the emancipation of women and I liked it very much" (p. 66).

4. First published in *Punch*, 26 May 1894, p. 252, this quatrain was republished in Ellen Jordan, "The Christening of the New Woman: May 1894," in *The Victorian Newsletter* 63 (spring 1983), pp. 19–21. I am grateful to Maureen Scobie for drawing it to my attention.

5. Jules Bertaut, *Le Paris d'avant-guerre* (Paris: Renaissance du livre, 1919), pp. 176–84.

6. For example, Paul Flat, *Nos Femmes de lettres* (Paris: Perrin, 1909).

7. For example, Emile Faguet, "Femmes auteurs," in *La Revue* (Ancienne Revue des Revues) XIVe an., vol. LXV, no. 13, 1 July 1903, pp. 19–24.

8. Françoise Picq, "Le Féminisme bourgeois: une théorie élaborée par les femmes socialistes avant la guerre de 14," in *Stratégies des femmes* (Paris: Tierce, 1984), pp. 391–406.

9. Louise-Marie Compain, "Les Conséquences du travail de la femme," in *La Grande revue*, 17e an., no. 10, 25 May 1913, pp. 364–76 (numbers at the foot of the page give 308–20. The title page lists p. 364).

10. Harlor, "L'Education de la volonté chez la femme," in *La Revue socialiste* 31, no. 184, April 1900, pp. 450–59.

11. Nelly Roussel, *L'Eternelle sacrifiée*, préface, notes, et commentaires: Daniel Armogathe et Maïté Albistur (Paris: Syros, 1979).

12. Hélène Brion, *La Voie féministe*, préface, notes, et commentaires: Huguette Bouchardeau (Paris: Syros, 1978).

13. Madeleine Pelletier, *L'Education féministe des filles et autres textes*, préface et notes Claude Maignien (Paris: Syros, 1978).

14. See Simone Bodève, *Son Mari* (Paris), for examples of women's attitudes.

15. Among the better writers in this vein were Miriam Harry, Gérard

d'Houville, Jeanne Landre, Daniel Lesueur, Camille Pert, and Georges de Peyrebrune.

16. Camille Pert, *Le Bonheur conjugal* (Paris: Librairie Universelle, 1905).

17. See, for example, Léopold Lacour, *L'Humanisme intégral* (Paris: Stock, 1897), and Jules Bois, *L'Eve nouvelle* (Paris: Léon Chailley, 1896).

18. For comparative documents, see Erna Olafson Hellerstein, Leslie Parker Hume, and Karen M. Offen, eds., *Victorian Women, a Documentary Account of Women's Lives in Nineteenth Century England, France and the United States* (Stanford: Stanford University Press, 1981).

19. Maité Albistur and Daniel Armogathe, *Histoire du féminisme français*, vol. 2 (Paris: Editions des femmes, 1977). For further bibliography, see Karen Offen, "First Wave Feminism in France: Network and Resources," in *Women's Studies International Forum*, vol. 5, 1982, pp. 685–689, and Jean Rabaut, *Féministes à la "Belle Epoque"* (Paris: Editions France-Empire, 1985).

SELECT BIBLIOGRAPHY

1. Primary sources: Prose writings c. 1898–1914

All references cited below are published in Paris unless otherwise indicated.

Bodève, Simone
  Clo, Bonvalot-Jouve, 1908
  La Petite Lotte, Bonvalot-Jouve, 1908
  Mon Mari, Bonvalot-Jouve, 1911
  Celles qui travaillent, Ollendorf, 1913
Colette, Gabrielle Sidonie
  Claudine à l'école, Ollendorf, 1900, with Willy
  Claudine à Paris, Ollendorf, 1901, with Willy
  Claudine s'en va, Ollendorf, 1903, with Willy
  Dialogue des bêtes, Mercure de France, 1905
  Sept dialogues des bêtes, Mercure de France, 1905
  La retraite sentimentale, Mercure de France, 1907
  Les Vrilles de la vigne, Vie Paris, 1908
  L'Ingénue libertine, Ollendorf, 1909
  La Vagabonde, Ollendorf, 1910
  L'Entrave, Librairie des Lettres, 1913
  L'Envers du Music-Hall, Flammarion, 1913
  Prou, Poucette et quelques autres, Flammarion, 1913
Compain, Louise-Marie
  L'Un vers l'autre, Stock, 1903
  L'Opprobre, Stock, 1905
  "En Feuilletant les catalogues," 1910 (*Brochure Bibliothèque Marguerite Durand*)
  "Les Femmes dans les organisations ouvrières," 1910 (*Brochure Bibliothèque Marguerite Durand*)
  La Vie tragique de Geneviève, Calmann-Lévy, 1912
  L'Amour de Claire, Calmann-Lévy, 1912
  "Les Conséquences du travail de la femme," *La Grande Revue*, May 1913
  "L'Initiation sociale de la femme," *La Grande Revue*, 1913
Coulevain, Pierre de
  Noblesse américaine, Ollendorf, 1896
  Eve victorieuse, Calmann-Lévy, 1901
  Sur la branche, Calmann-Lévy, 1904
  L'Ile inconnue, Calmann-Lévy, 1906
  Le Roman merveilleux, Calmann-Lévy, 1914
Delarue-Mardrus, Lucie
  Marie, fille-mère, Fasquelle, 1906
  Le Roman de six petites filles, Fasquelle, 1909
  L'Acharnée, Fasquelle, 1910

Comme tout le monde, Tallendier, 1910
Toute l'amour, Fasquelle, 1911
L'Inexpérimentée, Fasquelle, 1913
La Monnaie de singe, Fasquelle, 1913
Douce moitié, Fasquelle, 1913
Gyp
Sportomanomanie, Calmann-Lévy, 1898
Les Cayennes de Rio, Flammarion, 1899
L'Entrevue, Per Lamm, 1899
Les Femmes du Colonel, Flammarion, 1899
Les Izolâtres, Juven, 1899
M. de Folleuil, Calmann-Lévy, 1899
Balancez vos dames, Per Lamm, 1900
Martinette, Per Lamm, 1900
Journal d'une qui s'en fiche, Juven, 1900
La paix des champs, Juven, 1900
Trop de chic, Calmann-Lévy, 1900
(and 41 more titles before 1914)
Harlor
"L'Education de la volonté de la femme," *Revue Socialiste*, April 1900
Le Triomphe des vaincus, Bibliothèque des Réformes Sociales, 1908
Tu es femme, Plon, 1913
Harry, Miriam
Passage des Bédouins, Calmann-Lévy, 1899
Petites épouses, Calmann-Lévy, 1902
La Conquête de Jérusalem, Calmann-Lévy, 1903
L'Ile de volupté, Fayard, 1908
Mme Petit-Jardin, Fayard, 1909
Tunis la blanche, Fayard, 1910
La Divine chanson, Fayard, 1912
La Petite fille de Jérusalem, Fayard, 1914
Houville, Gérard d'
L'Inconstante, Fayard, 1903
L'Esclave, Calmann-Lévy, 1905
Le Temps d'aimer, Calmann-Lévy, 1908
Le Séducteur, Fayard, 1914
Landre, Jeanne
Cri-cri, roman passionnel, Offenstadt, 1900
Les Pierres du chemin, Offenstadt, 1900
Enfin seules!, Juven, 1902
L'Eternel masculin, Offenstadt, 1902
La Gargouille, Louis Michaud, 1908
Plaisirs d'amour, Michaud, 1908
Echalote et ses amants, Michaud, 1909
Contes de Montmartre . . . et d'ailleurs, Michaud, 1910
Echalote continue, Michaud, 1910
Camelots du roi, Michaud, 1911
Le Doigt dans l'oeil, Michaud, 1913

Lemaître, Mme Claude
  Ma soeur Zabette, Ollendorf, 1902
  L'Aubaine, Ollendorf, 1903
  Le Cant, Ollendorf, 1904
  Cadet Oui-oui, Flammarion, 1906
  Les Fantoches, Flammarion, 1907
  Marsile Gerbault, Flammarion, 1907
  Les Chimères, Flammarion, 1909
  Les Maris de Manette, Albert Maricaut, 1911
  Le Bon Samaritain, P. Lafitte, 1912
  Lina, histoire d'amour sous le second Empire, 1912
  Jeux de dames, Mericaut, 1912
Lesueur, Daniel
  Lointain revanche, 2 vol., A. Lemerre, 1900
  L'Honneur d'une femme, A. Lemerre, 1901
  Mortel secret, 2 vol., A. Lemerre, 1902
  Le Coeur chemine, A. Lemerre, 1904
  Le Masque d'amour, 2 vol., A. Lemerre, 1904
  La Force du passé, A. Lemerre, 1905
  Calvaire de femme, A. Lemerre, 1907
  La Nietzchéenne, A. Lemerre, 1907
  Le Droit à la force, A. Lemerre, 1909
  Du Sang dans les ténèbres, 2 vol., A. Lemerre, 1910
  Une Ame de vingt ans, A. Lemerre, 1911
  Au Tournant des jours, A. Lemerre, 1913
Marbo, Camille
  Christine Rodis, Stock, 1906
  Blassenay-le-vieux, Stock, 1907
  L'Heure du diable, Fayard, 1910
  Celle qui défait l'amour, Fayard, 1911, reprinted as *Hélène Barreaux*, 1926
  La Statue voilée, Fayard, 1912
Marni, Jeanne
  A Table, Ollendorf, 1900
  Vieilles, Ollendorf, 1901
  Le Livre d'une amoureuse, Ollendorf, 1904
  Théâtre de Madame, Ollendorf, 1906
  Pierre Tisserand, Ollendorf, 1907
  Souffrir, F. Juven, 1909
  L'Une et l'autre, P. Lafitte, 1909
Noailles, Anna, la Comtessa Mathieu de
  La Nouvelle espérance, Calmann-Lévy, 1903
  Le Visage émerveillé, Calmann-Lévy, 1904
  La Domination, Calmann-Lévy, 1905
  De la rive d'Europe à la rive d'Asie, Dorbon aîné, 1913
Pert, Camille
  Les Florifères, Simonis Empis, 1898
  Leur Egale, Simonis Empis, 1899
  Charlette, Simonis Empis, 1900

Mariage rêvé, Simonis Empis, 1900
Le Livre de la femme, Simonis Empis, 1900 (behavior manual)
Nos amours, nos vices, Simonis Empis, 1901
En Anarchie, Simonis Empis, 1901
La Loi de l'amour, Simonis Empis, 1903
Le Dernier cri du savoir vivre, Librairie universelle, 1904 (behavior manual)
Les amours perverses de Rosa Scari, Librairie artistique, 1905
Le Bonheur conjugal, Librairie universelle, 1905 (marriage manual)
L'Amour vengeur, Garnier, 1906
L'Outil, Ollendorf, 1907
Une Liaison coupable, Nilsson, 1907
Coeur d'orpheline, Ollendorf, 1908
La Femme dans la nature, les moeurs, la légende, la société, (in collaboration)
    Bong, 1908–10
L'Amour ingrat, Nilsson, 1906
Mirage de bonheur, Hachette, 1909
La Petite Cady, Juven, 1910
Le Drame de la maison des fous, Ollendorf, 1911
Cady mariée, Renaissance du livre, 1913
Le Divorce de Cady, Renaissance du livre, 1914
L'Incendiaire, Nilsson, 1914
Passionnette tragique, Renaissance du livre, 1914
Peyrebrune, George de
Les Passionnés, Lemerre, 1900
Une Expérience, Lemerre, 1901
Et l'amour vint!, Lemerre, 1902
Deux amoureuses, Lemerre, 1902
Une Sentimentale, Ollendorf, 1903
Les Trois demoiselles, Juven, 1905
Dona Quichotta, Hatier, 1906
Le Curé d'Anchelles, Mericaut, 1907
Le Réveil d'Eve, Mericault, 1909
Les Belles Martyrs, Mericault, 1911
Une Séparation, Renaissance du livre, 1913
Pougy, Liane de
L'Insaisissable, Librairie Nilsson, 1898
La Mauvaise part, Nilsson, 1899
Idylle saphique, Librairie de la plume, 1901; J. C. Lattès, 1977
Les Sensations de Mlle de la Bringue, Albin Michel, 1904
Yvée Lester, Aubert, 1906
Yvée Jourdan, Ambert, 1908
Prost, Yvette
Catherine Aubier, Armand Colin, 1912
Rachilde
L'Heure sexuelle, Marpon et Flammarion, 1898
La Tour d'amour, Marpon et Flammarion, 1899; Le Tout sur le tout, 1980
Contes et nouvelles, suivis du Théâtre, Marpon et Flammarion, 1900
La Jongleuse, Marpon et Flammarion, 1900; Editions des femmes, 1982
L'Imitation de la mort, 1903

Le Dessous, Mercure de France, 1904
Le Meneur de louves, Mercure de France, 1905
Son Printemps, Mercure de France, 1912
Reval, Gabrielle
   Les Sévriennes, Ollendorf, 1900
   Un Lycée de jeunes filles, Ollendorf, 1901
   Lycéennes, Ollendorf, 1902
   Notre-Dame des Ardents, Juven, 1903
   L'Avenir de nos jeunes filles, 1904
   La Cruche cassée, Calmann-Lévy, 1904
   Le Ruban de Vénus, Calmann-Lévy, 1906
   Les Camps-volants de la Riviera, Calmann-Lévy, 1908
   La Bachelière, Ed. de "Mirasol," 1910
   La Bachelière en Pologne, Ed. de "Mirasol," 1911
   Le Royaume du printemps, Hachette, 1913
Saint-Point, Valentine de
   Un Amour, Lib. Léon Vanier, 1900
   Un Inceste, Vanier, 1907
   La Femme et le désir, Vanier, 1910
   Une Mort, 1911, first published in *La Nouvelle revue*, 15 December
      1909–1 March 1910
Tinayre, Marcelle
   Avant l'amour, Mercure de France, 1897
   La Rançon, Mercure de France, 1898
   Hellé, Mercure de France, 1899
   L'Oiseau d'orage, Calmann-Lévy, 1900
   La Maison du péché, Calmann-Lévy, 1902
   La Vie amoureuse de François Barbazanges, Calmann-Lévy, 1904
   La Rebelle, Calmann-Lévy, 1905
   La Consolatrice and *L'Amour qui pleure*, Calmann-Lévy, 1908
   Notes d'une voyageuse en Turquie, Calmann-Lévy, 1909
   L'Ombre de l'amour, Calmann-Lévy, 1910
   La Douceur de vivre, Calmann-Lévy, 1911
   Madeleine au miroir. Journal d'une femme, Calmann-Lévy, 1913
Ulmes, Renée-Tony d'
   Vierge faible, Ollendorf, 1902
   Nices et ses environs, La Plume, 1903
   Sibylle femme, Ollendorf, 1904
   La Puissance de la mort, Lib. Léon Vanier, 1905
   Les Forces perdues and *La Vie invécue*, Vanier, 1906
   L'Ombre du soir, Miss Kate, Soeur Marie-Thérèse, Lemerre, 1907
   La Vie de Monique, Per Lamm, 1908
   Sibylle mère, Lemerre, 1909
   Les Demi-morts, Lemerre, 1912
   Le Jardin enchanté, Payot, Lausanne, 1910
   Nomades, Lemerre, 1910
   Pension de famille, Grasset, 1912
   Histoire d'une petite âme, Lemerre, 1913
   La Pension des oiseaux, Delagrave, 1914

Vivien, Renée
  Sapho, trad. Lemerre, 1903
  Du Vert au violet, Lemerre, 1903
  La Dame à la louve, Lemerre, 1904
  Une Femme m'apparut, Lemerre, 1904
Yver, Colette
  Les Cervelines, Juven, 1903
  La Bergerie, Juven, 1904
  Comment s'en vont les reines, Calmann-Lévy, 1905
  Princesses de science, Calmann-Lévy, 1907
  Les Dames du Palais, Calmann-Lévy, 1909
  Le Métier du roi, Calmann-Lévy, 1911
  Un Coin de voile, Calmann-Lévy, 1912
  Les Sables mouvants, Calmann-Lévy, 1913

For further bibliographical information on these authors, their minor writings, and contemporary reviews of their work, see Hugo P. Thième, *Bibliographie de la littérature française de 1800 à 1930 (Paris, 1933)*, Slatkine Reproductions (Genève, 1971), and Hector Talvert et Joseph Place, *Bibliographie des auteurs modernes de la langue française (1801–1975)*. Chronique des Lettres Françaises (Paris, 1928–75).

2. Secondary literary sources

a) Writings giving the flavor of the period and occasionally providing information

Bertaut, Jules: *La littérature féminine d'aujourd'hui* (Paris, 1909), *Le Paris d'avant-guerre* (Paris: Renaissance du livre, 1919).
Bethléem, Abbé Louis: *Romans à lire et romans à proscrire 1800–1914*, Lille aux bureaux de "Romans-revue" 1914.
Bonnefon, J. de: *La Corbeille des roses ou les dames de lettres* (Paris: Bouville et Cie., 1909).
Bonnefont, G.: *Les Parisiennes chez elles* (Paris, 1895–97).
Charasson, Henriette: "La Littérature féminine" in *Vingt-cinq années de littérature française*, ed. E. Montfort, Paris, Librairie de France, vol. 2, pp. 65–98, 1925.
Charenson, G.: *Comment ils écoutent*, ed. Montaigne (Paris, 1932).
Claretie, Léo: *Histoire de la littérature française*, vol. 5, "Les Contemporains 1900–1910" (Paris: Ollendorf, 1912).
Ernest-Charles, J.: *Les Samedis littéraires* (Paris: Perrin, 1903–1905).
Flat, P.: *Nos Femmes de lettres* (Paris: Perrin, 1908).
Gachons, Jacques des: "Les Femmes de lettres françaises," in *Figaro Illustré* (February 1910).
Larnac, Jean: *Histoire de la littérature féminine en France* (Paris: Editions Kra, 1929).
Mailloux, Auguste: *Ceux qui passent et ceux qui restent* (1ère série, Paris, Librairie de l'Institut Agronomique, ed. B. Alardie, 1908; 2ème série, ed. Mendel, Paris 1920).

Reval, Gabrielle: *La Chaîne des dames* (Paris: Crès, 1925).

Tissot, Ernest: *Nouvelles princesses de lettres* (Paris: Fontemoing, 1911).

b) Recent critical material on the authors cited

Colette: Andry Marc, *Chère Colette* (Paris: Presses de la Cité, 1983).

Brejaart, Marjo and Marjavan Buuren, "Amour et lesbianisme chez Colette," in *Analyses de textes* sous la direction de J. Plessen and A. van Zoest, *Cahiers de recherches interuniversitaires néerlandaises* 4–5, 1982, pp. 86–108.

D'Hollander, Paul, *Colette, ses apprentissages* (Montreal: Presses de l'Université de Montréal, 1978).

Dormann, Geneviève, *Amoureuse Colette* (Paris: Herscher, 1984).

Eisinger, Erika Mendelson and Mari Ward Mccarty, eds., *Colette the Woman, the Writer* (University Park: The Pennsylvania State University Press, 1981).

Harris, Elaine, *L'Approfondissement de la sensualité dans l'oeuvre romanesque de Colette* (Paris: Nizet, 1973).

Massie, Allan, *Colette* (Harmondsworth: Penguin Books, 1986).

Resch, Yannick, *Corps féminin, corps textuel* (Klincksieck, 1973).

Richardson, Joanna, *Colette* (London: Methuen, 1983).

Sarde, Michèle, *Colette libre et entravée* (Paris: Stock, 1984).

Stewart, Joan Hinde, *Colette* (Boston: Twayne, 1983).

Ward Jouve, Nicole, *Colette* (Brighton: Harvester Press, 1987).

Rachilde: Dauphiné, Claude, *Rachilde, femme de lettres 1900* (Paris: Pierre Fanlac, 1985).

Renée Vivien: Lorenz, Paul, *Sapho 1900 Renée Vivien* (Paris: Juillard, 1977).

To my knowledge there is no other recent material on any of the authors except Colette. The critical work on her is so extensive that I have listed only selected books published since 1970.

3. Historical sources

Adam, Juliette, *Idées anti-proudhoniennes sur l'amour, la femme et le mariage* (Paris: Dentu, 1861).

Albistur, Maîté et Daniel Armogathe, *Histoire du féminisme français* (Editions des femmes, 1977).

———, *Le Grief des femmes*, Anthologie de textes féministes du Moyen-Age à la 2e République (Paris: Hier et demain, 1978).

Alesson, Jean, *Le Monde est aux femmes*; s.l.n.d. (Brochure, Bibliothèque Marguerite Durand).

Aron, Jean-Paul, ed., *Misérable et glorieuse la femme du XIXe siècle* (Paris: Fayard, 1980).

Avril de Sainte-Croix, Mme G., *Le Féminisme* (Paris: V. Giard et E. Brière, 1907).

Bader, Clarisse, *La Femme française dans les temps modernes* (Paris: Didier, 1883).

Bell, Susan Groag and Karen M. Offen, eds., *Women, the Family and Freedom:*

The Debate in Documents, 1750–1950 (Stanford: Stanford University Press, 1983).

Benstock, Shari, *Women of the Left Bank* (London: Virago, 1987).

Bidelman, Patrick, *The Politics of French Feminism: Leon Richer and the Ligue Française pour le Droit des Femmes 1882–1891* (Historical Reflections, 1976).

———, *Pariahs Stand Up! The Founding of the Liberal Feminist Movement in France 1858–1889* (Westport, Conn.: Greenwood Press, 1982).

Bois, Jules, *L'Ere nouvelle* (Paris: Léon Chailley, 1896).

Boxer, Marilyn Jacoby, "Socialism Faces Feminism in France 1879–1913" (Ph.D. thesis, University of California, Riverside, 1975).

Brion, Hélène, *La Voie féministe* (Paris: Syros, 1978).

Clemenceau, G., *La "justice" du sexe fort* (Paris: Librairie de la Raison, 1907).

Collins, M. and S. Weil-Sayre, *Les Femmes en France* (New York: Charles Scribner's Sons, 1974).

Congrès international de la condition et des droits des femmes 1900 Paris (Paris: Imprimerie des Arts et manufactures, 1901).

Deraismes, Maria, *Ce que veulent les femmes* (Paris: Syros, 1980).

———, *Eve dans l'humanité* (Paris: Librairie L. Sauvaitre, 1971).

DuBreuil de Saint-Germain, J., *La Misère sociale de la femme et le suffrage* (Suresnes: J. Crémieu, 1911).

Evans, Richard J., *The Feminists* (London: Croom Helm and Barnes & Noble, 1977).

Farge, Arlette and Christiane Klapisch-Zuber et al., *Madame ou Mademoiselle: itinéraires de la solitude féminine 18e–20e siècle* (Paris: Arthaud-Montalba, 1984).

Hellerstein, E.O., L.P. Hume and K. M. Offen, eds., *Victorian Women, a Documentary Account of Women's Lives in Nineteenth Century England, France and the United States* (Stanford: Stanford University Press, 1981).

Kenenburg, B. de, *La Femme régénérateur* (Paris: Dupont, 1899).

Lacour, Léopold, *L'Humaniste intégral* (Paris: Stock, 1897),

Lecointre, Comtesse Pierre, *Etat de la question féministe en France en 1907* (Paris: Ecole professionnelle d'imprimerie, 1907).

Marquet, Jean, *La Condition légale de la femme au commencement et à la fin du XIXe siècle* (Nîmes: A. Chastanier, 1899).

Martial, Lydie, *La Femme et la liberté: La Femme intégrale* (Paris: chez l'auteur, 1901).

Martin, Marguerite, *Les Droits de la femme* (Paris: M. Rivière, 1919).

Martin-Fugier, Anne, *La Place des bonnes* (Paris: Grasset, 1979).

———, *La Bourgeoise* (Paris: Grasset, 1983).

McMillan, James, *Housewife or Harlot: The Place of Women in French Society 1870–1940* (Sussex: Harvester Press, 1981).

Minck, Paule, *Communarde et féministe (1839–1901)* (Paris: Syros, 1981).

Monod, Wilfred, *Masculin et féminin* (Paris: s.e., 1902).

Moreau, Thérèse, *Le Sang de l'histoire et l'idée de la femme au 19e siècle* (Paris: Flammarion, 1982).

Morsier, Emilie de, *La Mission de la femme: Discours et fragments* (Paris: Librairie Fischbacher, 1897).

Moses, Claire Goldberg, *French Feminism in the Nineteenth Century* (Albany: State University of New York Press, 1984).

Offen, Karen, "First Wave Feminism in France: Network and Resources," in *Women's Studies International Forum*, vol. 5, 1982, pp. 685–89.

———, "The Second Sex and the Baccalauréat in Republican France 1880–1924," in *French Historical Studies*, vol. XIII, no. 2, (Fall 1983), pp. 252–86.

———, "Depopulation, Nationalism and Feminism in Fin-de-siècle France," in *The American Historical Review*, vol. 89, no. 3 (June 1984), pp. 648–76.

Pasquier, Marie-Claire, et al. (collective book), *Stratégies des femmes* (Paris: Tierce, 1984).

Pelletier, Madeleine, *L'Education féministe des filles et autres textes* (Paris: Syros, 1978 [reprint]).

Périllon, Marie-Christine, *Vies de femmes: les travaux et les jours de la femme à la belle époque* (Roanne: Horvath, 1981).

Pope. Deborah, "The Development of Feminist Consciousness in Women's Writing in France in the First Half of the Nineteenth Century" (Ph.D. thesis, University of Bristol, 1979).

Poirson, S., *Mon féminisme* (Paris: E. Bernard, 1905).

Pottecher, Thérèse, "Le Mouvement féministe en France," in *La Grande Revue*, February 1910 and 1911.

Rabaut, Jean, *1900 Tournant du féminisme français* (Paris: Bulletin de la société d'histoire moderne, no. 17, 1983).

———, *Féministes à la Belle Epoque* (Paris: France-Empire, 1985).

Richer, Léon, *Le Code des femmes* (Paris: Dentu, 1883).

Roussel, Nelly, *L'Eternelle Sacrifiée* (Paris: Syros, 1979 [reprint]).

Terrisse, Marie C., *Notes et impressions à travers le féminisme* (Paris: Fischbacher, 1896).

Thibert, Marguerite, *Le Féminisme dans le socialisme français de 1830 à 1850* (Paris: Marcel Giard, 1926).

Thiebaux, Charles, *Le féminisme et les socialistes depuis Saint Simon jusqu'à nos jours* (Paris: A. Rousseau, 1906).

Thiesse, Anne-Marie, *Le Roman du quotidien: Lecteurs et lectures populaires à la Belle Epoque* (Paris: Le Chemin Vert, 1984).

Turgeon, Charles, *Le Féminisme français* (Paris: L. Larosa, 1902).

Turmann, Max, *Initiatives féminines* (Paris: V. Lecoffre, 1905).

Viviani, R., H. Robert, A. Meurgé et al.; *Cinquante ans de féminisme: 1870–1920* (Paris: Ed. de la Ligue française pour le Droit des femmes, 1921).

Zylberg-Hocquard, Marie-Hélène, *Féminisme et syndicalisme en France* (Paris: Anthropos, 1978).

INDEX

JENNIFER WAELTI-WALTERS, Professor of French and Director of the Women's Studies Program at the University of Victoria, has published on many topics concerning contemporary French and French Canadian literature and feminism. Her books include *Michel Butor, JMG LeClézio, Icare ou l'évasion impossible, Fairytales and the Female Imagination,* and *Jeanne Hyvrard.*